Freedom or Death!
History of the Chechen Republic of Ichkeria

Volume I
From the Revolution to the First Chechen War
(1991 - 1994)

Artwork: Eleonora Benedetti
First edition: February 2020
Second edition: October 2021
Independent publication
Bibliography available on www.ichkeria.net
Contacts: libertaomortechri@gmail.com

® Francesco Benedetti

FREEDOM OR DEATH!

History of the Chechen Republic of Ichkeria

VOLUME I

From the Revolution to the First Chechen War

1991 - 1994

FRANCESCO BENEDETTI

Introduction to the second edition

The idea of writing an essay on the history of the Chechen Republic of Ichkeria (ChRI) was born in the spring of 2018 when, as a passionate, after unsuccessfully looking for a monograph on the subject, I realized that no one existed. Obviously I am not talking about "books on Chechnya". There are many of those, even in Italian, and they mainly concerned with warfare, humanitarian disaster, terrorism and military tactics. What I could not find was a treatise that recounted the events of the self-proclaimed Chechen republic from a political point of view. In essence, there was not a single precise and accurate analysis of the social and political processes that had led Chechnya to secede from Russia, about how the new independent state was born and organized, and how it had evolved through sixteen years of history. My main interest was to reconstruct the state - building, to study the events of its main protagonists, to go deeper into the analisys of the structure of the state and its internal dynamics. Yet the literature on the subject (at least in English and Russian) is very vast, and there are numerous resources available on the web to deepen the individual aspects of the story in question. So why not summarize them in a single essay?

The following months of work made it clear to me why no one had embarked on such an undertaking until now. Approaching the study of sources on the subject is complicated to say the least, not only because they are mostly written in Russian, but because most of the official documents were destroyed during the two catastrophic wars that devastated the country or lies classified in the archives of the Russian Federation. Available for the researchers there are mostly memorials and journalistic, which, as is well known, must be carefully studied and verified in order to be considered reliable (especially those written during the war). The main difficulty I had to face, therefore, was to verify the numerous and fragmentary sources available, according to a research method more similar to ancient and medieval history than to that normally carried out by the contemporary researchers (who, on the other hand, often find themselves having to sort out the stacks of documents available) and the result, however satisfactory, it is far from definitive. For this reason I created the site www.ichkeria.net, on which I try to investigate issues regarding which, even today, uncertainties and contradictions remain.

The second edition of this book is also the first to be published in an English translated version. It is a translation that I have done personally, not possessing the necessary qualifications, and relying exclusively on my narrow personal skills. The result will certainly appear artisanal, but the costs for a professional translation of the work far exceed the budget at my disposal. I hope to be able to remedy in the future with a more "linguistically effective" version of the book. On the other hand, given the large number of visitors to the site from abroad, I thought it appropriate to try the path of translation even at the cost of incurring inelegant errors. I hope the reader can forgive me and be benevolent.

What the reader is about to read is the first of a series of volumes which I hope will be useful in deepening the history of independent Chechnya. This is a more precise and readable version of the previous one, published in February 2020 and afflicted by some deficiencies in form and legibility which I tried to remedy with a staggered solution, but above all based on the in-depth information published on the site, and which it will soon be implemented by specific publications that will be able to enrich the information kit with chronologies, biographies and thematic insights.

As I wrote in the preface of the first edition, the research work could not have taken place without the precious collaboration of Tamerlan Kasaev, to whom I dedicate the fruit of a work that, in some ways, can be considered "four-handed", and which I hope to have the pleasure of learning more in the following years.

Mission

This book contains material of historical and journalistic interest relating to the Chechen Republic of Ichkeria (ChRI). The purpose of this work is to collect in a single work a complete treatment on the subject, respecting the historical truth and without partisan political interest. It does not represent the views or positions of members of organizations that have been part of, or supported, the Chechen Republic of Ichkeria. This book does not propagate the constitution or the activity of political organizations, nor of criminal or terrorist associations, and the information published, which sometimes may refer to characters or organizations considered as such in some countries, is not intended to praise, glorify or justify criminal actions or that violate the laws of any state.

I unreservedly condemn the use of violence, intimidation and war as a means of resolving any dispute. I likewise condemn all forms of political and religious extremism, intolerance, racism and any other socially destructive thinking.

Francesco Benedetti

INDEX

CHAPTER 1 – *Vaynakh*..................10

The origins
    Crossroads of Empires
    From the Tsar to the Soviets
    Operation Lentil
    The sons of Ardakhar
    Soviet Chechnya
    Perestroika
    The resurrection of nationalism
    Chechen Glasnost

CHAPTER 2 – *From Zavgaev to Dudaev*..................57

    Radical reformists
    The situation in Chechnya
    The birth of parties
    The Congress
    The second session

CHAPTER 3 – *The revolution*..................98

The Gang of 8
    The insurrection
    Assault on the Soviet
    The Chechen Revolution
    Elections

CHAPTER 4 – *Independence*..................132

    The end of the USSR
    The new president
    The provisional government
    Building a state
    Political tensions in the Caucasus
    The cultural renaissance
    The opposition is reorganizing
    The 1991 balance

CHAPTER 5 – *The Republic*............................175

    The big sale
    The economic blockade
    Giving an order to the country
    The coup d'etat of March 31st
    The capture of the arsenals
    Exporting the revolution
    The war between Ossetians and Ingush
    The first Russian - Chechen crisis
    Dudaev against everyone
    The 1992 balance

CHAPTER 6 – *The Regime*............................237

The January negotiations
    Abkhazia on fire
    The constitutional reform
    The Mugadaev government
    The institutional crisis
    The coup d'état
    Dudaev's regime
    Assault on the White House
    The Zviadist uprising
    The Provisional Council

CHAPTER 7 – The civil war............................288

    The Chechen Republic of Ichkeria
        Unlikely alliances
    Dudaev seeks consent
    The opposition regroups
    The civil war
    The November Assault
    The ultimatum

CHAPTER 1

VAYNAKH

"It is difficult to be Chechen. It is a state of mind. The Chechen is in constant struggle for survival. He does not fight against his neighbors. Not a case in the history of a Chechen attack on their neighbors. But the Chechens have always had to defend their homeland, their culture and their customs.

The Chechen is always in search of his destiny. He doesn't live for himself! He always creates for his children. He dedicates his whole life to his children. He feels compelled to build a home for them, marry them and help raise his grandchildren.

The Chechen is a good friend. The Chechen is a dangerous enemy. He does not trust. It is funny. He likes to laugh at his mistakes, his failures. The Chechen does not call his wife by name, the Chechen does not caress his children in front of strangers. A Chechen will never caress his child in front of his parents.

The Chechen considers his home as his fortress. Therefore, always build a high fence around the house. His house must always be one meter longer than that of his neighbor. Chechens pay close attention to the house, its layout, its comfort, so that children feel at home forever. It's hard to be Chechen!"

Yan Chesnov

The origins

The homeland of the Chechens is the Caucasus, a wild land wedged between the Caspian Sea and the Black Sea and crossed from side to side by two mountain ranges: a higher one, located in the north and called the *Great Caucasus*, and a lower one, further south, the *Little Caucasus*. These two ridges form a barrier that can only be overcome by steep mountain passes, or by bypassing the hills along the coast. On the slopes of the mountains there are narrow valleys, carved out over the millennia by steep streams. To the south, beyond the Little Caucasus lies the *Armenian Plateau*, an expanse of barren hills. To the north, the vast Russian steppe opens up at the foot of the Greater Caucasus. The highest ridges, almost always covered with snow, draw a suggestive white crown on the dense forest that covers the plateaus. Just look at the majestic Mount Elbrus, its highest peak, to enjoy a setting worthy of a Tolkien story. It is no coincidence that humanity has set some of its best known myths here, such as the Greek one of Prometheus, or the Jewish one of Noah's Ark.

Meeting point between Europe, Asia and the Middle East, the Caucasus has been the crossroads of the greatest civilizations in history: great empires fighting for supremacy have contended for it without respite, and each of these has left its mark on religion, in architecture, in toponymy. The nature stingy of resources and the invasions of the conquerors have forged simple and lively peoples, accustomed to fighting for survival and therefore very attached to their origins and their specificities: just think that in this area as large as France coexist twenty nations, nineteen languages, seventeen states and three religions.

Set in this mosaic, Chechnya measures seventeen thousand square kilometers, more or less the same as

Galles, arranged to form a sort of rectangle one hundred and seventy kilometers long and one hundred wide. Its territory is very varied: traveling from north to south we meet a wide plain dominated by the steppe, which gradually gives way to a network of plowed fields, overlooking the banks of the main river of the country, the *Terek*, which crosses it from west to east, descending towards the Caspian Sea. After passing it, you enter its alluvial plain until you reach a chain of hills that marks its limit. Beyond these modest hills, called *Terek Ridge*, another wide valley opens up, crossed by another important river, the *Sunzha*. This too runs through the country from west to east, following a very articulated path full of bends that over the millennia has carved out a vast plain, the so-called *Chechen Plain*. Here are the most populous settlements, including the capital, *Grozny*, or as the Chechens called it *Solzha Ghala*. It is located almost in the geographic center of the country and is inhabited by nearly a third of the republic's residents. To the south of the plain there are numerous gorges, crossed by lively mountain streams. Going up them you reach the southernmost region of the country, rugged and wooded, dominated by the Caucasus mountains and dominated by the imposing *Mount Tebulosmta*, 4493 meters high.

The history of the Chechens begins about 6,000 years ago, when their ancestors came here from Mesopotamia. They were a hodgepodge of tribes who spoke a common language, called *Nakh* (literally "people"), from which their ancestral name of *Vaynakh* ("Our people") derived. They worshiped the typical gods of the ancient world, the spirits of nature, war, hunting and fertility. Over them reigned *Deela*, the supreme god, and over everything ruled *Taamash*, destiny. The pantheon of the Vaynakhs was similar to that of other pagan peoples, with whom it also shared the cult of heroes, such as the aforementioned Hellenic Prometheus (called *Pkharmat*) and monstrous creatures, such as giants (called *Nart*).

Once settled in the mountains, the Vaynakh tribes organized themselves into clans: some of them settled in the plains of Terek and Sunzha, devoted themselves to agriculture and were called clans of the plain, others remained on the highlands, dedicated themselves to breeding and were called mountain clans. Every summer the mountaineers went down to the valley to stock up on cereals and exchanged farm products with the farmers.

The peace of the Vaynakhs was shaken in the 6th century BC by the arrival of the *Cimmerians* and the *Scythians*, warrior peoples of Iranian origin who spread to the northern plains, forcing farmers to take refuge in the mountains with their southern brothers. Once recovered, the proto - Chechens went on the counterattack, forcing the Scythians to flee. It was not long, however, that new invaders arrived, stronger and more organized than the previous ones. They were called *Sarmatians*: their horde submerged the plains again, bringing death and destruction. Suffice it to say that the name of one of the main tributaries of the Sunzha, the *Martan*, originates from a Sarmatian word which means "river of the dead". Finally, after decades of conflict, this invasion also came to an end, and what remained of the Sarmatians settled not far from Chechnya, in today's *Ossetia*, giving rise to the people of the *Ossetians*.

For a few centuries the Vaynakh lived in peace, while in the south of the Great Caucasus Byzantines and Persians fought for hegemony by fighting bloody battles. When, during the 7th century AD, both empires were swept away by the advance of the Arabs, a power vacuum was created in the Caucasus which the locals took advantage of, constituting the first independent kingdoms. The most important of these was the

Kingdom of Georgia, which came to control the whole territory between the Great and the Small Caucasus. To protect themselves from the invasions of the Arabs and the peoples of the steppe, the Georgians sponsored the birth of small potentates perched on the mountains, which protected the access routes to the kingdom. Thus were born the first Vaynakh kingdoms: the *Kingdom of Durdzukhetia*, located in today's western Chechnya and Ingushetia (called in the cronicles of the time "protector of the mountains" and the *Principality of Simsir*, active in the South – Western Chechnya. Ruled by a king, called *Eela*, a class of lords (*Uzden*) administered the land in a system similar to our feudal pyramid. Free men, called *Halxoi*, had the right to bear arms, while servants (*Yalxhoi*) and peasants (*Lesh*) lived under their protection. At the base of the pyramid were slaves and prisoners of war, called *Yisarsh*.

During this period the Vaynakhs organized an articulated social system which in some ways may recall that of the Scots, the Basques or the ancient Germanic peoples. The family unit, made up of parents and children (called *Dezel*) was the basic unit. Most Dezel made up a kind of extended family called *Ts'a*, whose members collaborated in the cultivation of the common lands and in the breeding of animals. But the real cornerstone of the social structure was the *Teip*, whose name derives from the Arabic "Tayfa", and which identifies our most "familiar" clan. The teip was a confederation of families that could even number tens of thousands of people. It was governed by a *Mekh - Khel*, an assembly made up of the elders and most respected members of the community: it administered justice, assigned land to cultivate, it mobilized warriors in case of war and represented the teip in disputes with other clans. Each teip had a legendary ancestor and a founding myth, to which a sacred mountain was dedicated. On this mountain there were one or more towers, which served as both totems and shelters. The mountains of present-day Chechnya are littered with the remains of these tall stone towers, similar to bell towers, some of which are still perfectly preserved.

Finally, the elders handed down the folk story in long sheep parchments written in Arabic, called Tyaptari. In them, in addition to the historical accounts, the norms of customary law, called Adat, were also transcribed. It was a sort of unofficial civil code, a collection of moral guidelines that every good Chechen had to follow in order to be considered worthy of esteem[1]. Teip sometimes organized themselves into confederations, initially to serve contingent purposes (repel an invasion, face a particularly harsh winter, settle serious blood feuds, etc.) subsequently on a permanent basis. They were called *Tukkhum*, today there are nine and they collect about two hundred teips.

The teip system, the recourse to Adat and the central role of the elderly were the characteristics around which the nucleus of the Chechen nation was formed. Such a traditionalist society, fragmented into clans and used to resolving even the most delicate issues "in the family"

---

[1] The Chechen Adat was made up of three essential parts. the *Adamalla*, roughly translatable as being human, referred to the values of piety, compassion and benevolence. The *Konakhalla*, which can be translated as dignity, concerned the themes of honor and respect. Finally, the *Noxkhalla*, literally "Chechenity", was about belonging to the nation and the moral duty to defend it from enemies. Personal and family matters, property disputes, and so on were settled by resorting to Adat. When one community felt offended by another, the elders held an assembly during which the clan claiming to have been wronged publicly asked for satisfaction. If the accusation was particularly serious, the victim could declare a feud on his enemy's clan. In that case, if the accused's teip did not deliver the culprit or took his defense, bloody feuds could break out, which ended only when one of the two parties offered or granted forgiveness.

could hardly recognize the authority of a central state[2], which it probably didn't even feel the need for[3].

Crossroads of Empires

In 1237 the North Caucasus was submerged by the advance of the *Mongols*. After them it was the turn of the *Tatars* of Tamerlane, who conquered Southern Russia in 1350. In both cases the invaders could not get the better of the natives, and in the long run they had to give up, limiting themselves to colonizing the fertile plains along the Terek and the Sunzha[4].

---

[2] For this reason, even in the first half of the twentieth century the state authority was struggling to get respected. Anatoly Ivanov, former Minister of Finance of the Chechen Ingush Republic under the soviet rule, remembered this event: *I remember a case in which we were unable to catch a murderer because no one wanted to betray him [...] The representatives of the Prosecutor, the Militia, the KGB went to the elders saying to them: "Look what he did, look who he killed [...] help us take him, we must bring him to justice for his actions ". The elders thought, curled their beards for a while, then asked, "Friends, tell us. Will he be shot? " They replied: "This is up to the court of justice to decide, but we think he will be in prison for a long time, but he will not be shot." Later the elders said, "All right tomorrow morning at 9 will come with you." And of course, the next day exactly at 9 am the killer surrendered to the authorities. The elders had ordered him to do it.*

[3] As Kozh - Akhmed Nukhaev wrote, a very particular character of whom we will speak in the next chapters of this book: *Chechen individualism comes out of the awareness of freedom, and to prevent this from degenerating into selfishness we have incorporated ourselves into cells connected to each other by bonds of blood - the teips - which counterbalance individualism with collectivism [...] teips certainly do not recognize the state, just as the state does not recognize the teips. Teips are traditionally a guarantee of equality and equal rights among Chechens, regardless of their physical well-being or property. The teips are a brotherhood of free people who make up the Chechen nation.*

[4] Legend has it that Tamerlane, after yet another unsuccessful raid of his men on the mountains, hearing the mountaineers singing their folk songs late at night, came to propose an alliance to them, offering them one of his swords as a sign of respect for their steadfastness. According to what is said in Chechnya this saber would really exist and would have been handed down from generation to generation until, in 1944, the Soviet troops stole it and transported it to Moscow as a trophy.

The resistance of the Vaynakhs to these new invasions was stubborn and victorious, but the two small kingdoms of Durdzukhetia and Simsir did not survive the war. When the Tartars withdrew, the Chechens found themselves free, but without a state, and unable to reconstitute one. This power vacuum was filled by Tukkhums, who inherited its functions. As the invaders dispersed and abandoned their lands, the clans of the plains, who had had to evacuate to the mountains, were able to resettle in their ancient homes.[5].

The influence of the Mongol domination instilled new characteristics in Chechen society, starting with religion. On the expulsion of the Tartars, the Vaynakhs found themselves Muslims, albeit in their own way. For a long time they continued to call Allah by the same name as the supreme pagan god, Deela. If they had been left alone for a few generations, perhaps they would have given rise to an original cult of theirs. But this was not the case, since as soon as the Tartars had gone the Russians looked out over the Caucasus.

Russia was also a young nation, and like Chechnya it had just freed itself from Mongol rule, chasing the old invaders as they retreated and annexing their ancient kingdoms. The Tsar's avant-garde, the *Cossacks*, launched east and south, and soon reached the banks of the Terek. As they advanced from the north, two other empires fell on the Caucasus: the Ottoman one from the west and the Persian one from the east.

It was during a military expedition to those lands that the Russians and Chechens first came into contact. A

---

[5]This process was neither quick nor painless: for generations, in fact, the Mongolian populations had settled in those lands, and dislodging them was not at all easy. In some cases the Vaynakhs proceeded to assimilate them as "impure" teip. Those who did not want to bow to the new order were massacred or forced to migrate north.

tsarist squad, encamped near a village called *Chechana* (in Russian "Chechen – Aul") was attacked by the mountaineers who inhabited those lands and forced to flee. From that day the Russians started calling those people Chechens. In reality they had never called themselves that way: among them they used to call themselves *Nokhchi* (our people), and their nation they called *Nokhchi - Cho*, and they would continue to use these names for several centuries.

The arrival of the Russians, Slavs and Orthodox, once again unified the jagged system of teips and tukkhums in the defense of the community. Islam, which until then had penetrated in a rather superficial and approximate way, became the cultural bulwark of the resistance of the Nokhchi to the new invasion, and soon a dense network of religious communities was born, at the head of which the first Imams emerged. The most important of these was *Mansur Ushurma*, a *Sheikh* (a term derived from the Arabic that identifies a person who enjoys great respect) who proclaimed a holy war against the Russian "infidels"[6].

---

[6]The character is also interesting because, in addition to being the first Chechen national hero, according to some historians he could have Italian origins: he could be the Dominican friar Giambattista Boetti, born in Camino, in present-day Piedmont, on 2 June 1743. after a rather dissolute youth, Boetti had gone to Mosul, where he had led the local religious mission, earning a fair amount of credit (and also, apparently, a great patrimony) by virtue of the medical skills of which he was educated. In 1784 he theorized the foundations of a syncretic religion that blended Christianity and Islam, and after gathering an army of thousands of followers he headed for the Caucasus. The small army, strongly ideologized and, it seems, endowed with fanatical discipline, fought and won in Georgia, where he defeated the troops of the local King, Heraclius II, and forced the nobles to pay him substantial tributes, with which he built up an even larger army. Backed by funding from the Ottoman Sultan Selim III (the fabulous sum of 500,000 gold plates as well as cannons, weapons and ammunition is told) Boetti, who already called himself "Mansur" ("The Victorious") crossed the Great Caucasus , leading the war against the Russians.

Throughout the last quarter of a century of the 1700s, his *Gazavat* (a Turkish term that roughly means "offensive") kept the Tsarist army in check. In particular, in 1785 he managed to ambush a regiment of 2000 men near a ford on the Sunzha River, destroying it completely.[7].

The disastrous defeat convinced Tsarina *Catherine II*, then in power, to order the mobilization of a large army to put an end to Mansur's raids. However, it took another six years before Ushurma surrendered, besieged in the Turkish stronghold of Anapa. Arrested, he was taken to prison, where he died three years later. His sacrifice became a real founding myth for the anti-imperialism of the Caucasians. Mansur's death did not appease the rebellions to the Moscow crown but rather, it was a further inspiration: every spring the bands of mountaineers went down to the valley to attack the imperial garrisons and plunder their warehouses. Meanwhile Catherine II was succeeded by *Alexander I*, who sent his most valiant and cruel general, *Aleksey Ermolov*, to put an end to the guerrilla warfare[8].

The general built a series of fortresses to guard the valleys and along the main communication route of the region, the so-called Georgian Military Route. Some of them were built on the banks of the Sunzha, and for the

---

[7]The tsarist unit was commanded by another Italian of origin, Colonel De Pieri. His detachment, strong of 2000 men and 2 cannons, entered a gorge near the ford, when it was submerged by a sudden and devastating attack from both ridges. About 740 soldiers died, including De Pieri himself, torn to pieces a few meters from one of the two guns. Another 162 were the prisoners. The rest of the Russians withdrew in disorder, abandoning their weapons and ammunition.

[8] Ermolov was clear about the approach he used to restore order in North Caucasus: *I desire that the terror of my name protect our borders more than chains or fortresses, that my word be a more inevitable law for the natives than death. I will be inexorably strict. An execution saves hundreds of Russians from destruction, and thousands of Muslims from treason.*

construction of the largest of these the local population was entirely deported. The stronghold, completed in 1818, took the terrifying name of Grozny, in Russian "formidable", to enhance its impregnability. The Chechens still did not know it, but their hated enemy had just built their future capital and had given it a name that he would bitterly regret.

After fixing the rear, Ermolov set about the methodical destruction of any village that hosted the guerrillas, or that gave them support.[9]. Faced with Ermolov's advance, the Chechens appointed a new leader, in the figure of Imam *Ghazi Muhammad*[10]. He proclaimed his Gazavat and assembled an army, with which he stood up to the imperial armies for nearly twenty years. In 1832, exasperated by the strenuous resistance of the rebels, Tsar *Nicholas I* sent an army of twenty thousand men with the aim of pacifying the region at any cost. Again, the tsarists put the country to fire and sword, and finally managed to track down Ghazi Muhammad, forcing him to take refuge in his hometown, Gimry, and to besiege him. The rebels fought boldly, but

---

[9] Bloody massacres remain in historical memories, such as that of Dadi - Yurt, a prosperous agricultural village on the banks of the Terek. On September 15, 1819 the imperials surrounded the town, asking for its surrender. When the Chechens refused, the artillery razed it to the ground, and once inside the soldiers surrendered to a terrifying massacre. 400 people died among the defenders of the village, their wives and their children. Since 2009, Chechnya has remembered the bloody event by celebrating Women's Day, in honor of the young women who died in the massacre.

[10] Ghazi Muhammad (the Invincible) was born in 1795 in Gimry, in today's Dagestan. After studying the Koran together with his companion Shamil, he devoted himself to preaching, trying to convince the Chechen clans to abandon the Adat in favor of Islamic law, according to him able to unify the tribes and peoples of the Caucasus and to form a national consciousness. Appointed Imam in 1829, he launched a jihad both against the Russians and against the same Caucasian potentates who still resorted to Adat instead of Sharia. Until 1832 his followers managed to stand up to the Imperials, until they conquered Gimry and killed him in battle.

faced with the massive array of Russian artillery and their overwhelming number they had to abandon the field. Muhammad was killed, and the baton passed to one of his most loyal followers, Shamil, a young man of Avar origin[11] escaped the massacre. The new leader managed to rally the bands of mountaineers who opposed the Russian domination and organized a real political institution. Thus, was born the *Imamate of the North Caucasus*, a confessional state organized into 33 districts, administered by an official (*Naib*) and a judge (*Mufti*), who operated through a network of 510 *commanders* responsible for the collection of tithes and of the management of the armed forces. The Imamate was governed by the application of Islamic law, the *Sharia*, and recognized Arabic, the language of the Prophet Muhammad, as official idiom. Strengthened by this widespread organization, Shamil managed to give a permanent structure to the armed bands that until then had fought more like a disorderly swarm than a real army. Furthermore, through the establishment of a confessional state he succeeded in wiping out what remained of the residual pagan cults, and thus laid the foundations for the complete islamization of Chechens.

Against the Imamate Nicholas I he moved even more forces, and despite this it took at least another twenty years before the mountaineers were displaced from the plains and besieged on the mountains. Forced to find refuge in the gorges, Shamil tried to get help from the Ottoman Empire, but the government of the Sublime Gate could not do much: in those years, in fact, the

---

[11]Neither Shamil nor Ghazi Muhammad were Chechens. Both belonged to the Avar people, the majority ethnic group in today's Republic of Dagestan. The golden age of the Avars was between the 7th and 10th centuries AD, when one part migrated to Transylvania, carving out a powerful domain, while another horde conquered vast areas of southern Russia.

Turks were fighting the Crimean War, and they had no resources to send to the aid of the Imamate. Received a polite "spade" from his neighbor in Istanbul, Shamil came to ask for help from Queen Victoria of England who, together with the French and the Italians, was fighting the Crimean War on the side of the Ottomans.[12].

The British Empire's distress calls, however, also fell on deaf ears. As hunger and deprivation crippled the rebels, more and more mountaineers showed their willingness to come to terms with the Russians. For their part, they awaited the inevitable, limiting themselves to defending the fertile fields and preventing the rebels from coming down from the mountains. On September 6, 1859, Shamil decided to surrender. This time the Tsar tried to avoid turning him into a martyr: he allowed Shamil to live comfortably in a mansion on the outskirts of Moscow and gave him the opportunity to make the pilgrimage to Mecca, during which the miserly leader passed away in peace. His close associates, and even his sons, were drafted into the bureaucracy and the Tsarist army, going to constitute the first nucleus of a russified Caucasian ruling class and loyal to Russia. This policy of *appeasement* bore its fruits: for twenty years the Caucasus remained quiet, and the few rebellions that ignited remained local in scope, being easily suffocated by the imperial garrisons.

In any case, at the end of the 1870s, the fire of the revolt started to ignite again. A new Islamic preacher, *Albik Hajji*, succeeded in gathering an army of followers and occupied large areas of Chechnya, then poured into

---

[12]One of his passionate missives reads: *For years, O Honored Queen, we have been at war with Russia, our invader. Every year we must defend ourselves from the enemies that pour into our valleys. Our resistance is stubborn, we are obliged, in winter, to send our wives and children far away, seeking safety in the forests, where they have nothing, food or shelter against the severe cold. Yet, we are determined, it is Allah's will [...] we beg you, we urge you, O Queen, to help us [...].*

Dagestan. Again the tsarist army intervened in force, and between 1877 and 1881 reduced a large part of the country to rubble. The conflict caused tens of thousands of civilians and rebels deaths, but above all it interrupted the policy of tolerance adopted by Nicholas I after the surrender of Imam Shamil. The new Tsar, *Alexander III*, decided that coexistence between Russians and Caucasians was not possible, and ordered that the most rebellious among them be deported. The first to pay for this new doctrine were the Vaynakhs, who were deported en masse to Siberia and Central Asia. As we'll see, this radical measure would have "inspired" even more impressive and brutal actions during the 1900s.

In addition to the Chechens, the *Ingush* and the *Daghestani*, mountain peoples of the east, came under pressure the *Circassians*, the mountain peoples of the west. These were loaded en masse on fetid vessels and forced to emigrate to the Ottoman Empire, where they arrived decimated by the plague. To fill the gaps caused by the deportations, the Tsarist Empire sponsored a massive colonization of the region, sent a bevy of officials and promoted a vast modernization plan, building administrative offices, telegraphs, railways, wide roads that could be practiced all year round. The Caucasus became a viceroyalty, entrusted to a governor appointed directly by the Tsar.

From the Tsar to the Soviets

The advent of the industrial revolution, in the late 1800s, hit the newly pacified region. Some large oil fields were discovered around Grozny, and Chechnya soon became a major producer of black gold.[13]. The first

---

[13] Chechnya is one of the first places in the world where oil extraction has taken on industrial characteristics: the country's first

entrepreneurial class arose around the mining activity: the state orders for the construction of infrastructures and the wealth generated by the hydrocarbon trade produced the birth of a dynamic bourgeoisie, whose scions studied in Moscow or served in the Tsarist army. This nucleus of enriched citizens began to travel, to weave a network of commercial relations and political alliances, and some of its exponents reached the highest levels of the imperial hierarchy. For the first time a part of the Vaynakh society seemed to integrate with the Russian one, and it seemed that after centuries of war between the two peoples a relationship of trust and collaboration could be born. However, if the rich Chechen bourgeoisie began to have good relations with the center of the empire, the vast majority of the population remained hostile and suspicious, and badly digested the establishment of a modern state[14].

"modern" oil well was opened not far from Grozny in 1893, and since that time the Chechen subsoil has produced 420 million tons of crude oil. The discovery of vast superficial deposits, easy to drill and very productive, attracted the great European drillers (Shell in primis, but also French, German and Dutch companies) since the early 1900s. The owners of the local land were content to receive an annual rent in exchange for the right of the oil companies to exploit the wells. However, from the 10s of the 1900s some local entrepreneurs began to work on their own, building quite a fortune.

[14]Emblematic in this sense is the figure of *Abrek*, the brigand of honor. They were outlaws who by character or by necessity distributed part of the proceeds of their criminal actions to the people. Considered as bandits by the imperial authorities, they were idealized by the population because they attacked the state properties and those of the Cossack neighbors, then handing out the riches plundered to the poor peasants with whom they were hiding. The most famous Abrek of all lived between the late nineteenth and early twentieth centuries. His name was *Zelimkhan*, and he went into hiding in 1901 following a conviction for murder. After organizing a gang, he began to attack banks and post offices, emptying their coffers and distributing money to the mountaineers. His character became as popular as our Robin Hood: if he was the *prince of thieves*, Zelimkhan was the *ruler of the mountains*. To stop him, the Russian government arrested his family and placed a bounty of 18,000 rubles on his head, an exorbitant figure for the time. However, no

The development of industries did not only generate the birth of the rich bourgeoisie: at the same time a working class arose, with respect to whose claims the imperial government proved deaf and insensitive. In the second half of the nineteenth century the autocratic power of the Tsars, propped up on the great landed aristocracy and on the top cadres of the army, was violently shaken by the social upheavals unleashed by the bourgeoisie, flanked by workers and peasants. The imperial crown, initially reluctant to accept requests for social and political renewal, had to make some concessions, such as the *abolition of servitude* (1861) but the advent of reactionary emperors such as Alexander III before (1881 - 1894) and *Nicholas II* then (1894 - 1917) abruptly interrupted this phase of timid reforms. Social tensions began to increase again, and the first revolutionary organizations were born from the reformist front. In 1903, the maximalist current of the *Bolsheviks*, led by *Vladimir Lenin*, was born within the Russian Social Democratic Workers' Party. Initially a minority, the Bolsheviks increased their consensus on the ashes of the military defeats suffered by Nicholas II[15]. The starving and defeated masses were the human material with which the revolutionaries unleashed a wave of strikes and demonstrations that would take the name of the 1905 Revolution. The Tsar had to grant the constitution of a parliament, the *Duma*. However, once the revolts subsided, he began to weaken it to the point of paralyzing its activity and transforming it into a sort of imperial council.

---

mountaineer betrayed him, and he continued to rage until 1913, when the police finally managed to hunt him down and kill him.

[15] Between 1904 and 1905 Russia lost a war against Japan for the control of Manchuria, leaving on the field, in addition to the imperial prestige, fifty thousand dead, one hundred and twenty thousand wounded and eighty thousand prisoners.

Just nine years later the Empire found itself at war again, this time against Germany, Austria - Hungary and the Ottoman Empire. The Tsarist army suffered dramatic setbacks, and within two years Russia was faced with the real threat of being defeated again. The cities and the countryside became agitated again and the revolutionaries launched a frontal attack on the monarchy. In February 1917 a new revolution forced Nicholas II to abdicate, and in October of the same year the Bolsheviks took power.

The collapse of the monarchy rekindled the hopes of the Caucasian peoples to regain independence. On March 27, 1917, a few days after the Tsar's abdication, the first *Chechen National Congress* was held. It was animated by *Abdul "Tapa" Chermoev*[16], the young scion of a military family. His father was a general in the Tsarist army, and he himself had served in the Emperor's personal guard, before retiring to Grozny and successfully starting the oil extraction business. The Bolshevik revolution had found him again in the army, where he had been recalled following the outbreak of the Great War. Returning hastily to his homeland, he was convinced that only an independent Caucasian state

---

[16] *Abdul "Tapa" Madjid Bey Orsta Tchermoeff*, better known as *Tapa Chermoev*, was the first President of the North Caucasus Highlanders' Republic. The son of an army officer, he followed in his father's footsteps until he became part of the Tsar's personal guard. Thanks to the roles held by his father and himself, his family owned large land around Grozny, where prospectors found large oil reserves. Tapa Chermoev thus became one of the pioneers of the sector. Enlisted in the "Wild Division" (A cavalry unit made up entirely of Caucasian volunteers) in the First World War, at the outbreak of the October Revolution he returned home, where he tried to unify the Caucasian peoples in a state capable of actively opposing the spread of the Bolshevism. The North Caucasus Highlanders' Republic was born out of his energetic commitment but failed to gain international recognition at the Versailles Peace Conference. Lacking international support, the republic fell into the hands of the Red Army a few years later.

could save its people from Communism, of which he was a staunch opponent. A few days after the close of the assembly, the *Congress of the Mountain Peoples* was held, attended by representatives of almost all the peoples of the Caucasus. Chermoev tried to establish a unitary independence front, but his hopes were frustrated by the conflict that arose between the secular component of the Congress, in favor of the establishment of a secular republic, and the religious one, advocating a sectarian solution along the lines of the Imamate of Shamil.

The Bolsheviks entered into this diatribe, trying to bring the Caucasians to their side by exalting themselves in promises of autonomy and semi - independence among the most imaginative, even going so far as to guarantee the Islamic clergy the possibility of establishing Sharia law in the North Caucasus. The flirt of the revolutionaries was mainly motivated by the fact that a substantial part of the Russian army and bourgeoisie were forming a counter-revolutionary front. This had coagulated around senior officers such as generals Kornilov, Denikin, Judenic and Semenov, had formed his own army and with this attacked the provinces under the control of the Communists. In southern Russia the main obstacle to Lenin's victory was the Cossacks, always loyal to the crown and for this rewarded by the Tsars with large plots of arable land. The Reds promised the Chechens to distribute the land of the Cossacks, if the former allied with them. The Chechen peasants, galvanized by the promise of becoming landowners, sided with the revolutionaries and attacked their pro-Tsarist neighbors. These, for their part, tried to oppose the requisition of their properties, going to swell the ranks of the "whites".

While these events unfolded, Russia continued to be in arms against the Central Empires. It was necessary at least to close the external front, and the Bolsheviks decided to accept the onerous conditions of the enemy. On March 3, 1918, in Brest - Litovsk, Russia recognized its opponents control over Poland, the Baltic States, Finland, Ukraine and Transcaucasia (the region between the Great and Small Caucasus, currently occupied by Georgia, Armenia and Azerbaijan) . Seeing the Turkish army spreading just across the mountains, Chermoev made up his mind to put his political project into action. Thus was born the *Republic of Caucasus Highlanders*, with its capital in the Dagestani city of *Buynaksk* and Chermoev himself as President. It was a state that existed mostly on paper,

The intoxication of freedom did not last long: a few months later, in November 1918, the Great War ended with the defeat of the Central Powers. The Turkish garrisons garrisoning Transcaucasia withdrew, and Chermoev lost his main political supporter. The Republic of the Montanari remained isolated, and within a few weeks its territory was occupied by the "white" armies of General Denikin. The figure of Chermoev gradually lost its bite: in 1919 he was replaced at the head of the Republic first by a wealthy landowner, Pshemakho Kotsev, then by a former Tsarist general, Mikhail Kalilov, who preferred to dissolve it rather than fight his "colleague" Denikin, obtaining in exchange for the title of Governor of Dagestan. However, the separatists continued to operate, but credible enough to allow its leader to lead a delegation of ambassadors to Istanbul to gain recognition from the Sublime Gate.

Dreams of freedom did not last long: a few months later, in November 1918, the Great War ended with the defeat of Central Powers. The Turkish garrison withdrew from Transcaucasia, and Chermoev lost his main political supporter. The Highlander's Republic remained isolated, and within a few weeks its territory was occupied by the "white" army of General Denikin[17]. With the dissolution of secular power, the leadership of the resistance was assumed by the Islamic clergy. As we have already seen in its beginnings, the confessional party had opposed the constitution of a secular state. With the disappearance of the Republic of the Caucasus Highlanders, the Imams had a free hand in the proclamation of an *Islamic Emirate of the North Caucasus*, a confessional state inspired by the one established by Shamil seventy years earlier. The Emirate placed its capital in *Vedeno*, in the heart of Chechnya, and from there its guerrillas tormented the tsarists until, between the end of 1919 and the first months of 1920, the Red Army managed to repel Denikin and conquer the region.

At that point, many Chechens believed that the victory of the Communists would lead to the redistribution of the promised land two years earlier by Lenin and the establishment of Islamic law. In fact, as soon as the revolutionaries firmly took control of the Caucasus, they abolished the Emirate and established a mosaic of federated republics with the *Russian Soviet Federative Socialist Republic* (RSFSR), itself a member of the *Union of Soviet Socialist Republics* (USSR). Chechnya became, together with neighboring Ingushetia, part of the *Chechen-Ingush Autonomous Soviet Socialist Republic* (Chechen – Ingush RSSA). Land distribution was never mentioned again. Indeed, a few years later, in 1929, the Caucasus was chosen as the first territory of the Union destined to undergo *total collectivization*. The lands were expropriated

---

[17] The figure of Chermoev gradually lost its bite: in 1919 he was replaced at the head of the Republic first by a wealthy landowner Pshemakho Kotsev, then by a former tsarist general, Mikhail Kalilov, who preferred to dissolve it rather than fight his "colleague" Deniking, obtaining in exchange the title of Governor of Daghestan. However, the separatists continue to operate, fighting Denikin and his army.

from the owners, whether they were Cossacks or Chechens, and their lands were assigned to collective companies, called *Kolkhoz*, in which all citizens would have to work. The state would buy the crop at favorable prices, guaranteeing full employment in return. The project did not produce any tangible result except that of inflaming the Chechens, who had hoped for the victory of the Communists to finally become masters of the lands they worked, and who had instead lost even the few they had before the revolution.[18].

The uprisings against the regime kept Chechnya in turmoil throughout the 1920s and 1930s, and despite the Soviet police carrying out more than fourteen thousand arrests, Chechnya was never truly pacified. The rebels attacked public offices and collective companies, forcing the Soviet leadership to mobilize armed detachments to defend state infrastructure[19]. In 1939 this widespread revolt took on the connotations of an insurrection. At its head was the journalist and poet *Hassan Israilov*, whose arguments found fertile ground not only among the mountaineers, still enraged by the collectivization of their lands, but also among the intellectuals and the bourgeois, who in those years were undergoing a real and own decimation by the new leader of the USSR, *Josif Stalin*[20].

---

[18] Chechen resistance to collectivization was massive, according to historian Alexander Nekrich: *Chechnya did not have widespread private land ownership. Excluding some among whom this word had some sense, among those of the plains the sharing of land, water and forests was already in use, and the definition of Kulaki [wealthy peasants, persecuted by the Bolsheviks, ed.] Lost all meaning. Within a decade, collectivization resulted in the seizure of three-quarters of the arable land. However, the population boycotted the initiative en masse, refusing to work the common lands: just think that about 20% of the population never worked a single day in a Kholkhoz, while 46.3% worked just 50 in a year [...].*

[19] In 1938 alone, the Ministry of Interior recorded 98 *acts of terrorism* against local authorities. 44 of these caused fatalities among state officials.

[20] The Soviet dictator had initiated a series of measures, later called *purges*, to ensure the loyalty of the Communist Party and

Israilov succeeded in building a transversal front that brought together both religious leaders and those few intellectuals who had escaped persecution, as well as ordinary people who were fed up with Stalin's harassment, and in the spring of 1939 he took up arms against the government[21].

The rebels established their base in *Galanchozh*, a remote village perched in the mountains of the mountainous southwest. From here they began to launch raids against the towns downstream, managing to take control of large areas of the district of Shatoy. Their numbers, however, were insufficient to represent anything more than boredom to the regime, and their insurrection would have ended in yet another fiasco if Hitler's Germany had not invaded the Soviet Union.

Operation Lentil

While Israilov fought his little war against the USSR in Chechnya, the world was facing the tragedy of World

---

prevent its more moderate fringes from hindering its revolutionary programs. An essential part of these purges were the annihilation of any current that was not in line with his totalitarian vision of the USSR and the destruction of entire social classes guilty, he said, of plotting the counter-revolution. Between 1937 and 1939 the political police almost completely wiped out the Chechen intellectual class, and then raged on the same members of the CPSU and the army. Political violence pervaded the whole country: just think that, in the 1939 census, the Republic had almost ten percent fewer citizens than in 1937, net of the high natural growth rate of the population.

[21] As he proclaimed in a letter to the local First Party Secretary, Bykov: *For twenty years the Soviet authorities fought my people, trying to destroy them one group at a time. First the Kulaks, then the Mullahs and the "bandits", then the "bourgeois - nationalists". I am sure that the real goal of this war is the destruction of our entire nation. This is why I have decided to take command of my people in their liberation struggle.*

War II. In June 1941, Axis forces invaded Russia and were stopped at the gates of Moscow. In the summer of the following year, Hitler directed his sights on the Caucasus, trying to cut Stalin the oil supplies needed to move his armored divisions. The German avant-gardes reached the town of Malgobek, in the extreme west of the Chechen - Inguscia RSSA. Israilov issued an "appeal to the people" in which he invited the population to welcome the invaders as allies if they saw favorably the independence of the Caucasian peoples. For their part, the Germans tried to encourage the insurrection, in order to weaken the already tried Soviet defenses,[22]. However, there were contacts with the rebels, and Israilov seemed willing to collaborate with the new occupiers, making his men available against the anti-Nazi partisan resistance, in exchange for the promise of independence.

In February 1943, following the devastating defeat at Stalingrad, the Wehrmacht withdrew from the Caucasus, abandoning the Chechen rebels to their fate. Stalin's reaction was merciless. Towards the end of 1943, when Chechnya had returned to being the rear of the front, the Soviet dictator ordered the Minister of the Interior, *Lavrentji Beria* to deal once and for all with that turbulent people who, in the most difficult moment of the war, had not contributed adequately to the war effort of the USSR[23]. The question of the lack of loyalty shown by the

---

[22] *Operation Schamil* - Planned and implemented between August and September 1942, it involved sending small groups of commandos and saboteurs beyond the front lines. Their goal was to protect the oil infrastructure from planned destruction by the Red Army in the event of a withdrawal from Chechnya. In the summer of 1942 five groups of raiders, totaling 57 men, were parachuted over the front line. Some made contact with Israilov's anti-Soviet resistance, others occupied the refineries, assuming a defensive position pending the arrival of the German armored divisions. The failure of the summer offensive in the Caucasus and the formidable defense offered by the Russians in Stalingrad prevented the Axis units from advancing to Grozny.

Vaynakhs during the war was not very consistent, but it was also an excellent ideological umbrella to cover an "Ermolov-like" solution to the Caucasian problem at a time when the world was not interested in looking at what was happening in that corner of Europe.

Beria carried out Stalin's order with cynical professionalism: after bringing a brigade of NKVD agents to Grozny[24], ordered his men to collect evidence of the "betrayal" of the Chechens and their neighbors Ingush. The final report drawn up by the People's Commissars cited the presence of thirty-eight active religious sects, with about twenty thousand adherents, whose purpose was to overthrow the Soviet Union. Stalin's relentless executioner had already cut his teeth as a persecutor first in his native Transcaucasia (where he had administered the purges) then in Poland, and in the Baltic countries (where he had completed the purge of intellectuals and bourgeois) thus, after putting his military machine to the test by completing two "small" ethnic cleanings in Kabardino - Balkaria and in Karachai -

---

[23] Stalin's judgment did not take into consideration the sacrifice of tens of thousands of Caucasians in the battles that the Red Army had fought against the Germans: Chechens had been the first fallen of the Soviet army, heroically defended the position in the siege of Brest. Chechen was Khanpasha Nuradilov, a very skilled sniper during the Battle of Stalingrad and also Chechens would have been Movlad Bisaitov, the first soldier to meet the allies on the Elbe River and Hakim Ismailov, who together with his team was the one who hoisted the red flag on the ruins of the Reichstag. Over the course of the conflict, more than 1000 Chechens would be rewarded for their fighting actions.

[24] NKVD - *Narodnyj komissariat vnutrennich del* (People's Commissariat for Internal Affairs) was the organization responsible for state security during the Soviet period. Born from the ashes of the Tsarist imperial police, he took control of both detention facilities and branches of the police, including the notorious political police. The NKVD was the armed arm of Stalin's policy of terror. In 1946 the organization was transformed into the Ministry of Internal Affairs, while its political police section was renamed the State Security Committee, known as the KGB.

Circassia, he decided to develop that of the Chechens for the end of winter.

Between December 1943 and January 1944, one hundred and twenty thousand men between soldiers and NKVD officials were stationed in Chechnya, officially to support the reconstruction and prepare the harvest. Transport vehicles and freight trains were herded in military warehouses and railway stations, while soldiers set up garrisons across the country. In the night between 22 and 23 February, the so-called *Operation Lentil* began, which went down in history with the Russian term of *Chechevitza* and the Chechen term of *Ardakhar*: within a day three quarters of the entire Chechen people - Ingush were loaded onto trains goods and shipped to Central Asia. In the following days the same fate struck the last quarter. Anyone unable to move or resisting was executed on the spot.

Any resistance was useless. The villages in which they occurred were set on fire, and their inhabitants slaughtered. In the south of the country, where the snow was still deep and travel difficult, communists did not have too many problems forcing the populations to march in the snow to reach their destinations. The elderly, children and the disabled ended up shot or abandoned to their fate[25]. For those who got to the trains alive, a three-week death journey began. Crammed beyond belief in leaded wagons with no toilets, they set out on a three-thousand-kilometer journey across the snowy steppe, surviving on what little they had managed to take with them.[26]. Between 10 and 20% of the

---

[25] Particularly bloody was a massacre that many Chechens still remember today. In the village of Khaibakh, in the mountainous Galanchozh district, snow prevented any movement. But Beria's orders were clear and rather than disappoint his superior, the NKVD officer operating in the area, Colonel Gveshiani, ordered the elimination of anyone unable to cope with the march. Hundreds of people were gathered in a barn, where they were executed.

deportees died during the crossing. The survivors were dumped in bulk and forced to build themselves shelters and huts on the fringes of collective farms for which they would be the lowest form of labor. The Soviet government imposed compulsory stay on them. Every month the exiles would have had to report to the authorities and declare their presence, on pain of a 20-year sentence of forced labor.

Nothing remained of the Chechen - Ingushetia: the republic was dissolved, its districts were annexed to neighboring republics or transformed into Oblast, provinces without identity. All the cultural heritage of the Chechens was destroyed: mosques and Islamic centers were demolished, and their stones became building material. Even the stems that adorned the cemeteries were removed and used for the construction of houses, government buildings, even stables and pigsties. The *tyaptari*, the teip chronicles written on parchment and preserved by the elders, were burned or transferred to the Moscow archives. The depopulated country was filled with war refugees. From the regions most devastated by the conflict, hundreds of thousands of Russians were placed in a Grozny, which has now become a ghost town. Only a handful of survivors, who remained in Chechnya by chance or because they escaped their tormentors, continued to live in hiding in the Mountains. Israilov himself managed to escape arrest until December 24, 1944, when he was identified by the

---

[26] In a report to "Comrade Stalin" Beria wrote: *Between 23 and 29 February 478,479 people, including 91,259 Ingush, were concentrated and loaded onto trains. 177 trains have been filled, 152 of these have already been sent to the resettlement sites. […] 6,000 Chechens from the Galanchozh district still remain not rearranged due to heavy snow and the impracticability of the roads. However, their removal will be completed in the next two days […] During the operation 1016 anti-Soviet elements were arrested.* A few days later, in a second report, Beria reported that at the end of Operation Lentil, 650,000 people had been "successfully" deported.

police and killed in a shooting. For all the others, an ordeal began that would last thirteen years, until Stalin's death.

The deportees had to face the terrible conditions of nullity among populations who barely had to feed themselves. The death rate from disease and malnutrition soon reached dramatic levels. In the three-year period 1944 - 1947 alone, one hundred and fifty thousand people died, about a quarter of the population. The survivors lived in collective lodgings in which up to fifteen families were accommodated, mostly without stable employment and without resources. Those without a job wandered across the steppe in search of animal carcasses, or wild herbs, or tried to steal food from collective farms. Anyone who managed to get a job in one of these could hope to make ends meet:[27].

On hopes that the exile was a temporary punitive measure, and that sooner or later the central government would consider their guilt extinguished, the Supreme Soviet came to put a tombstone. In a special decree it was established that

In order to determine the accommodation regime for deported populations [...] it is to be considered perpetual, with no right of return [...].

The Chechens were forced to sign the decree one by one.

---

[27] In addition to food, there was a lack of clothes. In January 1945 the assistant to the President of the Assembly of People's Commissars wrote in his report: *The situation of the clothes and shoes of the special settlers has completely deteriorated. Even without taking into account all those who are unable to work, children are practically naked, and as a result disease causes high mortality rates. The absence of clothing prevents many of the healthy young people from being used in agricultural activities.*

The sons of Ardakhar

Deprived of their land and their customs, the Chechens tried to preserve their identity by handing down their stories orally and entrusting themselves to the elderly, who in the absence of anything else had become the only custodians of shared memory. Thanks to the traditions transmitted from generation to generation, Adat and Islam were kept alive in the uses and customs. The Soviet government tried to eradicate both, opening schools of ideological education and infiltrating the KGB among the Islamic communities, but the national sentiment of the Chechens did not fail and indeed strengthened in the resistance to the emancipation programs launched by the authorities. The distance from the homeland and the lack of written sources produced a simplified, idealized and mythologizing story, which would become the creed of that generation that would reach maturity in the early 1990s[28].

Among the hundreds of thousands of deportees who suffered the sad fate of exile was a child named *Dzhokhar*. He was born on February 15, 1944, nine days before Stalin ordered the deportation of all his people. Thirteenth son of Musa Dudaev, veterinarian, and his second wife Rabiat, he lived his childhood in a pariah community, considered unworthy to participate in the great socialist project, marginalized and closed in on itself. When his father died, leaving behind a large and resourceless family, his mother was allowed to move to the city of Shymkent in southern Kazakhstan, where the climate was milder and there was greater demand for

---

[28] As historians Carlotta Gall and Thomas de Waal have noted: *The experience of deportation was a collective experience based on ethnic criteria [...] Thirteen years of exile undoubtedly gave the Chechens, for the first time, the sense of a common identity. The proximity of the Chechens in the deportation has become legendary for themselves.*

labor. Dzhokhar, who had taken the dedication to study from his father, managed to complete primary school with merit[29]. With no higher education institutions available, he tried to support the family by working where possible, to bring home something that could alleviate his mother's fatigue. It was in this situation that the news of Stalin's death caught him. It was March 5, 1953, and the Chechens had been in exile for nine years.

The new Soviet leader, *Nikita Khrushchev*, launched a series of measures aimed at softening the iron fist with which the regime had governed the USSR in recent decades, which in the following years would take the name of *De-Stalinization*. The first step was to get rid of Stalin's loyalists, starting with the hateful Beria, who was tried and put to the wall within a few months to the delight of the Chechens and all the other deported peoples. The second was to forgive the enemies of the state that the tyrant had persecuted. From 1954, therefore, the status of *special settler* was revoked for all Chechens under the age of sixteen, allowing them for the first time to move from their forced home to work and study. In August 1955 this freedom was also recognized to teachers, to war decorated, to women married with Russians and to invalids. For all others the restrictions persisted, but the penalty for abusive abandonment of the settlements was reduced from 20 to 5 years of forced labor. The number of convictions dropped significantly, going from eight thousand in 1949 to just twenty-five in 1954.

Finally, on July 16, 1956, the long night of Ardakhar officially ended. By decree of the Supreme Soviet, the ban on returning to the lands of origin was officially

---

[29] Considering the fact that in those years only sixteen thousand Chechen children out of fifty thousand had access to some form of basic education, Dzhokhar Dudaev could say he was lucky to have had the opportunity to study.

lifted. On January 9 of the following year the Chechen – Ingush RSSA was re-established, to which all the districts that made it up were re-annexed except for one, that of Prigorodny, on the border with North Ossetia.

The Soviet government, aware that a mass return of Chechens would create many problems, tried to govern the phenomenon by setting up a sort of waiting list that would stagger the resettlement, but the impatience of Chechens and Ingushes to return to their homes was not negotiable and already in 1957, in the face of 17,000 authorizations, at least fifty thousand people returned home. During 1958 the exodus became torrential, with the return of 340,000 deportees, mostly without employment, education and economic resources, and by 1959 83% of the Chechens and 72% of the Ingush were on a permanent basis within the ancient borders. Local governments were unable to handle such a massive influx of people, and district governors asked Moscow for help.[30].

The ancient inhabitants of Chechen - Ingushetia turned into "immigrants in their own homes", ending up occupying the lowest positions of a social pyramid at the top of which were the Russians, to whom Stalin had given their houses and lands. This situation soon produced a sort of "apartheid" between the Russians, who held the monopoly of industry and administration, and the Chechens, who made up most of the agricultural

---

[30] Even in 1958, one year after Khrushchev's "forgiveness", only a fifth of Chechens had managed to obtain a home. For the others, makeshift lodgings remained in industrial complexes, in dilapidated huts or in the ruins of ancient farms on the plateaus and mountains. Even at the employment level, the situation remained critical for a long time: due to low schooling, most Chechens did not possess the necessary qualifications to obtain the best jobs in the country's factories and refineries, and the distrust with which local managers, all ethnic Russians, they looked at them made integration even more difficult. The school gap was very high: in 1959, compared to 8696 skilled workers of Russian origin, there were 177 Chechens occupying the same position,

labor or, at worst, were unemployed, forced to do seasonal work. underpaid and without protections[31]. It didn't take long before the friction between the two peoples escalated into violence: on August 23, 1958, an Ingush killed a Russian in a brawl. It was the spark that ignited an anti - Chechen pogrom during which dozens of people were lynched, some public buildings were set on fire and that only the intervention of the army was able to quell.

Obviously not all Russians opposed the integration of the Chechens. Many residents made some plots of their private land available to the new arrivals, and in the schools the teachers' efforts in the preparation of the young Chechens were great and selfless. The central government promoted the image of a Chechen - Ingushetia where cultural differences were respected and where different ethnic groups collaborated in the realization of socialism in peace and harmony. For this to be effectively achieved by Moscow, huge economic resources began to arrive for the construction of housing, schools, cultural centers and health services. In short, the budget of the Chechen-Ingush RSSA became dependent on the generous donations of Moscow, which came to represent even 80% of the public budget, triggering a phenomenon of financial dependence which, as we will see, would have given its bitter fruits thirty years later.

Soviet Chechnya

---

[31] The reader who wants to deepen the question of the Chechen economic system - Ingush in the Soviet period can find two detailed insights on the blog www.ichkeria.net entitled *The agricultural economy of ChRI*.

During the 1960s and 1970s, the general increase in the quality of life produced a well-being never seen before. Chechnya became a region with an industrial vocation: in 1969 there were 49 large factories capable of producing sugar, milk products, canned food, cement and electricity. However, the core business of the economy remained the production and refining of oil: Chechnya became the second largest extraction pole of the USSR, arriving in 1971 to supply 7% of the entire Soviet production, with an annual volume of 21,3 million tons of black gold extracted from the wells. A vibrant processing industry arose around the oil fields. Three large plants for the production of diesel, petrol and lubricants were added to the kerosene refineries (already established in 1910): in 1939 the first industrial refinery, *Sheripov*, was put into operation. This was followed by *Lenin* (1958) and *Anisimov* (1959). The opening of these three large refining centers allowed the Chechens to process not only their own oil, but also that coming from other regions of the USSR. The refineries could process up to 24 million tons per year, drawing supplies from the immense Siberian oil fields. Grozny, which until then had been a small to medium-sized city, experienced a real demographic explosion, going from 172,000 inhabitants in 1939 to 340,000 in 1970. The opening of these three large refining centers allowed the Chechens to process not only their own oil, but also that coming from other regions of the USSR. The refineries could process up to 24 million tons per year, drawing supplies from the immense Siberian oil fields. Grozny, which until then had been a small to medium-sized city, experienced a real demographic explosion, going from 172,000 inhabitants in 1939 to 340,000 in 1970[32].

---

[32] The reader who wants to deepen the question of the Chechen oil industry can find a detailed study on the blog www.ichkeria.net

To ensure a constant influx of skilled labor and support the integration between Russians and Chechens, the central government financed the construction of schools and colleges, so much so that at the end of the 1960s the Republic was able to reach an education rate above the Soviet average.[33]. The growth of cultural life went hand in hand: in the early 1970s there were 484 libraries, 400 cultural associations, 300 cinemas, three professional theater schools, two schools of applied art and a music school. 14 periodicals, 4 newspapers and two literary journals distributed around one million copies every day, almost one per inhabitant, while the local television station broadcast all day throughout the country. Participation in political activities and in the administration of the state also saw a clear recovery of the Chechen component over the Russian one: in the mid-1970s, 50% of deputies in local councils and a figure fluctuating between 12 and 19% of executives he was of Vaynakh origin. An amount still insufficient, but still much greater than ten years ago, when this barely reached 2%. In 1973, for the first time, a non-Russian was elected to lead the local Supreme Soviet[34].

It seemed that the conditions for peaceful coexistence among the populations that made up the ethnic mosaic of Chechnya were being manifested, to the greater glory of the socialist ideologues. This state of social calm was, however, very precarious: the shared memory of the deportation stirred souls under the slight patina of well-

---

entitled *The black gold of Ichkeria: Chechen oil.*

[33] In 1969 in Chechen - Ingushetia there were 569 secondary schools, capable of training 228,000 students, 289 specialization schools with 15,000 places available and two universities, one of which dedicated to the training of personnel for the oil industry, the Oil Institute of Grozny.

[34] It was the Ingush *Khazhibar Bokov*, elected on August 28, 1973, who held office until March 1990, being replaced by the Chechen *Doku Zavgaev*.

being that concealed all friction. To consolidate it, the Soviet regime intervened by proposing a new interpretation of the historical processes described so far, an artificial reinterpretation of the last three centuries of Russian-Chechen history in an integrationist function. The standard-bearer of this work of rewriting history was Professor *Vitaly Vinogradov*, author of the theory of Chechnya's "voluntary entry" to the USSR. He supported a revisionist thesis aimed at demonstrating how the elements of contact and collaboration between Chechens and Russians were by far the majority over the elements of division and conflict. According to Vinogradov, Russia, thanks to its cultural primacy, had emancipated primitive populations, leading them to civilization. The theory was quite odd, because it ignored or belittled the fact that for centuries Caucasians had openly fought the Moscow law, and it took all the professor's commitment and all the persuasiveness of the KGB to impose it on Chechen academics. If economic growth had continued to keep pace, the social architecture theorized by the communists would probably have led to some permanent results.

The arms race, the space race and all the other "races" that the United States was imposing on the USSR in those years began to wear out the economy. The Soviet Union spent enormous capital on maintaining its army, and the management of the political apparatus was equally expensive. The promotion of a sober and austere socialism was of little use: the ability of the central government to update its offer of rights, goods and services to the population was increasingly scarce. The economic machine, weighed down by an increasingly pervasive and inefficient bureaucracy, limited investments, and little by little the gap between Russians and non-Russians began to grow again. The most explicit reaction of the Chechens to this new departure from the economic and political summits was the recourse to civil and religious traditions: at the end of the 1970s, about five hundred mullahs were operating in the Republic, a veritable cultural protection network through which Adat developed in parallel with Soviet civil law. The ethnic consciousness of the Chechens, emphasized by Islam and the memory of the deportation, gave new impetus to the recovery of popular traditions, and during the 1980s these returned to predominance in the local culture. For its part, the communist leadership tried in every way to discourage social division: the publishing department of the USSR explicitly forbade any reference to the word "deportation" or "exile", but the memory of the exodus was still alive in the stories of the elderly who had survived, and the new generations expressed the desire to know, to know the truth[35] and to feel free to tell it in turn[36].

---

[35] Isa Kodzoev, leader of Ingush independentism which we will discuss in more detail later, explained his nationalist sentiment thus: It began when we were students at the pedagogical institute. All because we had been deported and wanted to know the truth. In 1944 my family numbered eleven. I buried them all, one by one, and went home alone. [...] After my first arrest in 1962 I told the judge that he was condemning me that I would fight Soviet power to the death.

[36] Interviewed in the early 1990s, a young militiaman named Ruslan said: *For me it all started at school. I knew from childhood what had been done to our people. But looking in all the textbooks there was no trace of the Chechens. There was talk of tribes, indigenous peoples, but not Chechens. We had a history teacher, Nazheda Nicolaevna. I asked her why the books cited the history of all peoples except ours, but I got a dirty look and no answer. The teacher's husband was a policeman, and a few days later he went to my father and told him I was asking too many questions. I knew that my grandfather was a Kulako, and that for this he was deported and died. His only fault was that he owned, together with his three brothers, two grain mills. They too were killed. My father was just nine when he was deported to Kazakhstan. He only got there with his mother, who died of hunger a month later. I always knew that if there was an opportunity I would fight. I was a born fighter.*

Perestroika

The gerontocratic leadership of Moscow responded to the need to change the system with deafening silence. The elderly and paranoid leader of the CPSU who succeeded Khrushchev, *Leonid Brezhnev*, seemed not to realize the gravity of the problem. Thus, while the USSR slipped into stagnation and accumulated a dizzying public debt, the state became rigid at all levels, corruption spread and the ruling class became more and more self-referential, unable to play the leading role that until then, with so much stick and with some carrots, he had covered. In particular, the Moscow government failed to make the country's economy, dependent on the export of raw materials, dynamize enough to compete with capitalist ones. Fluctuations in the prices of raw products, in particular of hydrocarbons, and the alternation of good and bad agricultural years produced frequent jumps in the economy. The government's response was to artificially calm prices by resorting to debt. The already tried public finances were being stressed by the rearmament race, in an attempt to keep the USSR in step with the United States.

In 1979 the Soviet Union invaded Afghanistan. What was supposed to be a blitz turned into an occupation conflict that tested not only the Soviet treasure but also the prestige of the Red Army. Precisely in Afghanistan we find that son of Ardakhar that we presented a few pages ago. *Dzhokhar Dudaev*, born a few days before the exile, had returned to Chechnya with his mother and his brothers immediately after Khrushchev's "forgiveness" in 1957. Having to bring home a salary he had found work as an electrician while continuing his evening studies. In 1962 he had managed to get accepted into the Tambov Air Force School. The diligence and the propensity to study had earned him the assignment to the 54th Heavy Bomber Regiment, at the Sjaykivka Air Force Base, in Kaluga Oblast. In 1968 he had taken the card of the Communist Party. The choice was not dictated only by the desire to climb the military hierarchy, which in those years did not look favorably on non-politicized elements (especially if of "suspicious" nationality like the Chechen one). Dudaev truly believed that a "reformed" socialism could overcome conflicts between peoples. In 1970 he had been transferred to the 1225th Heavy Bomber Regiment, stationed at the Belaya base. Within a year he had managed to enter the "Yuri Gagarin" Air Force Academy, attending the officer cadet course. After completing his studies he returned to Belaya, where six years later he obtained the rank of Deputy - Commander, then that of Chief of Staff and finally that of Regimental Commander. This had made him one of the few Chechens who mattered in the Soviet power hierarchy. During the invasion of Afghanistan Dudaev was deployed in command of the 185th Heavy Bomber Regiment[37]. In that capacity, at the end of the conflict, he was responsible for the orderly retreat of air units in his sector, earning a note of merit and being reassigned to command of an air force base for nuclear bombers near Tartu, Estonia.

---

[37] Many Chechens went into crisis when the Soviet Union, atheist or at most orthodox, began bombing the Afghan rebels, Islamic like them. In the Russian aggression they saw an attack on the freedom of that people, and the resistance of the Mujahideen as a re-edition of the revolt of Imam Shamil. Dudaev does not seem to have been of the same opinion, if it is true that he distinguished himself for the zeal with which he had the fortified villages of the guerrillas razed to the ground at least on two occasions. This information is however reported by the Russian Defense Minister Pavel Grachev and may not be true if we consider that this statement was issued at the outbreak of the First Chechen War, when the two were in command of two opposing fronts. The reader who wants do deepen the question che find an in – depth study entitled *Dudaev in Afghanistan: truth and lies* on www.ichkeria.net

Meanwhile Brezhnev was gone too, leaving *Juri Andropov*, a cautious reformer, in command of the Soviet Union. Under his short tenure, which lasted just sixteen months, tensions with the Western world increased, and his feeble attempts to rejuvenate the Soviet machine did not produce tangible results: military spending continued to rise, bringing the USSR one step away from collapse. Corruption and the black market became endemic problems, while the scourge of alcoholism spread among the demoralized and deprived ordinary people. After Andropov it was the turn of another gray official of the nomenklatura, *Constantin Chernenko*. His government was even shorter and irrelevant than the previous one: in his thirteen months of presidency, the elderly leader only managed to exacerbate tensions with the United States, ordering a boycott of the 1984 Olympics and further isolating the Soviet bloc. His death went almost unnoticed as, for some time, a new and interesting character, the 54-year-old *Mikhail Gorbachev*, had been making headlines.

This was a different leader from those who had preceded him. First of all, he was young: 54 years old, in a system devoted to old age, were relatively few. His charisma, his ability to empathize with people and, last but not least, his reformist thinking were the weapons with which he won his appointment as Secretary General of the CPSU, unanimously elected by an enthusiastic assembly.

His premise was honest: the cold war was being lost on all fronts and communism was in danger of collapsing on itself like a deflated balloon. His thesis was simple: the Soviet Union could not keep up with the West without possessing its own wealth and credibility. His plan, however, was nothing short of visionary. According to him, in order to achieve a "great economic leap" that would save the regime, a series of preliminary conditions had to be met: first of all, the end of the Cold War. If the USSR had stopped squandering its GDP on armaments and on the battlefields, it would have gained the freedom of maneuver it needed. To achieve this, it was necessary to resume negotiations with the West and initiate disarmament. For the West to be willing to reopen negotiations, however, the USSR would have had to look a little more like its opponent. The first step to trigger the happy chain of events hoped for by Gorbachev was therefore the realization of a "socialism with a human face", capable of giving a voice to the opposition and a new impetus to political life. Once the capital spent on armaments had been saved, it would have moved on to the creation of an economy based on market socialism: a vast plan of liberalization and the reintroduction of private property would have guaranteed greater productivity and constituted a class of entrepreneurs who would have led a big leap around the 2000s. The culmination of this restructuring (in Russian *Perestroika*) would have been the overcoming of the USSR into a new political entity made up of free and sovereign republics. The project was ambitious. In order to function, it was necessary for the Soviet people to understand and accept the need for change, giving the central government time to exploit each passage of the Perestroika as a function of the next.

The first measures were of an economic-social nature: Gorbachev invested enormous resources in the purchase of modern industrial technology from the West, however without the element of competitiveness, innovation lacked meaning. And indeed the updating of the industries was slow and ineffective. For these investments, the Soviet government had to resort to massive recourse to international credit. The expenses incurred went well beyond the budget, and shattered the coffers of the state, unable to cope with this gigantic pile of debts. The billions of rubles that left the internal economic circuit were added to the structural expenses for the purchase of cereals and other essential goods for the population. This resulted in high inflation, which made the ruble weaker and weaker on the currency market.

The USSR continued to spend more and more money trying to reverse a now irrecoverable economic collapse. No investment could have allowed the Union economy to support a gigantic army and an invasive party bureaucracy. But the new leader did not have the will to undermine the structure of power and was not yet willing to abolish the prerequisites of the Soviet regime: the planned economy and the one-party system. The result was that his economic plan exacerbated the shortcomings of the capitalist system without distributing the benefits: within five years the government, now devoid of liquid resources, lost the ability to maneuver. The periodic crises of over or under - production, which Moscow normally faced with generous pressure control,[38].

However, the most decisive interventions for subsequent events were those aimed at the democratization of society, called by historians *Glasnost* (Transparency). A series of measures ended under this name, from the release of political prisoners to the opening to dissent in the media, from the removal of restrictions on travel to the West to the recognition of the first non-communist associations. The loosening of control over the press and political initiative had an exponential effect: what could not be said before was shouted. Within a couple of years after the reforms

---

[38] At the fall of the USSR in December 1991, GDP would have been 17% lower than in 1980, and inflation 14% higher.

began, the political debate flared up, both in Russia and in the other countries of the Soviet bloc.

The resurrection of nationalism

In domestic politics, the decision to ease control over the press, to guarantee freedom to political opponents, to open state archives and to allow the development of independent news agencies generated a real political storm. While historians began to fill the so-called *blank pages* of the history of the USSR, that is, all those bloody facts that official historiography had buried in silence so as not to tarnish socialism, the first nationalist demands made their way among the people. The first republics to suffer the effects were the Baltic Republics, the richest and "western" ones of the USSR[39]. As in Chechnya, propaganda in these small nations had fabricated a myth of voluntary entry. In December 1986 the first major nationalist demonstration since the annexation took place in Riga, severely repressed by the police. Between 1988 and 1989 in all three republics civic movements compacted into a *Popular Front* that claimed independence and multi-partyism. Ten years earlier certain initiatives would have been bloodily suppressed, but Gorbachev wanted to give a signal of renewal and let the protest movements swell, gathering hundreds of thousands of supporters. Soon the phenomenon overflowed beyond the borders of the Baltic republics, affecting neighboring countries. Popular fronts were born almost everywhere,

With the rebirth of nationalism, the ancient territorial claims also arose, dormant but never dissipated. The

---

[39] Estonia, Latvia and Lithuania had been annexed to the Soviet Union in 1940, following the "Molotov - Ribbettrop" non-aggression pact between the USSR and Nazi Germany.

USSR was made up of more than a hundred subjects, many of which inhabited by small nations jealous of their identity. The explosion of nationalism produced the first local conflicts, and one of these ignited just a stone's throw from Chechnya, in the *Nagorno - Karabakh* region. This land was mainly inhabited by Armenians, but was part of the Azerbaijian Soviet Socialist Republic. The first frictions between Armenians and Azerbaijanis had already arisen after Stalin's death. The advent of Gorbachev sparked the claims of the Armenians, who were Christians, who feared a "cultural genocide" at the hands of their Muslim neighbors. Local intellectuals and politicians demanded that the schools be taught in Armenian, and that this be recognized on a par with Azerbaijani. By contrast, the Azeris claimed that territory as an integral part of their state and refused to grant Nagorno Karabakh such an autonomous status. Between 1987 and 1989 both fronts organized marches and demonstrations, while Gorbachev tried to bring the squares back to a negotiation. The protests soon turned into aggressions, and the first civilians began to displace.

On February 20, 1988, the fuse that would have sparked the conflict was lit: two Azerbaijani girls were raped by a group of Armenians. Two days later Azerbaijanis and Armenians clashed near *Askeran*. Two Azerbaijani boys died in the riots. A few days later, crowds of Azeris flocked to the town of *Sumgait*, a few kilometers from the Azerbaijian capital, Baku, indulging in three days of violence, rape and murder, in which at least 26 Armenians died. On March 1, the Soviet army entered the city and put an end to the riots, but the damage was already done, and in the following weeks the Armenian population's exodus from the country began. Between 1988 and 1989 hundreds of people were killed, and thousands forced to flee their homes.

Chechen Glasnost

The advent of Glasnost allowed for the first time the circulation of writings that recounted the deportation and other atrocities committed by the Soviets, bringing to the surface the memory of the Exodus and giving the first arguments to those who disavowed the theory of voluntary adhesion. In 1987, *Kavkaz* was born, the first cultural association dedicated to the preservation of the memory and identity of the Caucasian peoples. One of its main animators was *Bektimar Mezhidov*, a young law graduate, of whom we will discuss in detail in the following chapters. Kavkaz began to boldly refute the theses of Professor Vinogradov, introducing themes that until then had been categorically forbidden by the regime. In particular, he supported the position of academics who had been marginalized by universities because of their refusal to conform to the official historiographical position: first of all Professor *Hussein Akhmadov*, researcher at the Scientific Research Institute of Chechen - Ingushetia, author of numerous interventions contrary to Vinogradov's position and therefore sent, in 1985, to be a teacher in the small village of Dzhalka. A solid relationship of friendship and collaboration was born between Mezhidov and Akhmadov and would lead them to play central roles in independent Chechnya, as we will see later.

While the historical and cultural debate swept over the ruling class, the economic crisis wiped out the common people. The effects of Perestroika were making themselves felt strongly in Chechnya, exacerbating the structural shortcomings of society: in particular, the gap between Russians and Chechens had returned to increase, both in terms of income and in terms of access to work, education and services. This situation was made more hateful to the Chechens by the fact that the Russian-speaking minority was increasingly sparse, accounting for just a quarter of the total population. This was mostly urbanized in the capital, while the countryside was mostly inhabited by Chechens and Ingush. The two peoples, at the halfway point of the 90s, possessed some sad records: they were the least educated[40], the least employed, and the citizens with the highest infant mortality in the entire Soviet Union. The period of growth that Chechen - Ingushetia had experienced in the 60s and 70s was over.

A similar situation was recorded in the employment sector. The control of the most profitable economic activities was in the hands of the Russians, in particular those related to the extraction and refining of oil. Despite the country still producing 4 million tons of crude oil every year[41], that its refineries processed between 16 and

---

[40] In 1989 15.56% of Chechens did not possess any kind of school preparation, 13.32% had only a primary school qualification and only 25% could boast a diploma. Graduates represented just 5% of the population. according to the historian Dzhabrail Gakaev: *[...] Schooling in rural areas, where 70% of the indigenous population resides, records a very low level. There is a chronic lack of funds, teachers, services, textbooks [...] graduates from rural schools cannot compete with their parigrades who have attended schools in Russian cities. Consequently, the average education of Chechens is much lower than that of Russians [...]*.

[41] In the early 1980s, surface wells began to run out: by 1980 production had already dropped from 21 to 7.4 million tons per year, and five years later it reached 5.3 tons. Major technological investments would have been needed to revive the mining industry, but in those years the USSR was wallowing in insolvency, and the Soviet government decided not to allocate resources for drilling new wells and updating old ones. The drop in crude oil production had devastating effects on the local economy: at the beginning of the 1960s almost 70% of the budget of the Chechen - Inguscia RSSA was made up of oil revenues, and with the waning of this revenue item the Chechen treasury had to face the first liquidity crises. The Moscow government intervened by replacing the oil revenues with substantial financial transfers to the coffers of Chechen - Ingushetia: in this way the Kremlin prevented a disastrous economic crisis from affecting the republic but made the country dependent on aid from the central state. This welfare policy prevented the local economy

18 million tons and that the industrial center of Grozny was the first in all of Russia for the production of mechanical lubricants, almost all Chechens remained poor semi-illiterate farmers. Gorbachev's democratic opening brought their never dormant nationalism back to the surface, now further charged by the effects of the economic crisis.

The first protests against central power began in the spring of 1988 with a mobilization against the opening of a biochemical plant in *Gudermes*, the country's second city. A group of researchers led by engineer *Ruslan Ezbulatov* began holding meetings in which the dangerousness for the environment and for people of the production processes planned in the factory was disclosed.[42]. On May 22, the protesters gathered in an informal movement (so called by Soviet officials as it was not constituted within the Communist Party) and called a public demonstration for the next day. The result was a real mass rally attended by thousands of citizens. Some members of the CPSU tried to put a hat on the protest, taking the stage to speak, but were overwhelmed by the whistles and forced to leave. From that day on, almost every Sunday, for over four months, thousands of people gathered in Lenin Square in Grozny to demand that the biochemical plant be stopped. Meanwhile, the informal movement extended its influence throughout Chechnya.

---

from reconverting. Thus, while oil production was constantly decreasing (in 1990 4.2 million tons of crude oil were extracted, in 1991 4.1 tons, in 1992 3.6 and so on) the other economic sectors remained uncompetitive and unable to replace the old sources of income.

[42]Two years earlier, on April 26, 1986, the Chernobyl disaster had shaken world public opinion, and its echo had reached every part of the USSR. Since then, the Soviet authorities had relaxed their control over environmentalist popular initiatives, in order not to incur easy accusations of insensitivity to this issue. It was no coincidence, therefore, that the first anti-communist mobilizations took place under the umbrella of environmental protection.

Street demonstrations took place in Argun, Gudermes, Urus - Martan and Shali, and the first leaders began to emerge from the crowd. The first to emerge was the forty-year-old *Khozh Akhmed Bisultanov*, already enrolled in Kavkaz. Under his leadership the informal movement became a real political movement: inspired by what was happening in the Baltic Republics, Bisultanov formed the *Popular Front of Chechen - Ingushetia*.

Exquisitely political claims began to be added to the environmental protest: Bisultanov accused the leadership of the Republic of inefficiency, of disinterest in the needs of citizens and demanded that the gap in political representation between Chechens, Ingushes and Russians be bridged once and for all. Initially the regime reacted with the typical Soviet air, arranging the surveillance of the leaders and disavowing the Popular Front on television, branding it as an irresponsible and divisive force. The demonization of the frontists made them even more popular, and Bisultanov soon became the most acclaimed leader of Chechnya. Failing to tackle the problem, the government decided to go to de facto ways, ordering the arrest of Bisultanov and the other leaders of the Popular Front.

The popular victory against the Soviet police state gave way to a tumultuous process of democratic revival: now that the one-party system was reeling, everyone wanted to form a group, an association, a movement that would enrich the political landscape. At the end of 1988 the *Islamic Revival Party* was born, with the aim of bringing the values of Islam, denied and persecuted by state atheism, back to the center of the social life of Chechnya. Among its animators was the young journalist *Movladi Ugudov*, then a semi-unknown director of the dissident newspaper *Oriyentir*, but who would soon become one of the protagonists of independent Chechnya. In 1989,

Nijsho (literally "justice") was born, the association of Ingush nationalists led by the aforementioned *Isa Kodzoev*.

To contain the hemorrhage of consensus that was driving millions of citizens out of the CPSU, Gorbachev intervened by cracking down on the party, replacing the old veteran leaders with young administrators of more moderate views. The Chechen people demanded representation, and they were right: no indigenous had ever held one of the highest positions in the Party or in the state, which in Chechnya at that time were the First Secretary of the Party Committee and the President of the Supreme Soviet. The First Secretary was a Russian, *Vladimir Foteev*. The President of the Supreme Soviet was the Ingush *Khazhbikar Bokov*, whom we have already mentioned. It was decided to replace Foteev with an official of Chechen origin, so that both the Chechens and the Ingush would have their representative at the top of the Republic. The choice fell on an agricultural engineer, former Minister of Agriculture, *Doku Zavgaev* [43].

On February 7, 1989, the Regional Committee of the CPSU, in view of the planned rotation, published a statement in which, for the first time, it hoped for a radical political change[44]. For the first time in forty-five

---

[43] Born in 1940, he was a "son of the exodus", having been deported in 1944 along with his entire family. Back home he found a job as an elementary teacher, and then moved on to run a collective farm. In 1971 he embarked on a political career, first in the hometown district of Upper Terek, then in the central executive structures, as an agricultural production officer. He had held the functions of Director of the Association of State Farms, Minister of Agriculture, until he won the position of Second Secretary of the Party Committee.

[44] Published in the party organ, The Grozny Worker, it read: *The new political atmosphere, the Party's course towards democratization and the renewal of society, glasnost, allowed us to continue the work [...] to tell the whole truth about the illegal acts committed in the 1930s, 1940s and early of the 1950s, and of the illegal deportation of Chechens, Ingush and other peoples [...] the mass repressions that hit our peoples are a common feeling of every Soviet man, since it is difficult to find a family in our country who escaped this tragedy.*

years, the Chechens were able to freely talk about the tragedy they had endured. The seminars were attended by thousands of people, and the disconnect between the people and the leadership of the Republic seemed to be recomposed in the recognition of Stalin's sins. In July 1989 Zavgaev was appointed First Secretary of the Party, and the move seemed to be very happy: the Chechens enthusiastically welcomed the advent of one of their compatriots at the helm of the CPSU, and hailed the event as the beginning of an epochal turning point. . After decades of repression, it seemed that the Chechen people could take back their destiny.

CHAPTER 2

FROM ZAVGAEV TO DUDAEV

The Congress, proceeding from the natural, sacred and inviolable right of the Chechen people to self-determination, expressing the sovereign will of the Chechen people, aware of the historical responsibility for the fate of the Chechen people, as well as to create the necessary conditions for its further free development and comprehensive, taking care of the conservation and development of the Chechen ethnic group, respecting the rights and interests of all people of other nations

---

[...] *The plenum of the CPSU has decided to organize study seminars dedicated to the memory of the victims of Stalinist repressions for 17 - 18 February in the cities, villages and collectives.*

living in the republic, solemnly proclaims the state sovereignty of Nokhchi-cho.

From the Declaration of Sovereignty of the Chechen National Congress

Grozny, November 25, 1990

Radical reformists

The more time passed, the clearer it became that Perestroika was not working. The economic recovery was slow in coming and indeed, the economy had gone from stagnation to recession. The people were not interpreting Gorbachev's reforms as an opportunity to build a new socialism, but rather as an opportunity to get rid of the old one. Public opinion was divided in two: on the one hand there were the conservatives, supported by the bureaucracy, the party cadres and a part of the army who wanted to interrupt the reform plan in order to save the regime. On the other were the radical reformists, who instead pressed for an acceleration of Perestroika, and in order to see it realized they were willing to do without the USSR itself, if necessary. The first were gathered around *Egor Ligachev,* number two in the government. The latter were represented by Boris Eltsin, secretary of the Moscow section of the Party.

The clash between the two took place in September 1989, when Yeltsin put his resignation on the plate if the leader of the CPSU had not dumped Ligachev. Gorbachev did not feel like playing the requiem to the regime and kept his second in the saddle. Yeltsin did not take it well, but above all many Russians did not take it well, who saw in him the only man capable of saving them from the misery in which they found themselves[45]. A movement was formed around the radical leader that today we would define "anti-cast", which he intended to exploit to dismantle the system from within. Meanwhile the socialist regime was under attack from all sides. The worsening of the economic crisis inflamed the streets and gave arguments to those who, blaming the central government, demanded self-government. If the Baltic Republics had been the vanguard of the protest, now it crossed the whole Union, risking to blow the USSR into a thousand pieces. Gorbachev began to realize that he had wanted to do too many things all at once, but by now it was too late: the environmental protests had become democratic insurrections, led by the Popular Fronts. Within the fronts, then, new political subjects emerged, many of them of nationalist origin. The Soviets attempted to intervene by proposing autonomist reforms, recognizing local languages as official,

---

[45] In 1989 alone, industrial production contracted by 6%, inflation increased by 10% and the state began to resort to gold reserves to plug losses. The large commercial banks that Gorbachev wanted to turn to, to finance the modernization, smelled the smell of insolvency, began to refuse to grant loans.

sponsoring cultural revival and historical revisionism. That is, they tried to bring public opinion back into the Party enclosure. This run-up to popular favor, however, produced an equal and opposite effect: instead of strengthening consensus, the Soviet measures spread the belief that the system was failing. Independent associations multiplied and the protests took on a clear independence character.

The first to pass from words to deeds were the Estonians, led by the newly appointed leader *Vaino Valjias*. After deliberating the institution of the national language as the state language, on November 16, 1988 the Estonian Supreme Soviet promulgated a *Declaration of Sovereignty*, under which the laws of Estonia would be considered prevailing over those of the USSR. It was not yet a secession, but we were close to it. In the following days, Latvia and Lithuania also joined Estonia and similar initiatives were put in place in Georgia, Ukraine, Moldova and Belarus.

After the Baltic countries and the Caucasian republics it was the turn of the republics of Central Asia. In December 1986 there were violent demonstrations in Kazakhstan at the news that Gorbachev intended to replace the local President of the Supreme Soviet, *Konayev*, of Kazakh origin, with the Russian Gennady *Kolbin*. The protests had degenerated into urban warfare, with the death of two people and the wounding of another two hundred. The KGB intervened by arresting nearly five thousand people. In June 1989, inter-ethnic clashes broke out in Uzbekistan, which would soon bring the country one step away from civil war. In both countries Gorbachev replaced local leaders with figures appreciated by the population, but in this way he did nothing but accelerate the breakup of the USSR.

In the midst of all this, Yeltsin rode dissent and promoted further acceleration of reforms through his current, *Democratic Russia*. With this he wanted to challenge the conservatives in the first elections for a new political institution, designed by Gorbachev to further democratize the Union: the *Congress of People's Deputies*. It was a super - parliament composed of 2250 delegates, elected throughout the territory of the USSR, responsible for the appointment of the Supreme Soviet of the Union. The elections for the constitution of this new body took place between March 26 and May 26, 1989, and were the first in which candidates who were not members of the Communist Party could participate. For Yeltsin it was a triumph, as Democratic Russia won 600 seats, and the radical leader himself obtained 92% of the preferences in his constituency. His conservative opponent, Ligachev, was among the least voted candidates of all, along with representatives of the Soviet "old guard". The victory of the reformists gave the "light" to a new wave of demonstrations in Moldova, Ukraine and Belarus[46].

Meanwhile, inter-ethnic conflicts were intensifying. After Nagorno - Karabakh, of which we have already spoken, two other regions began to stir, *Abkhazia* and *South Ossetia*. Both were autonomous regions of the Republic of Georgia, and both claimed independence from Tbilisi. In March 1989 the Rector of the University of Shukhumi, the capital of Abkhazia, signed a Declaration of Sovereignty along the lines of that

---

[46]In Moldova, 16 newly elected nationalist deputies founded the Moldavian Popular Front, with which they brought three hundred thousand people to the streets demanding the re - institution of Moldovan as the official language and of the Latin alphabet instead of Cyrillic, once imposed by Stalin. In Ukraine, the sovereign Rukh movement moved towards the recognition of autocephaly for the Ukrainian national church. In Belarus, demonstrators began to publicly display their national flag, prohibited by law.

promulgated by the Estonians a few months earlier, together with a large number of exponents of the political and intellectual world. Only this time it was not a question of a rebellion against the Soviet bloc, but of a secession from another republic which, in turn, had declared its sovereignty. On September 20, 1990, after a series of street riots, South Ossetia also proclaimed its sovereignty, by promulgating a declaration of independence establishing the *Soviet Democratic Republic of South Ossetia*. The mechanism triggered by Estonia and tacitly accepted by Gorbachev was beginning to fragment the Soviet republics into a myriad of small ethnic states, in a process that, after the dissolution of the former Yugoslavia, would be called *balkanization*. And just as was about to happen in the Balkans, the central government in Georgia, then in the hands of the nationalist leader *Zviad Gamsakhurdia*, reacted by sending the army to suppress the uprisings. On 11 December, the Georgian National Guard besieged South Ossetia, preventing any movement to and from the region.[47].

The situation in Chechnya

As we have seen, Glasnost had produced the birth of informal alternative organizations to the CPSU, initially aligned with environmentalist positions and evolved into nationalist movements. To prevent dissent from overwhelming the Party, Gorbachev had tried to rejuvenate its leadership by promoting a crackdown on local leaders. In Chechnya, the choice fell on the former Minister of Agriculture *Doku Zavgaev*. He was considered

---

[47]The Georgian leader told the press: *The Ossetian people are garbage that must be expelled through the Roki [the mountain pass that connects Georgia to Russia, ed]. We will go to Ossetia and let the Ossetians submit and become Georgians, or, if they love the Russians so much, leave Georgia for Russia.*

a faithful official: he came from the village of Beno - Yurt, in Upper Terek, one of the most Russified districts of Chechnya located in the north, on the border with Russia. He was not a particularly authoritative-looking man, but the fact that he was Chechen was enough to make ordinary people appreciate him. He owed everything to the Party. Through the CPSU he had gone from working as a blacksmith in a collective farm to leading one of the most important ministries of the Republic. He seemed the right character to reassure the Chechens.

His appointment as First Secretary, however, was, in spite of himself, a detonator for nationalism. Convinced that the new leader would interpret the popular demands, the intellectuals were the first to get to work: having formed an *Association of Chechen-Ingush Intellectuals*, they organized for February 23, 1990, the anniversary of Ardakhar, a commemorative day entitled "The day of memory, the day of pain". Zavgaev was obviously invited to speak in front of all the newspapers. His speech began with the acknowledgment of the tragedy suffered by the Chechens at the hands of Stalin, something that until then had never been publicly declared:

We are gathered here today to commemorate the victims of repression, repression that had no basis. [...] Today we know that in the years in which Socialism was being built, Stalin was guilty of willfulness, he broke the Leninist principles in the politics of nationalities. This resulted in the infamous accusation of treason against entire peoples, which was followed by their deportation from the lands that had always belonged to them, the deprivation of a homeland, humiliation, through a real genocide [...]

Zavgaev's aim, however, was not to inflame the streets, but to bring dissent back into the Party. For this reason, once the epochal gesture of recognizing the crimes of socialism had been made, his speech turned towards a defense of its most humanitarian values:

Today, on this day of pain, we return with our thoughts to the steppes from Central Asia and Kazakhstan [...] we express our deepest gratitude to the thousands and thousands of Russians, Kazakhs, Ukrainians, Uzbeks, Kyrgyzs who have endured our tragedy [...] among all that tragic, humiliating and bitter we had to suffer, there are also moments of light, linked to people of different nationalities who in those terrible days gave us warmth, understanding and help. This is also our history, the history of relations between peoples [...]

Finally, commenting on the most recent events, in particular the nationalist uprisings that were driving entire republics into chaos, his speech became a call for moderation and the rejection of extremism:

Recent events [...] instead show us how deadly hostility between peoples can be. [...] Today we clearly understand that the success of Perestroika will depend on whether or not we manage to face the destabilizing forces that sow hostility among peoples. We say "no!" to interethnic hatred, we say "no!" to separatism, we say "no!" to all the forces that try to arouse mutual anger and suspicion among people of different nationalities, we say "no!" to nationalism! [...] The important thing now is to work, develop the economy and not allow extremists of any kind to lead people into conflict. It is the duty of every citizen [...].

The speech won the acclaim of the majority of public opinion, for its clarity and its sensibility. Zavgaev seemed to be able to interpret the dominant sentiment among ordinary people, and a front of consensus began to consolidate around him. Cleared by the words of the First Secretary of the CPSU, the revisionist debate on the crimes of Stalinism flared up[48]. By sponsoring the debate on the so-called blank pages of history, Zavgaev kept professors, academics and academics close to each other, and created the conditions for that generational change which the Party desperately needed in order not to be swept away by the democratization underway. In his personal political project there was, of course, the goal of lasting as long as possible, going through the crisis of the socialist system unscathed and acting as a point of reference for a new system: democratic, yes, multi-party, of course, but still dominated by his person, according to a semi - authoritarian model that would have represented the standard of the post - Soviet republics for a long time and which, in some cases, is still in force today.

The first problem, however, arrived early. As we have already said, heirs of the Vaynakh civilization are not only the Chechens, but also their Ingush "cousins", a population that hardly reaches 200,000 people and who lives between Chechnya and North Ossetia. They too, like the Chechens, had been deported, and on their return they had had to face the same difficulties, with one substantial difference: when Moscow had "forgiven" the Ingush, it had not allowed them to return masters of their entire land. A small district corresponding to the southwestern territory of Ingushetia had remained annexed to North Ossetia, because during the exile of the Ingush in that territory the capital of Ossetia, Vladikavkaz, was developed. with an imposing industrial district that now occupied a large part of that

---

[48]In July 1990 a long and accurate article by historian Nikolaj Bugaj entitled *The Truth About the Deportation of Chechens and Ingushes* caused a sensation due to the quantity and quality of historical sources cited. It summarizes unpublished documents, exchanges of information, transmissions of orders between Stalin and Berja. Official documents in which Stalin's establishment filed the succession of brutal actions in defense of the people carried out between the 30s and the 50s.

"unredeemed land". To avoid ethnic clashes, the central government had decided not to return the district, called *Prigorodny District*, to its legitimate Ingush owners. Now that Glasnost had allowed everyone to publicly vindicate their reasons, the Ingush were demanding that this historical wrong be righted. We have already mentioned *Nijsho*, the association of Ingush nationalists led by former dissident *Isa Kodzoev*. the Ingush wanted this historical wrong to be righted. We have already mentioned Nijsho, the association of Ingush nationalists led by former dissident Isa Kodzoev. the Ingush wanted this historical wrong to be righted. We have already mentioned Nijsho, the association of Ingush nationalists led by former dissident Isa Kodzoev.

While Zavgaev appealed to the Chechens asking them not to give in to nationalism, Kodzoev mobilized the streets precisely in defense of Ingush national sentiment. His reasons were based on the fact that, despite being part of the Chechen-Ingush RSSA, Ingushetia had remained on the fringes of economic and social development, having to endure for decades the fact that most of the investments, facilities and factories were concentrated Grozny, and therefore went to favor almost always Russians and Chechens, and almost never the Ingush[49].

Kodzoev's Nationalists pressed for Zavgaev to carry their demands to the central government, promoting the return of the Prigorodny District to Ingushetia. To prevent the problem from getting out of hand and to push the Ingush to dump the fiery Kodzoev, Zavgaev

---

[49] Gathered all the representatives of his little people in a National Congress, Kodzoev closed the assembly with this declaration: *The most important precondition for the preservation of any people is that it has its own form of national state [...] At the present time the main problem, the most serious problem for the Ingush people is the restoration of its autonomy. Without a positive solution to this problem, the people do not have, and cannot have, a full and normal life [...].*

solemnly promised to bring to the Congress of People's Deputies a law on the rehabilitation of oppressed peoples that recognized material compensation for the populations victims of Stalinism, to begin with the restitution of all land wrongfully stolen.

With the Ingushes calmed down for the moment, Zavgaev set about neutralizing the Popular Front. This, following Khozh Akhmed Bisultanov, was carrying out a series of demonstrations in which he called for the removal of the old party bureaucracy and the renewal of administrative offices. The importance of street mobilizations grew with the increase in unemployment: the effects of Perestroika were making themselves felt more and more heavily, especially on the weakest categories of the economic system. Among these were the seasonal workers, who among the Chechens were between one hundred and two hundred thousand people (10-15% of the population) and who now, left without subsistence, went to swell the ranks of the unemployed, and therefore of the demonstrators.

Zavgaev sensed that if he had managed to intercept the claims of all these people and if he had personally made them political guarantor, he would not only neutralize the opposition, but would also create a "private" consensus pool to be played in the eventuality, more and more concrete, that the USSR collapsed and that multi-partyism became a reality: at that point having a container of personal support to put in place would have allowed him to remain in the saddle even without socialism. So shortly after coming to power, the new First Secretary ordered the dismissal of 7 district secretaries, as well as many party leaders and local officials. The gesture was perceived as a revolutionary crackdown, and Zavgaev's indexes skyrocketed.

The replacement of the secretaries removed the main claim from the Popular Front and laid the foundations for its disappearance from the political arena. Now it was a question of giving a final push by settling the Ingush issue once and for all. On November 4, 1989, the Congress of People's Deputies approved a declaration on the recognition of the illegality of all criminal acts against peoples who have undergone forced deportation. It was not yet a rehabilitation law, but we were close to it, and its publication was greeted with enthusiasm by most of the citizens.[50]. Zavgaev was at the height of popularity, and in March 1990 he had two unique opportunities to capitalize on it in seemingly definitive political success. The first was the election for the renewal of the Supreme Soviet of the Chechen-Ingush RSSA. Candidate as the successor of the Ingush Khazhbikar Bokov, he succeeded in obtaining the support of the majority of the delegates, bringing together the highest executive office of the Republic in addition to the highest office of the Party. Passing from triumph to triumph, shortly after he managed to win a place in the Congress of People's Deputies, at the end of March 1990.

The statute of the Congress provided that every year one fifth of the seats would be renewed, to guarantee a constant updating of the political balance in the Union. The ongoing clash between the conservatives and the radical reformists made these renewals a real arena, in

---

[50] The actions carried out by Zavgaev to shore up his consensus also extended to the religious and social spheres. For the sake of brevity, we summarize them in the notes. At the confessional level, Zavgaev sponsored the birth of religious institutes and the opening of new mosques, sponsored the first official pilgrimage to Mecca since the USSR, promoted the establishment of an Islamic Council and the creation of two institutes of Islamic culture in Nazran and in Khulkaloy. On a social level, the new First Secretary promoted an ambitious social housing plan which nevertheless remained on paper and was never implemented.

which the various currents attacked each other with no holds barred. The strong man in Congress was, as we have seen, Boris Yeltsin, and once again his political proposal was hailed by millions as a great hope for Russia. Yeltsin proposed to establish the Presidency of the Russian Republic, removing the authority to legislate from the Supreme Soviet and effectively emptying the USSR of any effective power. The elections rewarded his proposal and a few days later the Congress deliberated the constitution of the Presidency of the Republic and the appointment of Yeltsin as President. He wasted no time, and immediately issued a Declaration of Sovereignty on the basis of which the laws passed in Russia would prevail over those passed by the Supreme Soviet. In this way the Soviet Union, which had already lost control over European states, and then over its own federated republics, also lost its center.

Zavgaev, a candidate in the ranks of the CPSU, managed to get a good position and get himself elected deputy. His run, however, was disturbed by another rising star of Chechen politics, Professor *Ruslan Khasbulatov*. He was a professor of law at the University of Moscow, authoritative and appreciated among intellectuals and held in great esteem by the nascent petty bourgeoisie. A member of Gorbachev's entourage, he oversaw numerous bills for him, earning a certain reputation both in the palaces of power and among the common Chechens. Zavagaev's growing popularity did not please Zavagaev at all, and he began to regard him as his main political opponent. The result was a series of squabbles of public relevance, so that in the congressional elections the challenge between the two became central to the political debate. In the end both were elected to the Assembly, but the bitterness between them persisted, heavily influencing, as we shall see, the Chechen events that would soon be unleashed.

The birth of parties

Contrary to what Zavgaev wanted, the exhaustion of the Popular Front did not lead to the disappearance of the opposition. Bisultanov's movement was the incubator of more structured political realities with more ambitious goals. In July 1989, the political-cultural association *Bart* (literally "Unity") was born from a rib of the Front. It was a nationalist-inspired grouping, and animated by a young writer, *Zelimkhan Yandarbiev*. His name was inspired by that of the famous "brigand of honor" we talked about in the first chapter, and this speaks volumes about the family background in which he grew up. Born in 1952 in Kazakhstan, he graduated in Grozny in 1981, and then devoted himself to poetry and literature, reaching leading roles in the cultural associations of the CPSU. Given his knowledge in journalism and academia, Yandarbiev was able in a short time to make contact with financiers and collaborators, who allowed Bart to regularly print a party organ (also called Bart) thanks to which to propagate the idea of an independent and sovereign Chechnya. It was during one of his trips to find financiers and supporters that the future leader of Chechen nationalism met Dzhokhar Dudaev.

He was in Tartu, where we had left him, in command of a nuclear bomber division[51]. When the two met,

---

[51]For what the Estonians remember Dudaev was highly appreciated by the common people: he made the military participate in civil life and made the provisions of the garrison available to the population during popular festivals. In June of that year, Estonia had reintroduced the national flag, and Dudaev had had a huge one thrown from the sky to celebrate the event, greatly unnerving the high commanders.

Yandarbiev realized he had found a perfect testimonial for his political campaign. The fact that Dudaev was a general was in itself something more unique than rare, given the difficulty with which the Chechens managed to climb the Soviet hierarchy. However, he had something more than just a nice uniform: he had a magnetic personality, a passionate speech and a natural authority, all qualities that if properly conveyed could have made the difference in a political landscape dominated by greyness and mediocrity.

Returning to his homeland, Yandarbiev found a rather fluid situation: Zavgaev had taken control of all the main structures of power, and the pervasiveness of his person was beginning to generate the first discontent. Within the CPSU itself, some personalities hostile to his figure began to work to constitute currents of opposition, and the recent quarrel with Khasbulatov had made this fact known to all.

The young nationalist intellectual thus decided to transform Bart into a real political party, an alternative to the CPSU but not as politically confused as the agonizing Popular Front.[52] Thus was born the *Vaynakh Democratic Party* (VDP), a nationalist organization that supported the country's full independence from Russia and was in favor of building a confederation of the peoples of the Caucasus.[53] Among the main points of his political

---

[52] In the early 1990s the Popular Front ran out of political drive and its main animators attacked each other for control of the movement. Bisultanov himself was accused of embezzlement in November 1990, only to be reinstated by Zavgaev at the helm of a public company and disappear from the political arena. Shortly thereafter, the Popular Front itself would split into numerous smaller groups, and then disperse.

[53] Hand in hand with the establishment of the Vaynakh Democratic Party, Yandarbiev animated the organization of the *Mountain Peoples' Congress*, a re-edition of the one organized by Tapa Chermoev in 1918 and animated by the same objectives. The Congress was held in Sukhumi, Abkhazia, and brought together all

program were the repudiation of state atheism and the reintroduction of religious law, as well as the reconstitution of the "Popular Council" of medieval memory, the so-called *Mekh - Khel*, of which we spoke in the first chapter. Initially presented as a "responsible opposition" to the Zavgaev government, the VDP soon became the main aggregator of dissent outside the CPSU.

In the wake of Yandarbiev's party, numerous other acronyms were born. The first was the *Green Movement*, an environmental faction led by professor of physical and mathematical sciences *Ramzan Goytemirov*. Shortly after, it was the turn of the *Dosh* ("Word") movement, an expression of intellectuals and a liberal orientation. On May 4, 1990, the *Chechen Social Democratic Party* was born, of which one of the members was *Timur Muzayev*, a brilliant journalist whom we will discuss in detail later. The moderate conservatives formed the *Movement of Civil Harmony*, in favor of multi-partyism and the maintenance of federal ties with Russia, while the Islamic Renaissance Party, founded two years earlier and now present on a permanent basis in Grozny, made its way among the radical parties. and surroundings, and the party of the *Islamic Way*, headed by former Interior Ministry official *Bislan Gantamirov*. The ethnic minority of the Cossacks, fearful of the growth of nationalist parties and fearful of a secession of Chechnya from Russia, founded their own movement, and so were Kodzoev and the Ingush radicals, who organized themselves in the *Ingush Democratic Party*.

---

nineteen Caucasian nationalities. The constitution of a unitary political party was discussed that would represent the instances of the Caucasians in Moscow, but the inter-ethnic frictions we have already mentioned prevented the idea from materializing. However, it was agreed on the establishment of a *Caucasus Peoples' Assembly* that would prepare the ground for the birth of a confederation of independent states.

As we have said, a lively political debate was also taking place within the Communist Party. The March 1990 elections to the Supreme Soviet had brought into the political arena strongly critical of the establishment. Among the newly elected critics of the official line was the aforementioned Hussein Akhmadov, a university researcher who was dismissed from Vinogradov because of his articles contrary to the theory of voluntary adhesion and now returned to the fore thanks to those same writings. In the "government" field, then, a figure made his way destined to be, albeit unwittingly, one of the "trojan horses" of independence: *Lecha Umkhaev*. This was a civil officer raised in state construction companies, and like many moderate exponents of the CPSU did not look favorably on the centralization of power that Zavgaev had achieved between the end of 1989 and the spring of 1990. His current was called *Sovereignty*, and aimed to incorporate not only the discontented communists, but also moderate nationalists who, at the time, remained outside the official political structures. For this to happen it was necessary for him to be able to keep one foot inside the Supreme Soviet and another among the "informal movements" that claimed representation and democracy. Thus it was that Umkahev proposed to hold a *Chechen National Congress* to which not only the representatives of all the parties, but the delegates of every single village in the country were invited.

The idea was a great success and was endorsed by everyone. It was supported by nationalist parties which, far from wanting to be cannon fodder in the power struggle between Zavgaev and Umkhaev, were counting on Congress to build a recruiting base, it was supported by intellectual associations.[54], who saw in the Congress

---

[54]In addition to the multiplication of political parties, 1990 saw

an opportunity to hold a major cultural event celebrating Chechen identity. It was even supported by Zavgaev, who hoped to take control of it and prop up his power even more firmly by basing it on popular sentiment, as well as on the authority of the Party and the state. Thus it was that when, in August 1990, Umkhaev proclaimed the constitution of an *Organizing Committee of the Congress,* enthusiastic adhesions came from all parts of the national political landscape. The Committee began its work on August 15th[55], publishing a declaration of intent[56] in

---

the birth of numerous intellectual associations, including the *Association of Ingush Scientists*, the *Association of Representatives of the National Intellectuality* and the *Association of Historical Researchers of Chechen - Ingushetia.*

[55] The *Organizing Committee* for the convening of the Chechen National Congress was officially constituted on August 15, 1990. Lecha Umkhaev, who had first put forward the idea, obtained the presidency. It was joined as executive members by *Yusup Soslambekov*, one of the leaders of the Vaynakh Democratic Party, the historian *Dalhan Khozhaev*, the professor and poet *Apti Bisultanov*, the writer *Musa Beksultanov*, the writer, poet and playwright *Musa Akhmadov*, the sportsman *Chingiz Zubairaev*, the historian and deputy of the Supreme Soviet *Yusup Elmurzaev* and professor of historical sciences *Ganga Elmurzaeva*, among many others. Both members of the Soviet nomenklatura and members of radical nationalism, such as Zelimkhan Yandarbiev, joined the Committee. In addition to these joined Hussein Akhmadov, of whom we have already spoken. To learn more about the subject, please refer to the specific articles published on www.ichkeria.net and to its sections *National Congress of the Chechen People* and *Nomenklatura*.

[56] The Declaration said: *The Chechen nation, which constitutes about 60% of the population of the Chechen – Ingush RSSA and 3% of the population of the RSSA of Dagestan, has been deprived of the material basis for normal development for many decades, and has been discriminated against even in its land . [...]The delay of the central government in solving the Chechen problem, the presence of over 230,000 Chechens forced to live outside their national state, the social and economic crisis that attacked Chechnya - Ingushetia, the need to relaunch the national language and preserving the spiritual and religious heritage, which has put on the agenda the problem of restoring the autonomy of Ingushetia, the aggravation of inter-ethnic relations in the country, poses a whole series of specific national problems to the Chechen people, such that without their resolution it is impossible to guarantee its development as a nation. Under these conditions a group of people's deputies, members of the state from all parts of Chechnya, formed an organizing*

which there were published a list of 13 objectives that the Congress set out to achieve: among these there were historical-cultural objectives, such as an account of the history and formation of the Chechen ethnic group but also political ones, such as the creation of mechanisms capable of guaranteeing integrity territoriality of Chechnya and the ethnic unity of the Chechen nation and above all the opening of a discussion on the idea of creating a sovereign Chechen republic[57].

The declaration of intent of the Organizing Committee was in some ways a programmatic charter. The idea of a sovereign republic was well rooted in both the moderate and radical components of the Committee. None of the organizers of the Congress appreciated the current state of political subjection of the country towards Russia. First of all because this translated into a sort of paradoxical social, cultural and political apartheid, for which the Chechens found themselves the poorest, least educated, least employed and least represented. The state of "autonomous republic" prevented the full development of Chechen culture, allowed the imposition of an artificial historical truth for the use and consumption of the ruling class, it prevented the Chechens from giving themselves a form of state that adhered to their traditions and their religion, it even prevented them from speaking their language freely or writing it in al alphabet that represented all its phonetics[58].

---

committee, taking on the responsibility of convening and holding a Chechen People's Congress.

[57] The full text of the declaration can be found at www.ichkeria.net in the *National Congress of the Chechen People* section.

[58] Before the advent of Stalin the theme of the alphabet to be used to correctly transcribe Chechen phonetics had been widely debated, and the need to use the Latin one emerged, considered more elastic than the Cyrillic one in relation to the articulated grammar of the Chechen language. With Stalin's rise to power and even more so with his deportation in 1944, Cyrillic was imposed as a state alphabet, in Chechnya as in all republics. The issue was

Faced with this fact, everyone, moderates and radicals, agreed, as can be seen from the Committee's program.

The conflict, in effect, was not over whether or not Chechnya should be a sovereign republic, but over what use of this sovereignty it should make. For the moderates, this would have allowed Chechnya to negotiate a new federative pact with Russia on an equal footing[59]. For the radicals, sovereignty would have been the premise of the country's full independence which, eventually, could have formed a Caucasian confederation with the other republics of the region, and free itself once and for all from Russian domination.

The Congress

The organizational machine set in motion. 1000 delegates would have participated in the Congress: 839 of these would have been elected by the Chechens on a district basis, in the number of 1 deputy for every 1000 inhabitants. To these were added 55 delegates representing the diaspora abroad[60]. Prominent personalities from the political, academic and scientific world would also have intervened. It would take at least 3

---

particularly felt in Chechnya, because Cyrillic prevented effective transliteration of many Chechen phonemes.

[59] As we said earlier, the point of arrival foreseen by Gorbachev's Perestroika was the overcoming of the USSR in a new confederal subject based on the free accession of free and sovereign republics. This subject would have been established with a federal agreement signed by each of the independent and autonomous republics that wished to sign it. The debate around this issue was very heated, since if only one of the republics in question had refused to sign the agreement, all the scaffolding behind it would run the risk of collapsing. As we will see below, Chechnya's refusal to pursue negotiations for the signing of the agreement will be one of the main reasons for the outbreak of the First Chechen War.

[60] On www.ichkeria.nett he list by territorial shares of all delegates to the congress is available. The list can be found in the *National Congress of the Chechen People* section.

days to complete the program. Financing such an important event, providing for the accommodation of all those present, their food and some form of recognition for the work done was not easy. Important funds were needed, and the Organizing Committee started looking for financiers. The result was excellent: thanks to the support of citizens, institutions and the foreign diaspora, the Committee managed to collect double the amount necessary. By mutual agreement, it was decided to set up a *Fund for the Revival of Chechen Culture* to which the surpluses would be conferred. The young writer Musa Akhmadov was appointed to the presidency of that fund.

Once the organization was structured and the liquidity to hold the meeting was found, the Organizing Committee began to design the organization chart of the executive bodies of the Congress, that is, of those offices that were to direct it, develop its contents in a political program and supervise on its implementation by the Supreme Soviet. In this way, an Executive Committee of the Congress (*Ispolkom*) was designed to act as a "government" and a coordination center that was responsible for translating the interventions of the speakers into motions and proposals to be put to the vote. The work would be overseen by a President and, in his stead, by two Vice-Presidents. The appointments of the leaders of the Congress would be made by the Executive Committee, which would begin to operate at the opening of the assembly.

In September 1990 everything was ready. Only one unknown weighed on the Organizing Committee: the presence of the Ingush neighbors at the Congress. Although, in fact, these were not technically Chechens, they belonged to the same ethnolinguistic family, and the two peoples were culturally so close that it was almost impossible to distinguish between them. The overwhelming majority of citizens of both nations were in favor of preserving the Chechen-Ingush state unity, and even if the evolution of the political situation seemed to lead to a completely different direction, the will to launch also prevailed among the members of the Organizing Committee. a political signal in a unified sense. The fact was that the Ingush, for their part, were struggling with the Law on the Rehabilitation of Oppressed Peoples, which in their hopes would lead to the reinstatement of the Prigorodny District. Uhmkaev and three other members of the Supreme Soviet decided to reassure the Ingush by organizing a summit meeting with the leadership of North Ossetia, in order to put the issue on the plate even before the Congress took place. The meeting was held in Vladikavkaz, the capital of the Ossetian republic. The Ossetians declared themselves willing to cede all the part of the Prigorodny district east of Vladikavkaz to Ingushetia, but not their capital, on which ¾ of the republic's industrial potential insisted. Both sides agreed to set up a joint commission that would begin negotiations as soon as possible. Umkhaev and his men thought they had reached a good compromise agreement, and headed to Nazran, capital of Ingushetia, to confront the local irredentist political forces. The Ossetian proposal ran up against the stubborn refusal of Kodzoev and the radical nationalists, who demanded the restitution of the entire district with no ifs and buts. Faced with this total closure of the Ingush, Umkhaev was left with nothing but to start the work of the Congress without their participation.

In view of the event, each speaker summoned his own: Zavgaev mobilized his court of officials and administrators, among whom were not a few relatives and numerous fellow villagers from Upper Terek, Umkhaev lined up the exponents of the intellectual and university world. Yandarbiev framed the leaders of his party, but he also worked to convince Dzhokhar Dudaev to intervene in Congress: he had made such a good

[61] Voice of Chechnya - Ingushetia, number 78 of 24 November 1990. The newspaper also published some excerpts from the most popular speeches:
Mahmud Wappi(Syria) Strong old man with short hair and gray mustache. [...] Speaks Chechen well, with a characteristic Arabic accent. Law. Of particular interest is the history of the peoples of the North Caucasus in the Middle East. [...] "We have an interest in everything that happens in the Soviet Union, mainly, of course, in the land of our ancestors. [...] Now I'm sure my people are starting the countdown to self-awareness and true national recognition. I hope the awakening of Chechen citizenship, language, culture, customs and traditions that have spanned millennia is coming. I wish it with all my heart. " Mahmud Wappi is a descendant of Chechens who emigrated from the Khasavyurt district. He has visited us many times and dreams of moving here. He is now retired. In Damascus he had a pretty good school with 500 students and three dozen teachers. He has four children. Adele and Islam are graduates of the University of Damascus, mechanical engineers. Arif and Imad are doctors, a therapist and a surgeon. [...]. Said Beno(Jordan) A road and housing construction technician, former Minister, and now owns a consulting firm. "On the agenda of the Congress I see issues of history, culture, inter-ethnic relations and the revival of ancient popular traditions. Of course, I did not participate in the writing and preparation of this program, but it fully fulfills my aspirations and hopes. I came to the congress not only to hear what was to be talked about, but also to personally take part in its work. I brought a letter to read here. In it, I propose to organize in Grozny a cultural center for relations with Chechens living abroad. I have the dream of collecting in this center everything that is written on the history of my people, on their culture, on their connections. This material can be found in the Soviet Union and abroad. And for this I will not spare my strength. " Abdulatip Beno(Jordan) [...] "Language unites people" he says. "And the strength of the people is only in unity. We probably would not have survived in our troubled lands if we had not sought unity and mutual support. [...] I am a soldier. I know how fatal the threat of ethnic hatred is. In no case should this be allowed, and there are already incidents in the [Soviet, ed] Union. The Chechens have never made sure to take what is someone else's; they stood out for their genuine hospitality. [...] "Abdulatip Beno is the first Jordanian Chechen to rise to the rank of General. He was a military attaché from his country in Moscow, has now resigned and is retired. Shamil Shaptukayev(New Jersey, United States) Contrary to the traditional belief that all Vaynakhs abroad, especially in a country like the United States, are "special" people, he has worked as an excavator all his life, and he knows how much worth the money. [...] "There are about 300 Vaynakh families in America [...] In their history, our people have never ignored the needs and concerns of our neighbors, they have always tried to help as much as possible. So we in the United States have created a special committee to strengthen ties with the Caucasian peoples. [...] "

impression on him on his last trip to Estonia, and with his high military rank he could have been a good forerunner for his speak.

On November 23, 1990 the city circus opened its doors for the long-awaited demonstration. The building was impressive, but not large enough to gather the flood of delegates, guests and spectators who thronged at its gates. Many citizens who rushed in at the last minute had to stay outside, and the organization installed loudspeakers to allow the excluded to hear the speakers. At 10:00 the notes of the opening hymn, written by the musician Ali Dimaev, resounded inside and outside the building. The official flag of the Congress was displayed on the central stage: a green banner of Islam crossed by two red bands and one white, surmounted by a crown of 9 golden stars representing the Tukkhum of the Chechen nation. The first day was dedicated to greeting the authorities, issues of historical and cultural interest and the interventions of the representatives of the Chechen diaspora. The newspaper "Voice of Chechnya - Ingushetia[61]"Reported the salient passages in an article of the following day:

Yesterday the National Congress of the Chechen People opened its proceedings. Participants include representatives from all cities and regions of the Republic, guests from neighboring regions and independent republics. The diaspora of the Chechen communities living in Central Asia, Moscow, Leningrad and other cities of the country (of Russia, ed.), As well as our comrades from Jordan, Syria, Turkey and the United States also arrived at the Congress. [...] The audience is packed. Many of those who want to attend the work of the Congress are left outside the building. Speakers were installed on the street for them.[...] 10 in the morning. Play the Chechen anthem. The first to speak are the popular poet A. Suleymanov, the famous writer A. Ajdamirov, Professor K. Chokayev of the State University. The President of the Supreme Soviet of the

Chechen-Ingush RSSA (Zavgaev, ed.) Gives a short opening speech. The opening procedure ends, and the members move on to the practical work. The first block of reports is dedicated to the history of the Chechen people. This broad topic is treated by historian I. Akhmadov and Vice-President Elmurzaev. There are many dramatic pages in the ancient history of the Chechen people. They are the Caucasian War, the period of the Civil War, the years of the so-called collectivization. Of course, the most terrible tragedy is the Ardakh of 1944. The history of the Chechens has been mystified, rewritten by order of the authorities. [...] The speakers and moderators of the debate discussed the social and economic situation in detail. It was pointed out that Chechnya - Ingushetia, once the most developed Republic of the Northern Caucasus, is now far behind other regions of the USSR in terms of material well-being, social and spiritual development of its population. [...] "

The second day began in political confrontation between the various souls of the Congress. Zavgaev, who received the opening speech, referred to the delicate situation in which the Soviet Union found itself, appealing to the calm and moderation of the Chechens, asking for their confidence in managing the delicate transition from the socialist system to multi-party democracy. Then it was Umkhaev's turn, and his speech was more heated. After a long opening on the history of the Russian - Chechen conflicts, his speech turned on the need to rebuild relations between Grozny and Moscow starting from a mutual recognition of difference and co - dependence, opening a debate that did not see Chechnya as a periphery of empire, but as a partner in a new, major political project. The debate remained heated but calm until Yandarbiev, in the middle of the day, pulled out his "ace", making the Major General of the Aviation Dzhokhar Dudaev stand on the podium. When Dudaev spoke, his speech was overwhelming. Having overcome by a leap the prudence of Zavgaev and the moderation of

Umkhaev, he faced with passionate prose the theme of the awakening of traditions, he spoke of how to give substance to the project of an independent and sovereign Chechnya. His conclusion, then, was exciting: looking up at the sky with dreamy eyes, he solemnly declared:

We will create an independent Chechen state, we will create an army that knows how to defend it, and that knows how to defend our freedom!

No one knew him before that speech. The next day all Chechnya praised him. For the nationalists it was a triumph (even if Yandarbiev would have preferred to have achieved it) for Umkhaev a half fiasco, mitigated only by the fact that it was even more so for Zavgaev, who intervened in Congress to take control and ended up being put in shadow from that half-unknown officer who had stolen the show. The last of the three days of Congress was dominated by the figure of Dudaev, and the agenda was dictated by the political proposal he proclaimed.

Following the General's promise, DVP leader Yusup Soslambekov proposed that the Executive Committee of

---

[62] Unfortunately, there is no authentic copy of that document left[62], and the only source we can draw from is a recording of Democratic Party leader Vaynakh (VDP) and Congressional Executive Committee member Yusup Soslambekov. It is possible that the final document did not differ much from the version below, which is a transcript of his speech to Congress. A transcript of that recording is available at www.ichkeria.net in the *National Congress of the Chechen People* section.

[63] The newspaper Voice della Chechnya - Ingushetia would comment as follows in the next edition: *The Chechen National Congress will go down in history as a significant turning point in the path of the nation's spiritual, moral and cultural awakening [...] the three days of Congress will be forever inscribed in the annals of the Chechen people. Justice, Freedom, Unity. These are the slogans of the Congress, these are ideals close to each lover of their homeland. [...]*

the Congress promulgate a *Declaration of Sovereignty* and ordered the Supreme Soviet to accept it[62].

On the evening of the third day the assembly broke up with thunderous applause[63]. To give continuity to the work of the Congress it was decided to set up an Executive Committee to coordinate the activities of the various work commissions that had been organized during the three days, and to prepare a second session to be held by the summer of 1991. Dudaev was called to the presidency, ousting the favorite Umkhaev, former president of the Organizing Committee. However, being Dudaev on duty in Estonia, and not being able to deal directly with the daily activities of the Committee, it was decided to appoint two vice-presidents, expressions of the two souls of the assembly: the moderate one, a follower of Umkhaev, and the radical one, represented by Yandarbiev . The two leaders thus became the executive authorities of the Committee. For Zavgaev there was no "spoils".

In an attempt to regain lost ground, the First Secretary called an extraordinary session of the Supreme Soviet. On the streets, people were talking about Dudaev and independence, and Zavgaev had to take matters into his own hands before the nationalists monopolized the debate. Not being able to oppose the Declaration of Sovereignty and not wanting to be torpedoed, he took the initiative and presented "his" Declaration of Sovereignty to the Soviet. Following the indications of the Congress, the Soviet would replace the Chechen - Ingush Republic RSSA with an independent and sovereign Chechen - Ingush Republic. The motion was anything but symbolic: if in fact the states that had launched similar declarations until then were independent entities, united with Russia in the USSR assembly, Chechnya - Ingushetia did not have the status of an independent republic, but of an autonomous republic united with Russia by a relationship of juridical subjection. The declaration presented by Zavgaev, therefore, not only cast doubt on Chechnya's participation in the Soviet Union but subverted the relationship it had with the Russian "mother republic". generating a juridical short circuit quite similar to a real secession. Faced with the initiative of the First Secretary, most of the historical members of the Supreme Soviet raised lively protests: the long debate preceding the vote revealed how an action of this kind could have generated a civil war, or even an armed intervention by Moscow to protect the territorial integrity of Russia. In the end, however, the draft Zavgaev submitted won the majority of votes. or even an armed intervention by Moscow to protect the territorial integrity of Russia. In the end, however, the draft Zavgaev submitted won the majority of votes.

The document, while aligning itself in principle with the positions expressed by the National Congress, and defining Chechnya - Ingushetia as a state independent and sovereign, differed in both form and substance:

The Supreme Soviet of the Chechen Republic - Inguscia, which expresses the will of the people, aware of the historical responsibility for the fate of Chechnya and Ingushetia and of their national sovereignty, respecting the rights and interests of all ethnic groups living in the Republic [...] solemnly proclaims the state sovereignty of the Republic [...] and declares the decision to create a democratic rule of law "

First of all, the interests of all ethnic groups residing within the borders of the republic were guaranteed, openly rejecting the prospect of an ethnic Chechen state in favor of one *multi-ethnic, legal and democratic state*. This concept was also reiterated in point 3 of the declaration, which said: *The holder of sovereignty and the source of state power in the Chechen Republic - Inguscia is its multinational people [...].* Article 7 then made it clear that no party or organization could in any way replace legitimate government structures: *No political party, public organization [...] can speak on behalf of the people of the Chechen Republic - Inguscia. Only the Supreme Soviet, the highest authority in the Republic, has the right to speak on behalf of the people [...].* Therefore, no body, not even a national congress, could have aspired to replace the established authority.[64]. And with that the Ingush were also settled. Or at least so Zavgaev believed, underestimating the fact that they saw the independence of the Republic as smoke and mirrors, fearing that once the separation took place Moscow would never support their irredentist ambitions. He had proof of this a few days later, when he met the leaders of political organizations to discuss the next steps to be taken to follow up on the Declaration of Sovereignty. On that occasion the Ingush representatives expressed all their disappointment at a considered gesture*unhappy and inappropriate. Zavgaev tried to recover them to his cause, reminding them that the question of a secession was absolutely out of the political calendar, and that the declaration had the sole purpose of placing on the plate of federal negotiations a bargaining chip with which to "buy" Prigorodny* .

In doing so, however, he set himself against the DVP nationalists, who intended to pursue the goal of full independence, and who did not fail to covertly threaten the First Secretary. Yandarbiev, who spoke on the matter, declared:

---

[64]The text quoted: *The Republic confirms the just request of the Ingush for the restoration of national sovereignty and the need to solve the problem of the return of the territories that belong to them, stolen following the repressions of Stalin, in the Prigorodny District and in part of the territory of the Malgobek District, as well as the right bank of the Ordzhonikidze (Valdikavkaz). The Union Treaty will be signed by the Chechen Republic - Ingushia after the question of the return of the alienated territories to Ingushetia has been resolved.*

> *We thank Zavgaev and the institutions of the Chechen-Ingush RSSA for such a decisive step, which they took in the political struggle for the independence of the Chechen people. [...] To achieve this it is necessary to consolidate all the political forces of the people [...] we did not expect such courage and determination on your part. You and your deputies have proved to be much better than expected.*

His speech, however, ended with a clear warning:

> *If the Supreme Soviet continues to show itself as a supporter of state sovereignty, if it acts in the direction of concretizing the content of the Declaration, we are ready to be its most loyal and disinterested allies [...] But if it secretly or explicitly betrays the declaration adopted, thereby betraying way the interests of the Chechen people who responded trust in it, the VDP will start the most ruthless of struggles [...].*

From day to day Zavgaev became increasingly clear that his choice to pursue dissent by bypassing it with a move of great political impact had placed him in an even more delicate position than before: the various forces that made up the jagged Chechen-Ingush political landscape were conflicting with each other, and it was increasingly difficult for the First Secretary to keep them all at bay: the Chechens wanted independence and the Ingushes. they wanted to negotiate a new federative pact. Everyone, in any case, could not bear that only he was in power, and they railed against his government, whose clientelist aspects and populist attitude were not lacking. At the end of 1990 all the parties in favor of his removal from power gathered in the *National Movement of the Chechen People:* both the radicals of the VDP and the moderates of Umkhaev, who in the meantime had formed his own political movement called *Daimokhk* ("Homeland"), converged there. This great popular coalition launched its first mass demonstrations in December 1990: in those months the last bars of the confrontation between Iraq and the United States for control of Kuwait were being consumed. The Chechens supported the Iraqis, Muslims like them, and sided en masse on the side of the dictator Saddam Hussein. The government responded with police charges to unauthorized demonstrations organized by VDP militants, in a climax that increased every day.

At the beginning of 1991 it was clear that Zavgaev no longer had control of the squares, and that his effective authority was only in the palaces of power. The favor of the common Chechen had abandoned him, and the center of gravity of Chechen political life had passed from the Supreme Soviet to the National Congress, whose militant expression was the National Movement. Here, the clash between moderates and radicals was in full swing: the former pushed to make Congress a sort of shadow parliament and the Executive Committee its shadow government. The latter, on the other hand, tried to bring the confrontation back to legitimate institutions, where they had greater support and more favorable numbers. Umkhaev and Yandarbiev competed for leadership, but neither could prevail over the other. The tip of the balance in this matter would have been the "honorary president" Dudaev. It was him that the Chechens had looked to since November 1990: his duties of service had forced him to return to service in Estonia, but he could soon take the field and keep his promise to return.

So the two Vice-Presidents went to Tartu. They both thought the General was a malleable character, but they soon realized they didn't understand what he was made of. Dudaev procrastinated for a few weeks. Then, at the end of March, he dissolved his reservations and returned to Grozny, taking the leadership of the Executive Committee. He supported Yandarbiev's line, who begged him to return to his homeland and convene a second session of Congress in which to declare the Supreme Soviet lapsed, with respect to Umkhaev's line, which instead wanted to stall and buy time to strengthen his position, perhaps conquering the mandate of negotiator in the talks between Chechnya and the central state. The support that Dudaev gave to Yandarbiev, however, was not unconditional: he demanded the leadership of the radical front.

Once Dudaev sided with the National Movement, there was no more match for Umkhaev. He, like many of his followers, was organic to the Supreme Soviet, and the events that followed one another, both in Chechnya and throughout the Soviet Union, were undermining the credibility of this institution. It was easy, therefore, for Yandarbiev to present him as a "fifth column" of the Zavgaev regime in Congress, and push him and his men to the margins of the Executive Committee.

The second session

While the complex political match between Zavgaev, Yandarbiev and Umkhaev was taking place in Chechnya, in Moscow the confrontation between Gorbachev and Yeltsin was reaching the decisive clash, represented by the presidential elections, scheduled for June 12, 1991. If Nikolai Ryzhov, the Gorbachev's candidate, had won, Yeltsin would have disappeared from circulation and the radical reformists would have suffered a bitter defeat. If Yeltsin had won, the Soviet Union would have disappeared. The latter, for his part, blew the fire of popular anger, leading an electoral campaign based on the acceleration of reforms and the dissolution of the

Union. One of its most important areas of consensus was represented by the autonomous republics and by those that had declared their sovereignty, and towards them his slogan was *take all the sovereignty you can swallow!* With such an invitation, it was clear that anyone who hated the centralist methods of the USSR and the Russian population in general would support his candidacy.

In January 1991 Yeltsin made a stop in Estonia for his propaganda tour. In Tallinn he appealed to the Soviet garrisons not to oppose the claims of local nationalists, obtaining the support of General Dudaev. The two did not know each other yet, but the general went to the Radio to share Yeltsin's appeal, declaring that he would never allow his men to shoot peaceful demonstrators. A real friendship was born between the two[65]. The rumor began to circulate in the presidential candidate's entourage that the regime's top officials wanted to shoot down the plane on which he was traveling. Terrified by the idea, he decided to return to Moscow by car: Dudaev then made his personal car available to him, making sure that he returned unharmed. The radio statement in which Dudaev publicly declared his insubordination was enough to convince his superiors to resign him. Thus it was time for him to leave the Red Army and return to Chechnya to lead the National Movement.

Meanwhile in Grozny, Zavgaev was trying to regain the initiative, scoring at least some concrete results. The process that began on November 4, 1989, with the declaration promulgated by the Congress of People's Deputies on the recognition of the illegality of all criminal acts against peoples who have suffered forced

---

[65]Among the Soviet high commanders this meeting was experienced with great apprehension. In the Party offices it was commented: *Now Yeltsin not only supported the rebels, but also gave them the nuclear bombs!*

deportation should have already ended with the adoption of a rehabilitation law. of oppressed peoples, but the goal still seemed far away. The Ingushes had lost faith in him and had become agitated again. In early April 1991 there were the first clashes with the Ossetians and the Cossacks, with dead and wounded[66]. Zavgaev intervened both indirectly, holding meetings with moderate representatives of Ingush nationalism, and directly, delivering a public speech in which he declared:

"The dramatic events that are taking place in various areas of the country [...] instill deep alarm for peace and harmony in our common home. Irresponsible elements [...] who deal with political hooliganism [...] try to lead us on the shameful and bloody path of inter-ethnic conflict [...] If we set out on that deadly road, which is proposed to you by instigators, political adventurers, social demagogues, , inhabitants of a small republic, we will be involved in a huge tragedy of blood, which no nationality, no citizen can bring anything but pain and suffering."

The situation was becoming explosive, and the First Secretary had to find a solution that would avert an inter-ethnic confrontation. Isa Kodzoev and the radical nationalists held permanent garrisons in Nazran, and even in Ossetia the situation was heating up. Worried by the threats of the Ingush, the Ossetian Supreme Soviet proclaimed a state of emergency, mobilizing the militia of the Ministry of the Interior. Finally, on April 25, the *Rehabilitation Law for Repressed Peoples* was officially approved by the Congress of People's Deputies[67]. The

---

[66]In the village of Kurtat, in the Prigorodny District, there was a brawl between young Ossetians and Ingush, who vied for a plot of land that until 1944 had been owned by an Ingush family, and which was then assigned to an Ossetian. Numerous injuries had been registered. A few days later some Ingush clashed with a group of Cossacks: 8 people died and another 15 were injured.

[67] The Rehabilitation Act was a long and complex document. We will dwell on the most delicate passages, referring to articles 2, 3 and 9: *Art. 2 - Peoples are recognized as victims [...] towards whom, according to the criterion of national belonging, a policy has been pursued at the state level of slander and genocide, accompanied by their forced deportation, the distribution of their national-state formations, the remaking of territorial borders and the imposition of a regime of terror and violence in the places of deportation. Art. 3 - The rehabilitation of peoples victims of repression implies the recognition and realization of their rights to restore their territorial integrity [...]. Art. 9 – The damages suffered by the peoples who are victims of repressions by the State will be compensated [...].*

[68] In his speech on the occasion of the promulgation of the law, Zavgaev said these words: *The Supreme Soviet, by approving the law, accepted all our indications and corrections. The necessary conditions are created so that all those who suffered repression during Stalinism can return to the places of their centuries-old memory [...] not a few efforts have cost the delegation to reach the exclusion of the point that proposed the solution of the territorial question only according to the municipality agreement of the interested parties. Such a point would have practically excluded the possibility of a complete restoration of trampled justice* . Zavgaev referred to the proposal made by the Ossetian delegation to proceed with the restoration of the territories only by mutual agreement with the current occupants.

[69] In the note drawn up by the Ministry of Nationalities, he read: *People are worried about the possible revision of the borders of republics, between regions, between provinces, between inhabited centers. A dangerous situation is being created in the relations between the RSSA of North Ossetia and the Chechen-Ingush RSSA (and within the latter between the Chechen and the Ingush side). In fact, in 1957 Ossetia returned only 4 of the 5 provinces that had been annexed to it in 1944. Within the borders of Ossetia, the District of Prigorodny and some plots of land remain, on which the Ingush have claims. Vice versa, three provinces confiscated from the Stavropol Krai were attributed to the Chechen-Ingush RSSA [...] the Akkinzy of Dagestan [a population of Vaynakh origin living in the nearby Daghestani RSSA, ed.] they demand the restitution of the previous geographical denominations, that their ancient houses be freed, but today they are inhabited by Lakl and the Avars, deported against their will [...] if the law were observed to the letter, the Autonomous Republic of Germans of the Volga should be restored, a decision considered negatively by the populations of Volgograd and Saratov [...].*

[70] The choice of date was certainly not accidental: a few days before the elections, no candidate, much less Yeltsin, would have dreamed of responding to a political action by Congress by threatening armed retaliation or asking for the arrest of his delegates. Moreover, given the overwhelming superiority of Yeltsin over the other candidates, a statement in a sovereign sense would have been fully in line with what has been said more than once, and certainly he could not have taken his word back without losing credibility.

of emergency and Zavgaev was able to breathe a sigh of relief: he had achieved his first real political victory. He could not have known, then, that it would also be the last.

Upon approval of the law, Zavgaev was pleased that the institutions had accepted the criterion of restoring territorial integrity, as requested by him to protect the rights of the Ingush.[68]. In reality, as it was written, the law could lead to very little concrete. Already in July the Ministry of Nationalities pointed out that the application of the law would force local governments to rearrange entire populations to restore the ancient rights boasted by oppressed peoples. To right the wrongs done at the time with the deportations, in essence, new deportations should have been carried out[69]. It was not long, therefore, that Zavgaev's apparent triumph deflated in the face of the inapplicability of his proposals.

Meanwhile Dudaev had returned to Chechnya, and together with Yandarbiev was preparing to take control of the Executive Committee of the Congress (the so-called *Ispolkom*). Both were convinced that it was necessary to transform Congress as soon as possible into a platform of political action not parallel to the Supreme Soviet, but against it. Yandarbiev and the radicals imposed themselves in organizing the second session of the Congress. It was supposed to take place between 8 and 9 June 1991, 4 days before the Russian presidential elections took place[70]. If the first Chechen National Congress had been a kind of people's assembly and had been guided by the desire to testify to national identity in all its forms, the second should have been the gathering of the National Movement. A purely political, indeed, revolutionary event. For this reason Yandarbiev decided that it would be held in a structure with a high symbolic value such as the dramatic theater of the city, one of the most beautiful buildings that Grozny could then offer. The event should have once and for all incensed Dudaev and his followers as the political leaders of the nation, which is why Congress should have shown a granite audience, faithfully aligned with the positions of its leaders. Thus, for the most part, delegates of proven nationalist faith were summoned to the gathering, and Umkhaev himself, leader of the moderate faction, he found himself deprived of his right to access the assembly and to intervene. Of the nearly 900 delegates elected at the first session, only 400 were reconfirmed, while another 200 were accredited without having received any popular mandate. What would be discussed at the congress, which was pompously renamed the National Congress of the Chechen People (OCKhN) was easy to imagine: two weeks earlier, on May 25, Dudaev had publicly declared that the Supreme Soviet had lost all political legitimacy following the Declaration of Sovereignty, and that no body could have inherited its powers better than the National Congress. On June 8, the second session of the Congress began. In front of an audience largely made up of his followers, the General pompously declared:

> *"The revenue vital to any empire are the colonies, one of which is our Chechnya, which has been cruelly exploited for a century and a half. The imperial machine, with the help of the apparatus of violence, has deprived our people of religion, language, education, science, culture, natural resources, the right to freedom and life. The Chechen people have chosen their own path by unanimously deciding to establish a sovereign state, entrusting the responsibility for the implementation of the decisions of the Congress to the Executive Committee. "*

Lecha Umkhaev, who had barely managed to be readmitted to the assembly with a handful of followers, was able to speak only to see that the audience he was addressing had no intention of following him. After accusing Congress of betraying its political mission, he presented a declaration signed by thirteen members of the moderate current[71] in which, with bitterness, he testified to the failure of his project[72].

---

[71] The document was signed by Umkhaev and his supporters, among whom we find some characters who would have written the immediately following history of Chechnya: Yusup Elmurzaev, delegate of Urus - Martan who would have fought for all his life the Dudaevites, Adani Osmaev, exponent of the old guard of the CPSU, Magomed Gushakaev, who would become Vice - President of the independence parliament in November 1991 as well as others (G. Elmurzaev and S. Khunkerkhanov), also deputies to the Supreme Soviet. In addition to them, representatives of both the Soviet and the Congress signed the congressional delegates Yunusov, Ibrahimov, Akhmadov, Satikhanov, Dzhanaraliev, Arsunkayev, Guzhayev, Bakaev, Gamaev Daduev and A. Khadyrov (who has nothing to do with the famous Akhmat Kadyrov which we will talk about later).

[72] *"[...] The congress designated as its main objective the search for ways to further consolidate and build a Chechen sovereign state [...] To ensure constant monitoring of the decisions taken by the Congress, the Executive Committee was elected, entrusted with the functions of research of the modalities of implementation of the decisions of the Congress through the legislative and executive authorities. From the earliest days of its work, the Executive Committee [...] has divided itself into two distinct positions regarding the policy aimed at achieving this goal. The first position was characterized by a tendency clearly aimed at creating parallel power structures, and an attempt to impose one's own beliefs, declaring them the only correct and representative of the will of the people [...] The Executive Committee of the Congress, which has been defined as the highest legislative and executive body, has recently opposed the Supreme Soviet and the government. There are situations in which the political ambitions of some representatives of the sociopolitical movements, primarily the VDP (Vaynakh Democratic Party) divide the National Movement for the Restoration of the Chechen State and cancel the efforts to realistically and legally solve this problem. At the same time, the social base of the movement is shrinking significantly. The Executive Committee itself is being moved beyond the constitutionally admissible form, requesting the dissolution of the Supreme Soviet and the transfer of the functions of government to the Executive Committee itself. [...] Now there is no doubt that we are pushing the path of a coup, and we do not have the right to observe all this in silence. [...] This meeting cannot be called "Second Congress" because the re-election of the delegates did not take place and, above all, the Congress agenda was not made public. [...] We members of the Executive Committee, representatives of the Organizing Committee which participated in the preparation of the Congress and the*

The leadership of the Executive Committee passed to Soslambekov and Akhmadov, both loyal to the radical line. On the evening of June 8, at the end of the first day of Congress, Dudaev stepped onto the podium and gave a long speech, of which we publish the most important passages:

By replacing the word "colony" with "autonomy", with a complete distortion of the very concept in which statehood looks like a hoax, the imperial machine that uses the apparatus of violence - the army, the KGB, the Ministry of Internal Affairs, the prosecutor's office - the CPSU has taken away from our people religion, language, education, science, culture, natural and material resources, ideology, media, art, work, the right to freedom and to life. [...] The main method is the fight against the Islamic faith, as the most powerful weapon capable of uniting peoples, to resist and affirm against any force, any faith, any ideology. [...].

The Executive Committee responsibly acknowledges and brings to the attention of the delegates the fact that the Supreme Soviet of the Chechen Republic has not only not taken a single step towards the establishment of sovereignty, but has also cynically subjected the will of the people to political bargaining between the country and Russia [...]. Furthermore, the Supreme Soviet has made every effort to erode and cancel the right to independence it had declared, so as to [...] receive a nod of approval from its masters [...]. The main efforts of the Supreme Soviet were aimed at paralyzing the activities of the Executive Committee. [...].

In accordance with the law recognized by international law, the Supreme Soviet of the former autonomy (as a colonist) have lost their rights to legislative power in Chechnya since

convening of its delegates, express our strong disagreement with the attempt to use the podium of the Congress to divide our people and divide its actions aimed at achieving the primary objective: the building of a sovereign Chechen Republic as a part of a renewed union [...].

November 28, 1990 [...]. In such a situation, the legislative power must be administered by the Executive Committee of the Congress which, without having control of the state, cannot yet administer the executive and judicial powers. [...]. The question today is one: do we want to be free or voluntarily accept our destiny as servants? Today we must finally make our choice. If someone tells me today that the consciousness of the masses is not mature and that more time is needed, this is pure hypocrisy. [...].

The following day the Executive Committee closed the second session of Congress in a crowd, before which the final deliberations were read, condemning the cowardice and political inability of the old apparatus to manage an updated system, the fear to lose material privileges and power from the ruling elite in the transition to democratic forms of government and the implementation of the will expressed by the delegates to create an independent sovereign state was hoped for[73].

The die was cast. With the resolution of 9 June 1991, the National Congress of the Chechen People declared the independence of Chechnya. At the time, nobody paid much attention to it: after all, the OKChN was not a recognized institution either in Chechnya or abroad. Zavgaev, from the Supreme Soviet, simply ignored the declaration, branding it as the extravagance of a group of exalted people. The news came quietly in Moscow, since the presidential elections had, unsurprisingly, monopolized the square, and no one seriously cared about Chechnya or its National Congress. Yet that declaration would have had decisive consequences for the future of the small Caucasian republic and for that of Russia itself.

---

[73] The full text of the resolution is available at www.ichkeria.net in the *National Congress of the Chechen People* section.

Ispolkom, now monopolized by radical nationalists, immediately set to work, sending the Supreme Soviet a proposal for the adoption of a new constitution that sanctioned the full independence of the country, a law on citizenship that would allow the Ingush to secede and, if they wished, to remain part of Russia and to hold free presidential elections by the following 15 September. Any treaty with Moscow would not have been signed before the recognition of the Chechen nation's right to independence and a peace treaty ending three centuries of occupation. The Ispolkom then decreed that the independence government should hold a public trial to condemn those responsible for the genocide of the Chechen people, and to identify the means by which Russia should have compensated the victims. Finally, the Executive Committee endowed itself with a *Presidium* (a sort of government) to which key figures alligned to the nationalist turn of the congress such as Yusup Soslambekov, Zelimkhan Yandarbiev, Hussein Akhmadov, Bislan Gantamirov and Movladi Ugudov were called (we have introduced each of them in the previous chapters).

As we said, in Russia the echo of what happened in Grozny came rather muffled. Sergei Stankevich, Secretary of the Moscow Soviet and supporter of Eltisn, asked and obtained a meeting with the exponents of Ispolkom, urging them to moderate the terms and to accept a collaborative and negotiating approach to the issue, in order to avoid an escalation that could have lead, in extreme cases, to the *use of force*. But the presidential elections were upon us, and Yeltsin was not prepared to ignite controversy in one of the constituencies that, on paper, could give him more satisfaction. For their part, the separatists initially tried to boycott the electoral round, considering it an act without legal value now that the country had declared itself independent. However, they still did not have control of the structures of the state, nor the political strength to impose such a decision. On June 12, therefore, the elections were held regularly, and Yeltsin obtained the overwhelming majority of the consensus both among the Chechens (76.7%) and among the Ingush (85%). This triumph went to strengthen the national result, which saw him win the race for the presidency with 57% of the votes against Gorbachev's candidate, Nicolaji Ryzhov, who got just 16.8%.

CHAPTER 3

THE REVOLUTION

If we are really serious about freedom, if we are serious about building our own independent state, we must be fully aware of the great difficulties we will face. We will be strictly measured. We will have to face deprivation, and Russia will probably try to crush our aspirations for freedom by force. If today we are not ready for these tests, if we fear the possibility of a war, it would be better for us to wait, not to embark on a direct confrontation with Russia. But if we have truly decided to establish our state, if this is our conscious choice, and you have the will and the courage to go through all the trials that await us on this path, I will take on myself the responsibility of being your leader.

Dzhokhar Dudaev, November 1991

The Gang of 8

With Yeltsin's victory in the presidential elections, Gorbachev's position became desperate. The local governors dumped it and began to divide up the republics as if they were personal fiefdoms. Around the Soviet leader remained only the senior officials, members of the party's old guard, who had never believed in him too much and who now considered him a weakling, a naive dreamer who had ruined sixty years of Socialism. Yeltsin, on the other hand, was living his most radiant moment. He had swept the elections and unloaded the Soviet bandwagon. But the knots of his impetuous policy of "sovereignty for all" would soon come to a head. The strong message that had allowed him to win all those votes was the invitation to all the autonomous republics to take all the sovereignty they could swallow. This slogan, repeated like a mantra in all the squares of Russia, was a time bomb.

The countdown of the timer was moving quickly towards a very specific date: August 20, 1991. On that date Gorbachev would present the new *Union Treaty*, the agreement between sovereign republics that would lead to the overcoming of the USSR and the constitution of a confederation of independent states. At that moment all political relations between Moscow and its provinces would be called into question. The territories with a Russian majority would certainly have joined the Treaty without too many problems. But how would all the autonomous republics in which the majority of the population was not Russian behave? It was about thirty territories scattered throughout the Eurasian continent, many of whom had a lot to say about the methods by which the central government had appropriated their natural wealth and exploited them without returning them adequate benefits. To renegotiate all these relations would have meant dragging Yeltsin into a quagmire of head-to-head negotiations from which the newly elected president would certainly have come out with broken bones.

Thus, while Yeltsin undermined the USSR, Gorbachev undermined Russia. In this game of slaughter, no one seemed to take into account the Communist Party officials, dumped by the former and abandoned by the latter. There was an entire ruling class hidden among offices, commissions and assemblies who could do nothing but sign papers and who lived in terror of being swept away by events. Thus, when Gorbachev set the date of the signing of the Treaty of the Union for August 20, 1991, for many officials of the CPSU it was the signal that their world was about to disappear. For months, the intellectuals of the regime had been appealing to the population about the risk of a dissolution of the socialist dream[74], and among the higher echelons of the administration there were rumors about the need to stop reforms and restore order in the state.

---

[74] On July 21, 1991, an appeal appeared in the Sovetskaya Rossiya newspaper that appeared to be an invitation to insurrection. The article, entitled A Word to the People, read: *A huge unforeseen calamity has taken place. Our homeland, our land [...] is dying, it is falling into darkness [...] and this collapse is taking place in silence, with our assent. [...] Brothers, we are waking up too late, when by now our tears and our blood will be needed to extinguish the fire that devours it [...] We will allow civil discord and war a second time in this century, we will accept to throw ourselves back into millstone that will crumble the backbone of Russia? [...] Let's unite to stop the chain reaction of the disastrous collapse of the state, the economy, the people, to contribute to the strengthening of Soviet power, to its transformation into a genuinely popular power, and not into a manger for the hungry new rich, who are ready to sell everything for their insatiable appetite [...] Soviet Union, this is our home and stronghold, built with enormous efforts of all peoples and their nations, which saved us from misfortune and slavery at the time of the horrible invasions! Our beloved Russia is asking for help! [...]." who saved us from misfortune and slavery at the time of the horrible invasions! Our beloved Russia is asking for help! [...]." who saved us from misfortune and slavery at the time of the horrible invasions! Our beloved Russia is asking for help! [...].*

On August 4, Gorbachev retired to his dacha in Crimea for a short period of rest before the signing of the Union Treaty. Taking advantage of his absence, eight great notables of the party carried out a coup d'état to oust him. What was later called the gang of 8 was led by *Gennady Yanaev*, Vice President of the USSR. Together with him conspired *Valentin Pavlov*, Prime Minister of the Soviet Union, *Boris Pugo*, Minister of the Interior, *Dmitri Yazov*, Minister of Defense, *Vladimir Kryuchkov*, Director of the KGB, *Oleg Baklanov*, President of the Defense Council, *Vasily Starodubtsev*, President of the Union of Peasants and *Alexander Tizyakov*, President of the Association of State Enterprises. Gathered in a *State Emergency Committee*, the conspirators sent emissaries to parley with Gorbachev, trying to get him to cancel the conference. Upon their refusal, they carried out a military coup d'état.

At dawn on August 19, after kidnapping the Soviet leader from his home and cutting off all communications, the Gang of 8 declared a state of emergency, suspending all civil liberties and mobilizing the security forces. Yanaev proclaimed himself President as army units flocked to Moscow to take control of the ministries. The State Emergency Committee assumed full powers, declaring Gorbachev incapacitated. While the first parliamentarians were placed in custody, armored units positioned themselves near the White House, the seat of Parliament, where Yeltsin had arrived in the meantime, accompanied by Ruslan Khasbulatov, who in the meantime had become President of the Russian Supreme Soviet.

The reaction of the newly elected President was immediate and vehement: he condemned the coup d'état, appealed to the population and the army, proclaiming a general strike. Throughout Russia, people took to the streets, and thousands of civilians gathered around the Parliament building, who erected makeshift barricades to resist a possible military blitz. Within hours, international condemnations began to arrive: American President George Bush railed against the coup leaders, and so did the European chancelleries. In the evening the army began to deal with Yeltsin, and over the next day the coup was wrecked. As hundreds of thousands of people demonstrated in the streets in support of the President, he harangued the crowd standing on the bulkhead of a tank, waving the order to dissolve the State Emergency Committee. In the afternoon of August 21, the crisis subsided, and in the following hours the authors of what would be called August Putsch were arrested. Gorbachev returned to the leadership of the USSR, but the fate of communism was sealed. Over the next four months, what was left of the Soviet Union melted like snow in the sun. Between 21 August and 30 November 1991 all Soviet republics declared their full independence, and a month later the USSR itself ceased to exist.

Among the volunteers crowded around Yeltsin's tank in the confused days of the August Putsch was *Shamil Basayev*, a twenty-six-year-old Chechen boy. He was born in 1965 near Vedeno, one of the oldest villages in Chechnya. His family belonged to the *Yallorhoy* teip, a mountain clan. This made him a "true Chechen" and in this sense his family could boast a certain pedigree. His grandfather had fought in the ranks of the Islamic Emirate proclaimed at the end of the First World War. His father, Salman Basayev, had been deported in '44. To make the Russians understand how strong his attachment to his people was, he named his son Shamil, in honor of that Imam who had kept the Russians in check for three decades. After graduating from high school, Shamil had been drafted as a ground auxiliary in the Air Force. After his service he had unsuccessfully tried to enter the law faculty at Moscow State University. Failing to be admitted, he had turned to the Institute for Land Management, and this time he had managed to enter, but within a year he had been expelled due to insufficient mathematics (or more likely because there almost never went). He ended up as a bouncer in restaurants, in 1988 he was hired by a small Chechen entrepreneur, Supyan Taramov, apparently after a recommendation from a family friend. In June 1991, after a couple of failed attempts to open his own business and, apparently, finding himself persecuted by creditors, he returned to Chechnya.

During his Muscovite period he had carried out Islamic studies, finding in religion a decisive stimulus to his spiritual maturation. He had therefore linked Islam to the radical nationalism of Yandarbiev's VDP, developing a disruptive ideological mix. Between 1989 and 1990 he had frequented nationalist circles and participated in the activities of the Confederation of Peoples of the Caucasus, for which he had been involved in setting up a sort of police service by recruiting volunteers from among his acquaintances in the surroundings of Vedeno. In the days when the Gang of 8 was carrying out his unsuccessful military coup he was in Moscow and decided to join the defenders of Parliament. Gathered a few friends and a handful of hand grenades, he headed, with his first "brigade" to the White House, and climbed the barricade.

The insurrection

The August Putsch took Zavgaev completely by surprise. Arriving in Moscow on the 18th to attend the signing of the Union Treaty, a few hours before the Gang of 8 went into action, the First Secretary found himself displaced. For nearly two days he avoided taking sides, making himself untraceable. In Grozny the local officials, left without direction, behaved according to their conscience. Some received the orders of the Emergency Committee but did not pass them on, others "fell ill" or avoided presenting themselves. Only the President of the Grozny City Council, *Kutsenko*, openly sided with the coup leaders.

Those who had no doubts from the early hours of August 19th were the exponents of the National Movement. Already in the middle of the day hundreds of militants were in the streets to protest against the coup d'état. KGB officers intervening to quell the riots arrested Yandarbiev, but released him shortly after, when an angry mob stormed the Security Services Headquarters[75]. The protests escalated the next day, becoming real street clashes. The first firearms began to appear in the crowd, while the militiamen of the Ministry of the Interior, sent to quell the revolt, sympathized with the civilians. On the afternoon of August 20, the Executive Committee of the Congress could publicly declare that it had taken control of the city squares.

Kutsenko, the only significant authority left in Chechnya and a supporter of Yanaev's restoration, publicly requested the intervention of the army. Armed units were activated throughout the country, while reinforcements flocked from Dagestan and the Stavropol Territory. These army movements caused panic among ordinary people, frightened by the specter of a new deportation.

---

[75] According to Dudaev's wife, Alla Dudaeva, in his memoirs, the general personally placed himself at the head of the insurgents, and threatened to occupy the palace and arrest all officials who were there if Yandarbiev was not promptly released. This version is however denied by other speakers, who speak of a much more friendly conversation between the two.

The Ispolkom urged the military detachments not to move from their barracks and threatened to respond with weapons to any further action. Only late in the evening, when it was now clear that the coup was failing, did Zavgaev and his men finally show up at Grozny airport. The President of the Chechen-Ingush Supreme Soviet had stalled until the end, partly because he was an opportunist, partly because he honestly didn't know what to do with it. If he had supported the coup leaders and the putsch had failed, he would have been fired by Yeltsin within twenty-four hours. If he had condemned him and this had been successful, the Gang of 8 would have sent him to make photocopies in Novosibirsk. So he had decided to slip away until it was clear who was the owner of the field. On the evening of August 20, Yanaev and his followers were about to flee, surrender or commit suicide, and Zavgaev called an extraordinary session of the Supreme Soviet for the next day.

The meeting took place in a fiery atmosphere: the deputies of the Supreme Soviet were besieged by opposition demonstrators, who demanded their immediate resignation. There was a rumor among the nationalists that the Emergency Committee had planned a new deportation, and that the prisons had been emptied to make room for men, women and children.[76]

---

[76]In a subsequent interview, Dudaev recounted: *The union of the nation began with the Emergency Committee. When the Supreme Soviet and other power structures fully supported the Committee's program, we sensed the serious danger of the physical elimination of our people, of a new genocide. In the first frantic hours of the Putsch we did not notice what threatened us. But those who had lived through 1944 came from all corners of the Republic and said: Dzhokhar, this is the repetition of '44. [...] We unanimously accepted the decree of non-submission signed by Yeltsin. On the morning of August 19th, Ispolkom had already approved the decree, protests were already taking place at 10 am. The KGB men had begun to arrest our leaders [...] In those hours it was clear to us that the local authorities were ready to drown the Chechen people in blood. On August 19, in the evening, a demonstration of a hundred thousand people made a decision: the Supreme Soviet must be dissolved. A few hours later the situation was under our control. In every village and in every province, armed*

The "scenario of 1944" feared by the nationalists was absolutely not in place, and the Gang of 8 had not planned any deportation, but in those confused days any doubt became certainty. Zavgaev presented a motion condemning the Putsch, but the conservative wing of the Soviet demanded the approval of a provision of the same tenor also against the National Movement, considered a divisive and irresponsible force. This infuriated even more the people crowding outside the building, which in the meantime had grown to the point of completely filling Lenin Square, the main square of the city.

On the afternoon of August 22, Dudaev took the podium in front of tens of thousands of people. While demanding the dissolution of the Supreme Soviet and the resignation of the "mafia" Zavgaev, he obtained the popular investiture of leader.[77]. The Chechen General had carefully prepared his script: from the previous day, through his friend and ally Bislan Gantamirov, leader of the Islamic Way movement, he had brought a certain quantity of small arms, pistols, hand grenades and ammunition to Grozny.[78]. With the newly arrived

detachments began to form to oppose the Emergency Committee. [...].

[77]Hussein Akhmadov, a member of the Executive Committee of Congress and later President of Parliament, recalled those moments thus: *When the Putsch was put in place the republican authorities were bewildered. They supported the coup leaders and the people realized it. The National Congress, on the other hand, knew what to do. He spoke out against the Putsch and supported Gorbachev, and took the lead in the protests. The demonstration was massive, at least one hundred thousand people gathered in front of the Palace of Culture. And this human mass was ruled by Dudaev, and recognized no one else but him.*

[78]Gantamirov had contacts with the officials of the Ministry of the Interior, as well as with the business world and, through this, with that of organized crime. These contacts would have led to elements notoriously mafia to occupy key roles in the secessionist movement. This is the case of Khozh - Akhmed Nukhaev, a well-known "entrepreneur" in the field of the resale of stolen cars, financier of the nationalists since the time of Bart (for whom he paid the press). Having entered Dudaev's circle, he would have supported his political activity until he became a close collaborator of his.

weapons Gantamirov armed a hundred militiamen, who until then had carried out the order service of the demonstration. Framed by an improvised National Guard, the volunteers were placed under Dudaev's orders. They were little more than a gang, but enough to force the Republic's bewildered defenses.

On the evening of August 23, the National Guard raided the state TV building, and in a couple of hours the nationalists were able to broadcast Dudaev's proclamations across the country. Within twenty-four hours, the demonstration became a movement of revolt: armed militiamen roamed the city, while the new idol of the crowds harangued the demonstrators in front of the seat of the Council of Ministers, the so-called Sovmin. In an attempt to regain the situation, Zavgaev ordered the soldiers of the Ministry of the Interior to intervene and disperse the crowd. Many of them, however, were young Chechens who worshiped Dudaev, and ended up fraternizing with the demonstrators, either joining them or merely guarding the building's entrances. For the First Secretary it was a moral slap and a political disaster:

Among the militiamen of the National Guard was Shamil Basayev, the young man from Vedeno who had lined up in defense of Yeltsin. When it became clear that the August Putsch was failing, Basayev rushed back to Chechnya, and having learned that a voluntary force was forming to defend independence, he got his hands on a rifle and some hand grenades and introduced himself to Gantamirov. He had already formed three platoons, entrusting the command to three veteran NCOs from Afghanistan. Shamil had no military experience but he had a weapon, and at that moment a rifle was worth more than any shoulder strap. Of the 150 volunteers who showed up, in fact, there were few who possessed a rifle capable of firing. His was enough to get him the rank of Captain of the Third Platoon.

Assault on the Soviet

In early September, the echo of the August Putsch began to fade in Moscow and the main Russian cities, and Yeltsin was able to return to rest his gaze on the turbulent peripheries of the empire. Chechnya had gone into a state of turmoil, but the Russian president did not give too much weight to the alarming reports from the local Supreme Soviet. He was convinced that all that noise was nothing more than an anti-caste regurgitation as had been seen so many at that time in the USSR. He thought that it would be enough to replace Zavgaev with someone else to be able to calm the hearts of the people and restore Chechnya - Ingushetia to social peace. So he thought of *Salambek Hadjiev*, a professor who had made headlines a few months earlier, when he was appointed Minister of Chemical and Oil Industry of the Soviet government. Born in Kazakhstan, Hadjiev had earned a position in academia, graduating from the Grozny Petroleum Institute and then working on it until he became its director. A prolific researcher, he was a member of the Academy of Sciences, as well as one of the leading experts in the petrochemical sector in all of Russia. Known for being a moderate anti-militarist (he was head of the Committee for Chemical Weapons and Disarmament) he represented in all respects the "mature" alter ego of the leader Dudaev. Yeltsin appreciated him because he could speak to both intellectuals and entrepreneurs, had a modern vision of the state and was a hard worker. He seemed to have all the credentials to compete with the General, who had his nice uniform, good rhetoric and little else on his side. The idea of replacing Zavgaev with Hadjiev also pleased the President of the Supreme Soviet Khasbulatov, who, as we have seen, certainly did not like the current First Secretary. Hadjiev, on the other hand, was a man of high intellectual qualities like him (who was a professor) and like him he had a moderate and reformist vision. Arranging one of "his" people in power in Chechnya would also have been convenient for him in terms of elections, so he worked to ensure that the change took place as soon as possible.

Khasbulatov then headed to Chechnya to secure a painless changing of the guard. His notoriety, now that he was at the top of the Soviet state, his culture and his political ability would have allowed him to oust his hateful rival and to install a viable alternative that averted civil war and favored his position. However, there was to be reckoned with the nationalists, who grew up in the shadow of the crisis and rebelled during the coup.

To vanquish them, Khasbulatov drew up a plan. From his point of view, the nationalists were an amalgam of disillusioned, desperate and opportunists, held together by a vanguard of young idealists unable to rule the beast they were raising. Faced on the terrain of political debate, most likely they would have ended up being reduced to a residual fraction. Only the context, according to him, allowed them to occupy the scene. Despair and lack of alternatives were the ingredients of the mixture that threatened to break out the revolution. To neutralize the threat it was necessary to "change the air": the opposition had strengthened against Zavgaev and his corrupt regime, getting him out of the way was the first step. There was to replace him with someone who had good numbers. And Hadjiev seemed the right one. The solution, however, he could not descend from above. It was necessary to establish an alternative consensus front to Dudaev and for this it took time. The nationalists had conquered the streets riding the wave of the institutional crisis. Getting them bogged down in a political diatribe by letting time pass, while the situation normalized, would have deprived the *Dudaevites* (as the supporters of the General began to call themselves) the ground under their feet. As socio-political conditions stabilized, the desperate would be less and less desperate, the disillusioned less and less disillusioned. People would have listened to those who called for calm and reforms rather than revolution and war, and the radicals would be marginalized. Finally, with a good democratic election, the moderates would have won and the revolutionaries would have lost.

A perfect plan, in theory, which, however, was based on two significant variables. The first: that Dudaev and his people were too afraid to force their hand, thus leaving the initiative to him. The second: that the situation in Moscow did not degenerate further. And Khasbulatov, unfortunately for him, could not control either the first or the second. Yet somewhere we had to start and so, from 23 August, the President of the Supreme Soviet went to Grozny, accompanied by Hadjiev, with the intention of killing Zavgaev. In a turbulent meeting of the Presidium of the Supreme Soviet, to the First Secretary who begged him to authorize the proclamation of a state of emergency and to disperse the opposition, Khasbulatov replied that the use of force was absolutely to be avoided, and that the solution of the crisis should be political, which meant only one thing: resignation.

Having cornered Zavgaev, he went to test his opponent. His first conversation with Dudaev seemed to be promising: the General welcomed him with affability and agreed to his proposal to dissolve the Supreme

Soviet and replace it with a provisional administration to ferry the country into the elections. Satisfied, he returned to Moscow convinced that he had brought home a good point. The real goal, however, was achieved by the leader of the nationalists. Discovering Khasbulatov's cards, he was now clear that no one would raise a finger to defend the legitimate government of Chechnya - Ingushetia: a casus belli would be enough to force the hand and take control of the institutions. Thus, while Moscow was toasting to the happy solution of the crisis, in Grozny the Dudaevites took control of the city and besieged the government, now without an army to defend it. Nevertheless, Zavgaev did not intend to give up. His abdication could only have been imposed by a vote of the Supreme Soviet, and almost none of the deputies had any intention of endorsing it, considering that a moment later the Soviet itself would be dissolved. Thus the situation remained at a standstill for a few days, with the government not resigning and the nationalists not abandoning the streets.

Between 28 and 30 August Dudaev began to test Moscow's reactions: the National Guard broke into numerous public buildings, occupying them and displacing anyone who opposed them. Not a breath came from Moscow. Then the General ordered the establishment of armed patrols to guard the streets, and once again there was no reaction. Chaos was taking over the country and nobody seemed to care that much[79].

---

[79] The riots that broke out following the August Putsch had led to the paralysis of government departments, which was beginning to show its first harmful effects on everyday life. On August 28, about 400 inmates from the Naursk penal colony rose up, attacking the garrison of garrison, setting fire to the watchtowers, devastating the service rooms and occupying the prison facility. Two days later fifty of them, armed with handcrafted knives and weapons, occupied a wing of the building. All the others had escaped, dispersing among the demonstrators

On September 1, Dudaev called the third session of the Congress. The National Guard presided over the assembly. Armed volunteers erected barricades all around. A group of militiamen entered in the *Sovmin*, occupied it and lowered the flag of the Chechen-Ingush RSSA, hoisting the green banner of Islam in its place. There was no trace of the moderates: ousted in the June session, they were now unable to influence public opinion in any way. The scene was all for the great leader, who exhorted Ispolkom to declare the Supreme Soviet lapsed. The delegates promptly agreed to the proposal and declared the Executive Committee the only legitimate authority in Chechnya. Once again, the reactions from Moscow were tepid, and mostly superficial. Khasbulatov himself, underestimating the gravity of the situation, he thought that Zavgaev's replacement would be enough to split the nationalist front in two. Now, according to him, it would be sufficient to force Zavgaev to leave and replace him with Hadjiev, or someone else, to put the radicals in the minority. In reality, what was happening in Grozny was something much more serious than the political game that Khasbulatov thought he was playing. Dudaev had almost all public opinion on his side, he had his armed guards and was setting up a real government.

This was absolutely clear to the First Secretary, and it was even more so when on September 3, ignoring the directives of Moscow, he attempted to introduce a state of emergency through a resolution of the Presidium of the Supreme Soviet: no police or army department answered the call. While many of the Interior Ministry Militia men had already changed sides, those who had not taken a position simply avoided moving. Defeated again, Zavgaev remained holed up in the *House of Political Education*, where he had barricaded himself with his followers. Finally, on the evening of September 6, the National Guard also broke in there: a handful of men led by the Vice-President of Ispolkom Yusup Soslambekov entered the building. It is not known whether it was a premeditated action or the rise of agitation, the fact is that the crowd followed the militiamen and began to devastate everything. The deputies were beaten and silenced. Soslambekov placed in front of each of them a sheet and a pen and ordered them to write their resignations in their own hand. One by one, all the deputies signed. Under the threat of being executed on the spot, Zavgaev signed a waiver in which he "voluntarily" abandoned all public offices. Only the President of the Grozny City Council, *Vitaly Kutsenko*, refused to sign. When questioned by Soslambekov, he replied: *I will not sign. What you are doing is illegal, it is a coup!* Moments later Kutsenko flew from the third floor, crashing to the ground. He would later be hospitalized, where he would die in excruciating suffering[80]. The moderates condemned the assault, disassociated themselves publicly and withdrew from the National Movement, constituting an alternative *Round Table* to

---

[80]It is unclear whether Kutsenko threw himself from the palace in a panic attack or was deliberately ousted. According to some, it was he who threw himself downstairs, beating his head against a cast iron manhole. Other versions speak of a guard of Dudaev, or of Soslambekov himself, who would have thrown him against a window when he refused to sign his resignation. Even regarding his hospitalization, the testimonies are conflicting. According to some, the angry mob attacked him, filling him with kicks and spit. Others, like Yandarbiev himself in his memoirs, say that Kutsenko was promptly picked up and taken to hospital, but he refused to be examined by any Chechen doctor for fear of being finished. As there were no Russian doctors available, he ended up in a coma, only to expire a few days later. However, the investigation into Kutsenko's death would not have established any responsibility. The official version reported by the Prosecutor's Office was that the President of the Grozny City Council voluntarily threw himself downstairs, frightened by the crowd.

Congress. Zavgaev was driven out of Grozny and took refuge in *Upper Terek District*, his native land. In Grozny, Ispolkom began to operate as a real government, setting up commissions, issuing decrees and occupying public buildings.

In Moscow the news of the insurrection was received almost with disinterest. It took four days before a government delegation, made up of the Secretary of State, *Barbulis*, and the Minister of Press and Information, *Poltoranin*, arrived in Chechnya to try to resolve the crisis. With Dudaev, the two tried a "Soviet" approach: in the roaring years of the USSR, when a person represented a danger to the Party and could not be sent to a gulag to clear his mind, he was promoted and kept good. Poltoranin and Barbulis thought that if they offered Dudaev a leading role, he might take the chance to get out of that mess in exchange for a good job and a hefty pension. Unfortunately for them the General wasn't just smarter than they thought, but he was also more courageous and determined, and he really believed in an independent Chechnya. So the meeting ended in a stalemate.

Khasbulatov meanwhile had returned to Chechnya, where he hoped to resume negotiations with Dudaev where he had left them. The meeting between the two was resolved with a new draft agreement: the "fallen" Supreme Soviet would be dissolved, and in its place a "provisional" Soviet would be established to deal with ordinary administration pending new elections. Representatives of Congress would also have participated in this executive. Comforted by the apparent concession of the nationalist leader, the President of the Russian Supreme Soviet spoke to the masses thronged in Lenin Square. In front of a large crowd (who even spoke of a hundred thousand demonstrators) invited everyone to calm down, asked for the demonstrations to be stopped and put all the blame on Zavgaev, ordering him in absentia not to show up unless he wanted to *be taken to Moscow in an iron cage*. Finally, when an extraordinary assembly of the Supreme Soviet was convened, he induced the deputies to resign and to establish a Provisional Soviet of 32 members, some from the old assembly and some from the ranks of the Executive Committee. The last act of the Chechen-Ingush Supreme Soviet was a decree calling for new elections for the following 17 November.

Once again it seemed that the situation had been recovered at the last minute, and Khasbulatov set about returning to his duties in Moscow not before Dudaev had fully recommended that the agreements be respected. He did not even have time to land in the Russian capital, which was greeted by a resolution of the Executive Committee of the Congress, just made to vote by Dudaev, in which Ispolkom recognized the Provisional Soviet as an expression of the will of the Congress, and warned him to go against the will expressed by it[81]. The declaration also contained an electoral calendar different from the one agreed: fearful that normalization would weaken their position, the nationalists decreed that elections would take place on

---

[81] The text of the declaration, organized in sixteen programmatic points, began by condemning the Supreme Soviet, guilty of having lost the right to exercise legislative power, of having committed a betrayal of the interests of the people and of having wanted to favor the coup d'état. Some of the main political exponents of the Congress were appointed to the Provisional Soviet (Hussein Akhmadov as President, as well as other nationalists chosen from the ranks of the VDP). The Soviet would have operated in compliance with the mandate entrusted to it by Congress: if a crisis of confidence had occurred, this would have been rejected by the Executive Committee and promptly dissolved. The solidarity *of parliaments around the world* and of the countries that have just left the USSR was also invoked, in opposition to *the attempt by the imperial forces to continue the genocide against the Chechen people*.

October 19 and 27, respectively for the institutions of the President of the Republic and Parliament. Nobody in Moscow knew for sure which president and which parliament they were talking about: the Constitution of the Chechen-Ingush RSSA did not provide for any of these institutions. From the tone of the declaration it was now clear that the National Congress intended to proclaim full independence.

The Chechen Revolution

The matter was even clearer when on the day of the first convocation of the Provisional Supreme Soviet, only 13 of the 32 appointed deputies managed to attend the assembly. Most of the representatives of the old Soviet were blocked by the National Guard and dissuaded from attempting further tests of courage. The "purged" Soviet elected Hussein Akhmadov as President. He wasted no time, and on the first occasion he convened an extraordinary session in which only the representatives delegated by the Congress participated, solemnly proclaiming the birth of an independent Chechen republic, and transferring the powers to the Executive Committee, of which he himself was Vice-President. The deputies left outside shouted the coup and disheartened Akhmadov, but they got nothing but a declaration of solidarity from Khasbulatov. The latter, from Moscow, could not help but acknowledge the failure of his political project.

While in Grozny Dudaev took control of the institutions, in Ingushetia the autonomist tensions had not subsided: on the contrary, the fear that the secessionists would take power and drag them too into a civil war terrified the population.[82]. The August Putsch

---

[82] An Ingush girl who lived in Grozny until 1994 recounted those

had rekindled the controversy between the moderate nationalists and the radicals. The latter, led by Kodzoev and in favor of continuing on a path parallel to the one the Dudaevites were following, held a "National Congress" on September 15, during which they proclaimed the birth of the Autonomous Republic of Ingush, federated with Russia. On the same day, Kodzoev met with Dudaev, who gave him the widest reassurance regarding the right of the Ingush to secede and establish their own state within the new Russian Federation. The moderates, still convinced they could save the Chechen-Ingush condominium and keep Dudaev out of power, called a "counter-congress" for October 10, but Kodzoev took them on time, meeting on the 1st of the month with Hussein Akhmadov and signing a joint declaration in wich the Chechen Executive Committee and the Ingush National Congress decreed the secession of the two entities into two distinct republics.

The forced dissolution of the Chechen-Ingush ASSR instilled some courage in the deputies of the Provisional Supreme Soviet who had been expelled from the assembly, so that they tried to oppose by declaring Akhmadov and Kodzoev's decree "illegitimate", but they were soon joined by the Guard National who, dispensing slaps and blows, dispersed them again.

The August insurrection had now become a real revolution. But for this to be successful, the secessionists needed to arm a real army. Human material, as we have

---

moments in an interview: *In Grozny they started organizing demonstrations in the streets [...] They were demonstrations for independence, people shouted:" We want to be independent! "," Get Chechnya out of Russia! " [...] Not a word about Ingushetia. Then it became clear that Russia would not let Chechnya go, and that there would be an armed confrontation. Everyone suspected it. This was before the start of the war, and even then many weapons were shot among the people. Then Ingushetia broke away from Chechnya and remained part of Russia, understanding that being with Chechnya meant facing a war [...].*

seen, was not lacking. But how to arm it? There was only one way. Take it to regular forces. The military warehouses were heavily manned, and the National Guard wouldn't last two hours with what little they had at their disposal. The Ministry of the Interior and the KGB building, on the other hand, were empty and semi-deserted. The first was occupied on the afternoon of October 3, but there wasn't much left inside. For the attack on the second, however, a real night blitz was organized. According to what was reported by the Polish pro-secessionist journalist (later fighter) *Miroslav Kuleba* in his book *The Empire on its knees*:

On October 5, the young National Guard received an order: suddenly take over the KGB building in Grozny. It was the last institution of the republic subordinate to Moscow. A detailed plan was developed. In this was clearly visible the hand of Shamil [Basayev, ed.] Who later became a brilliant strategist. At that time only 50 people remained in the unit, of which only 34 were armed. The KGB building was captured without firing a shot. The young men who attacked him were armed with 4 old machine guns, two light machine guns, some mostly hunting rifles and some pistols as well as about fifty grenades. [...] The assault had been successful, and the attackers could taste their first victory, when several hundred excited people came running from the square.[83].

---

[83]The ease with which the secessionists took control of the public offices is indicative of the disarray in which the state apparatus suffered. In the case of the attack on the KGB building, General *Aslambek Aslakhanov*, commander of the Russian Interior Ministry Militia, said in an interview released in 1993: *The KGB building in Grozny [...] was able to withstand a siege of two / three months and an artillery bombardment. Its communications and technological equipment were designed to control the entire North Caucasus. However [...] during the assault, there were just 4 employees inside, and only one of them was armed. The attackers took the building within minutes. I'm sure all this was the result of an agreement.*

With the taking of the KGB building, the National Guard got their hands on the first Soviet military arsenal: 100 submachine guns, 12 assault rifles, 4 sniper rifles, ammunition and large quantities of grenades. But it was only the tip of the iceberg of what, after careful research, Basayev would have found in an underground warehouse: as he himself reported later:

There was everything: there were five thousand grenades, six hundred thousand cartridges, 525 Kalashnikov assault rifles, 76 machine guns, 9 anti-tank grenade launchers, 20 light grenade launchers, 50 binoculars, 50 night visors, 50 helmets equipped with thermal devices, a huge quantities of medicines, camp kitchens, tents, mattresses, blankets, uniforms for six hundred people.

Now the revolutionaries could arm their army. In addition to this, they had access to the gigantic mine of information contained in the archives of the state secret services. Millions of pages of documents, lists of informants, of military warehouses, of codes and everything else that could be useful to the police in identifying and monitoring political opponents. It was at this point that the Chechen insurrection began to be taken seriously in Moscow.

Yeltsin gave a televised speech in which he denounced *the seizure of state structures, radio and television, through which local institutions and the Supreme Soviet are discredited*. But the intervention came when the situation was now firmly in the hands of the Dudaevites, who were now armed to the teeth. At this point, putting him out of action would have required at least an armed intervention, which at that moment for the USSR was equivalent to unleashing an unmanageable uproar. The Russian president then sent his deputy, *Rutskoi*, to negotiate with Dudaev. The nationalist leader promised to restore the Provisional

Supreme Soviet and allow free elections, but retained full control of public buildings and streets, reserving the right to resume the initiative at any time.

On October 7, the Supreme Soviet reunited in a funeral atmosphere. The deputies passed a motion condemning the Executive Committee, well aware that this would be their first and last statement. And in fact a few hours later a flood of nationalist militants, coming from the just concluded congress of the Vaynakh Democratic Party, broke in and scattered them for the umpteenth and last time. The Executive Committee disavowed the agreement for the Soviet elections scheduled for November 17 and called new ones for a Parliament and a President of the Republic for October 27. To those who quietly pointed out that such institutions did not exist and that there was no electoral law applicable to this consultation, the secessionists responded by appointing an improvised electoral commission.

The Russian parliament decided to pass a resolution in which it stated that the *federal bodies and their employees* were *under seizure* and that *the lives, rights and property of citizens* were *in increasing danger*. The Provisional Soviet was recognized as the only legitimate authority, Hussein Akhmadov was sacked from the office of President of the Assembly and ordered all illegal armed formations to surrender their arms and disband. It was not yet a state of emergency, but we were close to it. The Congressional Executive Committee responded as if the secession had already taken place. In a statement that had the appearance of a state decree, he declared that the action of the Russian parliament was to be considered *a serious interference in the internal affairs of the Chechen Republic, on a par with an armed attack*.[84]. Yandarbiev, just confirmed as

---

[84]The statement by the Executive Committee defined the

leader of the DVP by the October 7th congress, did even more, urging all Chechens of Islamic faith to declare a *Ghazavat* (the holy war launched by Imam Shamil) against the Russian infidels. Tens of thousands of people gathered in the square, demanding that Ispolkom distribute the weapons seized from the KGB. Probably neither Dudaev, nor Yandarbiev, nor the majority of Chechens believed that it would really lead to a conflict. The whole USSR was in turmoil, states of emergency followed one another almost every week in at least one corner of the collapsing Soviet empire, without ever producing anything concrete. It had been like this in the Baltic countries, it had been like that in the republics of Eastern Europe, it would have been like that in Chechnya as well. This feeling was encouraged by yet another mess of the Russian Supreme Soviet which, on October 10, issued a 24-hour ultimatum to the secessionist armed groups and once it expired did absolutely nothing to follow up on its threats. Evidently Khasbulatov and Rutskoi were still convinced that it

---

resolution of the Moscow parliamentarians as *provocative, aimed at creating a context of unpredictable consequences and fratricidal bloodshed for the sole purpose of preserving colonial rule over the Chechen people, the peoples of the Caucasus and their natural wealth.* It was to be regarded *as a crude and provocative interference in the internal affairs of the Chechen Republic, which should be regarded as a declaration of war, the entire responsibility of which lies with the President of the Supreme Soviet of the RSFSR and the so-called Provisional Soviet.* In light of this, Ispolkom decided to *declare the mobilization of all males between 15 and 55 years old in a national militia, to bring the National Guard of the Chechen Republic to a state of alert and to withdraw all Soviet military personnel of Chechen nationality.* The declaration ended with a heartfelt appeal: *Understanding historical responsibility for the fate of the peoples of the Caucasus, taking into account common interests, the Executive Committee of the National People's Congress of Chechen appeals to all peoples of the Caucasus to defend honor, freedom and independence. The hour of the decisive fight has come! the Executive Committee of the National Congress of the Chechen People appeals to all the peoples of the Caucasus to defend honor, freedom and independence. The hour of the decisive fight has come! the Executive Committee of the National Congress of the Chechen People appeals to all the peoples of the Caucasus to defend honor, freedom and independence. The hour of the decisive fight has come!*

would be enough to raise the tone to lead the Dudaevites to more mild advice. After all, according to them, the secessionists were *no more than two hundred, two hundred and fifty desperate terrorists.*

Evidently they were wrong. The general mobilization of Dudaev and Yandarbiev's Ghazavat brought at least fifty thousand people to the streets. Freedom Square, the main aggregation center of the city, was filled with people until it burst. The moderates for their part went down Lenin Square, renamed by the revolutionaries *Sheikh Mansur Square* in honor of the Chechen national hero, to testify their opposition to the escalation. Their garrison also came to count tens of thousands of people, making the situation explosive to say the least. For a week the two political fronts swelled their ranks without coming to a physical confrontation. More and more serious threats continued to come from Moscow. On October 16, Yeltsin defined the separatists as *a gang of criminals who terrorize the population* and ordered the deployment of the army on the borders of the republic. It was a big mistake.

During the August Putsch one of the main arguments used by the nationalists to take control of Grozny was the deployment of armed forces to the country's borders. In 1944 this was followed by deportation, and the fear that the tragedy would repeat itself had compacted the Chechens around Dudaev. The military maneuvers launched by Yeltsin ignited the passion of all Chechens. The leader of the Executive Committee harangued the square, and on state TV warned citizens that Russia would soon invade the country *as hostile forces are massing in North Ossetia and Dagestan, preparing an attack on the republic to strangle the revolution.* He also stated that Moscow was planning *a continuation of the genocide against the Chechen people* and that in response tens of thousands of young

Chechens were enlisting in the National Guard. Hussein Akhmadov echoed him, marking Yeltsin's ultimatum *the last breath of the Russian empire* and *the desire to trample the democratic forces of the Chechen Republic.* Upon hearing of the deployment of federal units on the border with Ingushetia, he further declared that *any action attempting to undermine the democratic process underway in the Republic would be considered a continuation of the genocide against our people.*

Elections

On October 19, Yeltsin again ordered the dissolution of the National Guard, giving the Dudaevites three days to clear the government buildings and allow the resettlement of the legitimate authorities. If his demands were not met, Russia *would take all necessary measures to normalize the situation, to guarantee the safety of the population and to protect the constitutional order.* Once again Grozny did not receive any answers, nor did Dudaev lower his tone. This time, however, the Russian President was serious: on 20 October he ordered the troops massed on the borders of Chechnya to prepare to enter the country. It seemed like it was the end but, incredibly, the federal departments received no orders to move forward, either the next day or the day after. Something was wrong in the Russian army's chain of command.

Meanwhile in Grozny the secessionists were carrying out preparations for the elections on October 27th. The field was entirely in their hands, and most of the moderate candidates who had ventured to present themselves were withdrawn from the competition. On the eve of the vote, of the original thirteen candidates only four were present on the ballots, and three of them had a purely decorative role, as it was obvious to anyone that the winning man at the start was Dzhokhar Dudaev.

In fact it was a plebiscite loosely disguised as free elections[85]. The whole democratic and liberal constitutional arc had decided to boycott them, the same had been done by the Russian authorities. The media was in the hands of the separatists, under the skillful direction of Movladi Ugudov[86], appointed President of the *Information and Media Commission* of the National Congress and became the "Minister of Propaganda" of the radicals.

On October 27, the elections took place in a climate of general euphoria. The result, taken for granted from the start, was fully confirmed: General Dzhokhar Dudaev was elected with 90.1% of the votes, and the coalition that supported him, composed of the VDP and Islamic Path, obtained almost all the seats in parliament.[87].

---

[85] As the anti-Dudaevite journalist Timur Muzaev wrote: *Basically the elections were conducted by a social organization whose leader was running for the position of Head of State.*

[86] We have already talked about Ugudov, but we briefly summarize his biography. Born in Grozny (or according to others around Shali) in 1962, he had moved to St. Petersburg to try to become a journalist, his great dream. Having failed to graduate, he had found a job as a factory accountant. In 1988 he was one of the founders of the Islamic Revival Party, and in December 1990 he enthusiastically joined the National Movement. Here he made available his passion for journalism, quickly becoming the communications manager of the Executive Committee of the Congress.

[87] The report from the ITAR - TASS news agency, published the next day, read: *Last night in the center of Grozny there was a loud fire from machine guns and other firearms, pistols and shotguns, fortunately in the air. Supporters of Dzhokhar Dudaev expressed their joy in a particular way, having learned that according to preliminary data he was elected as President of the Chechen Republic. Late at night, the 47-year-old General held a small press conference. Dudaev stressed: "We must demonstrate to world civilization that, having become freer, we will be more needed not only for our neighbors, but for all other nations." Speaking of foreign policy, he said: "In my foreign policy I will follow the principle of open doors, equality and mutually beneficial cooperation with all republics and states will be our values and the norm in the international arena ". Speaking of domestic politics, he noted that he will pursue the priority of civil peace, harmony and prosperity of all people living within the territory of the Chechen Republic, regardless of religion, race and social status. He also stressed that he is a staunch supporter of a single Chechen state - Ingush: "The Ingush are our blood brothers, and this does not require any proof. As soon as the*

Parallel to the presidential elections were also held those for the constitution of the Parliament. Of the 41 seats provided, 32 deputies were elected in the first instance. The other 9 would be appointed after the ballots, scheduled for the following month[88].

According to data released by the Electoral Commission, 72% of those entitled voted. The opposition stigmatized the results, stating that the turnout had not exceeded 10/12% and that the consultations had only taken place in 70 of the 360 sections provided. The electoral round, effectively, was studded with irregularities of all kinds: first of all, the electoral law had been written and approved by an organization, the National Congress, legally unable to do so. In compiling the lists of those entitled to it, this had excluded the Ingush, who were formally citizens of the republic, and had included the Chechens of the diaspora, who were not. Secondly, the institutions for which they were intended were not recognized by any Constitution. Third, the election campaign, which took place in just two weeks in the presence of armed militiamen in every corner of Chechnya, it certainly could not be said to be regular. The elections were held in a state of martial law, under the constant threat of armed conflict, and moderate candidates were forced to withdraw from the

---

Ingush population deems it necessary, it will be possible to hold presidential elections also on its territory ": As for relations with Russia, Dudaev said the Chechen Republic is ready to build relations with Russia on the principles of equality, mutual benefit and consideration of the interests of both sides."

[88] The composition of the Parliament, the committees appointed by it and all the information available on the subject are available on the website www.ichkeria.net in the *Parliament* section. As readers interested in learning more about the subject can verify, the available data are fragmented and constantly updated. The destruction of Parliament's archives during the First and Second Chechen Wars and the seizure of the surviving material by the Federal authorities led to the disappearance of most of the official documents of the Chechen Republic of Ichkeria.

competition. Regarding the conduct of the voting operations, it was carried out arbitrarily: some ballot boxes were publicly displayed in the square, and citizens voted in front of a large mass of people, many of them armed, on easily recognizable ballots. According to the opposition, then, numerous VDP militants voted several times, exhibiting other people's documents or not exhibiting any at all. Cases were found in which these showed up at the polling stations with packs of ballots collected who knows where,

Immediately after confirming the victory, Dudaev spoke to the nation, reading his first official decree, entitled On the Declaration of Sovereignty of the Chechen Republic. This was officially published on November 1st, and it read:

Guided by the Declaration of State Sovereignty of the Republic and the will of the citizens of the Chechen Republic expressed by the general political elections, we declare the Sovereignty of the State since November 1, 1991[89]

The Declaration of Independence gave rise to a diarchy: on the one hand the remnants of the Provisional Soviet, supported by Moscow and the moderate opposition, which continued to prepare for the November 17th elections as if nothing had happened. On the other hand, the self-proclaimed *Republic of Nokhchi - cho* (from here on we will continue to call it the "Chechen Republic" for practical purposes) headed by Dudaev, who had already held his elections and was beginning to operate as an independent state[90].

---

[89] Any reader wishing to learn more about the content of the decrees and laws we have received can consult the translations on the site www.ichkeria.net in the *Documents* section.

[90] ITAR - TASS journalist *Sherip Asuev*, author of the memorial book *So It Was*, commented in a note from those days: *In Grozny they*

In Moscow it was now understood that the situation was really serious. In particular, there was a fear that the Chechen insurrectionary intoxication would spill over into the whole Caucasus, and from there into every republic that had something to complain about in Moscow, triggering a chain reaction that could lead the nascent Federation to civil war. On November 2, when still in Grozny there was shooting in the air to celebrate independence, the Russian Supreme Soviet issued a declaration condemning the elections that had just taken place, declaring them illegal and considering all the acts produced by the government of Dudaev as illegitimate.[91]. The situation remained stalled for another five days after which, on the evening of November 7, Yeltsin decided to pass the decree on the introduction of a state of emergency in the Chechen Republic - Inguscia. As long as the state of emergency had decreed Zavgaev there was little to worry about: the now fallen leader had neither the political nor the military strength to follow up on his threats. But Yeltsin's state of emergency was something else because, on paper, the Russian President would have only had to lift a finger to have the country occupied militarily and put an end to the secession.

Once again, however, the intervention of the Russian leader came late, and above all wrong. Proving that he did not understand the character of the Chechens very well, Yeltsin returned to threaten a military invasion. Just

---

are already accustomed to the independent meeting of two groups of adversaries. Now, apparently, there will be two parliaments [...] the Provisional Supreme Soviet does not recognize the elections that have just taken place legitimate. And the Executive Committee of the Chechen Congress, and the President of the Chechen Republic Dzhokhar Dudaev do not recognize the opposition's right to organize new elections scheduled for November 17. The stalemate increases by the hour. Both groups are known to be well armed.

[91]In response, Dudaev declared: *All my life I have dreamed of seeing my people independent. [...] The direction is now taken: it is the path of an open political struggle based on international norms of statehood and independence [...].*

as in August and October the danger of being deported again had filled Dudaev's consensus tank, the introduction of the state of emergency made him overcoat. Everyone, even his moderate opponents, rallied against military intervention[92]. Intellectuals, such as *Musa Temishev* and *Abdu Vazuev*, opposed to separatism, declared solidarity with Dudaev[93]. Rumors began to circulate among the Chechens that the introduction of a state of emergency was the antechamber of a new deportation. They were convinced more than all the elderly, who had experienced the occupation and its dramatic consequences[94]. The opposition seemed to dissolve overnight, as the National Guard distributed weapons to volunteers and Dudaev proclaimed full mobilization. The home front was all with him. On the evening of November 8, the newly installed Parliament granted him full powers.

Within half a day, the small armed gang that had stormed government offices swelled to thousands. Gantamirov took a group of them with him and deployed them around the Khankala military base, a large

---

[92]Hussein Akhmadov, meanwhile appointed President of the newly elected Parliament, declared: *the introduction of a state of emergency has affected all citizens of the Chechen Republic. From that moment on, the Russian leadership would have had to deal not with a political group, but with an entire nation ready to make any sacrifices to defend freedom.*

[93]Temishev declared: *I am against Dudaev, but if the Russians came here I, Musa Temishev, would be the first to attack them, as would any Chechen. Vazuev, on the other hand: If the tanks arrive here, in Chechnya, he will join me in the fight.*

[94]The historian and sociologist Georgi M. Derlugian, with respect to this, wrote: *It is necessary to seriously consider the psychological imprint left by a genocide on those peoples, whose reactions of self - protection might otherwise seem excessive. This observation is valid for Armenian and Serbian Christians, for Israeli Jews, as much as it is for Chechen Muslims. It is not a question of civilization or religious traditions, it is rather the urgency to overcome the trauma of a collective victimization linked to the past and to ensure survival in the future: the powerful feeling of "never again!". Precisely because the collective emotions of post-genocide syndromes are excessively strong, they are usually useful for the political advantage of extremists.*

airport complex not far from Grozny, where Yeltsin was expected to land the federal army paratroopers. Everywhere, in the rest of the country, people armed themselves with what they found, took to the streets and prepared to resist the imminent invasion.[95]. Meanwhile, the solidarity of parties and institutions was coming from the neighboring republics. On November 10, the Confederation of Peoples of the Caucasus, of which we have already mentioned (but we will talk more about it later) took the side of the separatists, declaring the mobilization of all the volunteers available to defend Chechnya.

The determination and sense of national unity that the Chechens were showing were certainly granite, but they could have done nothing against one of the most deadly armies in the world if an unexpected rescue had not come to their aid: that of the President of the USSR Mikhail Gorbachev. He was still formally the head of the Union, and as such he was the only one authorized to mobilize the armed forces. And as it was easy to guess, he had no intention of pandering to his main political opponent now that he was in trouble. He publicly proclaimed his intention not to support armed intervention, and so did many senior Soviet officials, including Interior Minister *Barannikov*.[96]

---

[95] In one of its issues, ITAR - TASS reported. *The decision to impose a state of emergency has relieved the masses. Tens of thousands of people invaded the streets and squares of Grozny. Within a few hours the city turned into a fortress. According to unconfirmed data, rail traffic is blocked. The National Guard controls military and civilian airports. With President Duduev's decree, the state of emergency was lifted throughout the country, and martial law was declared. The general mobilization has also been resumed [...] Now the center of Grozny is a human sea. The entrances to the city are blocked by the National Guard. People continue to pour in from the villages, many are armed. The police and the army do not seem to follow up on the state of emergency.*

[96] In an interview released years later, Khasbulatov recalled the words that Gorbachev maliciously addressed to him when he refused to support the state of emergency: *once Yeltsin refused to introduce a state of emergency in Lithuania... do you remember how indignant*

Yeltsin was left with only riot policemen. And with those he certainly could not face thousands of militiamen armed with submachine guns. To further complicate matters, on the evening of November 9th a commando of three Chechen terrorists, including Shamil Basayev, seized an Aeroflot plane bound for Yekaterinburg and hijacked it to Ankara. Arriving at the airport of the Turkish capital, Basayev asked for the withdrawal of the state of emergency and a safe conduct to Grozny in exchange for the delivery of the hostages. The Russian President, who was due to present himself to the United Nations in a few days and who was having a bilateral meeting with American President Bush, was left with nothing more than to back down. Otherwise, he confided to one of his collaborators, *we will be the ones who bombed villages in Afghanistan and annihilated Chechnya with tanks!* On the evening of November 10, the state of emergency was withdrawn, Basayev and his followers landed safely in Grozny and the whole world knew little Chechnya's struggle for independence. Long articles on the hijacking and insurrection appeared in Western newspapers. The photo of the hijackers who enthusiastically greet the crowd upon their return to Grozny went around the world. It was the first "media action" in the history of Chechen independence, and it was a complete success Basayev and his followers landed safely in Grozny and the whole world knew of little Chechnya's struggle for independence. Long articles about the hijacking and the insurrection appeared in Western newspapers. The photo of the hijackers who enthusiastically greet the crowd upon their return to Grozny went around the world. It was the first "media action" in the history of Chechen independence, and it was a complete success[97]. The fact that the West was so

he was?

sensitive to the spectacular blitzes convinced Basayev and the fiercest separatists that to attract the attention of Europe and the United States, their actions would have to be read in the newspapers and seen on TV.

In Grozny, meanwhile, Dudaev was the undisputed leader of the country. On 9 November he had received the official investiture of President of the Republic, swearing on the Koran before the highest religious authorities. The ITAR - TASS report on the ceremony reads:

The swearing ceremony of the first President of the Chechen Republic took place under the roar of gunfire, thanks to God, in the air. Dzhokhar Dudaev. In parade uniform, in the presence of the elders of the Republic and a large audience, he swore on the Koran to serve the people faithfully and to fulfill his duties as President [...] Immediately after the ceremony, the President gave an exclusive interview with our correspondent. "I want" he said "that all the peoples of the country and the world know that the Chechens do not want a confrontation with anyone." The Russian leadership, according to Dudaev, tries in vain to aggravate the situation of the Republic. "The Chechen people" says the President, "have firmly decided to be independent, and we do not want to go back on this [...]."

---

[97] The reader who wants to deepen the history of the plane hijacking operated by Basayev can consult the deepening *Basayev's first "feat": the hijacking of Ankara* on the website www.ichkeria.net.

CHAPTER 4

INDEPENDENCE

We were born in the night, when the she-wolf gave birth in the morning, at the roar of the lions, we were given our names,
our mothers nursed us in eagles' nests, our fathers taught us to tame a stallion

We were devoted to our mothers, our people and our homeland, and if they need us we will respond bravely, we have grown free, together with the mountain eagles, we have overcome difficulties and obstacles with dignity

The granite rocks will melt like lead, before we lose our nobility in life and struggle, the earth will be destroyed by the scorching sun, before we appear without honor before the world

We will never show ourselves submissive to anyone, death or freedom - we can choose only one path, our sisters heal our wounds with their songs, the eyes of the beloved push us to the feat of arms

If hunger knocks us down, we'll chew the roots, if thirst tortures us, we'll drink dew from the grass

We were born in the night, when the she-wolf gave birth, God, Nation and Country, we are devoted only to them.

Hymn of the Chechen Republic of Ichkeria

The end of the USSR

The Communist Party, pillar of the Soviet Union, was officially "suspended" by the Supreme Soviet on August 29, 1991, four days after Gorbachev himself resigned from his presidency. Yeltsin's liberal - radical party remained the masters of the square. A week later the government fell, making way for a Council of State that would ferry what was left of the USSR to a new leadership. The former First Secretary of the party still hoped that the current transition would leave socialism with some chance of survival, but hardly anyone else believed in it besides him. Yeltsin certainly did not believe it, as he intended to shake off that political wreck as soon as possible. Even the states that had lived under its government for sixty years no longer believed it: after Estonia, Latvia, Lithuania, Georgia and Armenia, which had declared themselves independent in the spring of 1990, during the coup d'état and in the days immediately following left Ukraine (August 24), Belarus (August 25), Moldova (August 27), Kyrgyzstan (August 31) Uzbekistan (1 September) and Tajikistan (9 September). Hopes of reviving the Soviet carcass vanished when, on September 5, the People's Council of Deputies also decreed its own dissolution, depriving the Union of its main legislative body.

In this process of unstoppable disintegration it was essential to save, at least for the moment, the planning of the economy. In a system in which the whole process of production and distribution of services was centralized, suddenly blocking the machine would have brought Russia back to the Middle Ages. For this reason, Gorbachev established *a Committee for the Operational Management of the Soviet Economy* that would continue to operate the system. This emergency government, headed by *Ivan Saliev*, lasted a hundred days, during which the last act of Soviet history took place: on December 8, Yeltsin gathered the presidents of Belarus in the town of *Belavezha*, not far from Brest. and Ukraine, which together with Russia and the defunct Transcaucasia had founded the USSR. Here the three heads of state signed an agreement in which it was acknowledged that the USSR, *as a subject of international law and geopolitical reality, was ceasing to exist* and the foundations were being laid for a future international agreement that would lead to the birth of a *Community of Independent States*. Gorbachev shouted at the coup[98], but no one lifted a finger to block the initiative. On December 12, the Russian Supreme Soviet ratified the Belavezha Accords and recalled the deputies from the Supreme Soviet of the USSR. On December 21, the former Soviet republics ratified the *Protocol of Alma - Ata*, with which they formed the *Commonwealth of Independent States*, "accepting" at the same time the resignation of Gorbachev as President of the Soviet Union even if he had not yet resigned. On December 25, he formalized his decision to interrupt the activities of President of the Union of Soviet Socialist Republics, delegating his residual powers to Yeltsin and leaving the political arena forever. At 11:40 pm that evening, the USSR officially ceased to exist.

The Soviet empire passed away, but his ghost soon came to claim revenge. Carrying a centralized and one-party system towards democracy and the free market was a titanic undertaking, never attempted before. Yeltsin was convinced that a gradual transition was not possible, and

---

[98] In a public statement Gorbachev declared: *The fate of a multinational state cannot be determined by the will of the leaders of the three republics. The issue should only be decided by constitutional means with the participation of all sovereign states and taking into account the will of all their citizens - The declaration [...] is illegal and dangerous, it can only aggravate chaos and anarchy in society [...]*.

the Perestroika disaster seemed to prove him right. Instead, he supported the need for a decisive shift towards the free market, and in this he made his own the theses of *Egor Gajdar*, a young liberal-inspired economist. Behind him, a bevy of Western "advisers" sponsored by large international investment groups were pushing for a "shock therapy" that would insert the Russian economy into the free market as soon as possible. Gajdar's recipe, on paper, was simple: the state should have disposed of all non-essential properties, should have let prices fluctuate and allow the private initiative of a new class of entrepreneurs to drive the economy towards natural competitive growth. The faster the state let go, the faster the healthy forces of the economy and finance could play their part. The omnipotent "law of the market" would have done the rest, bringing the system to a balance between supply and demand.

While Moscow was witnessing the requiem of the regime, the revolution had taken place in Chechnya. The statue of Lenin that overlooked the square of the same name in Grozny had been demolished, and in its place was erected a monument depicting a wolf, animal-guide of the Chechens. This symbol, which for some time stood out at the rallies of the National Congress, surrounded by nine stars representing the nine Tukkhum of the Chechen nation, had become the state emblem of the Republic. The national flag had also been made official: a green rectangle symbolizing Islam, crossed by a red band, a symbol of the blood of the martyrs enclosed between two white bands, a symbol of purity.

Not everyone supported the secession. A large part of public opinion, especially educated ones, was inclined to consider Chechnya as an entity in contact with (if not really "inside") the Russian Federation. When they spoke of independence they did not always mean a political reality, but the freedom to profess their religion, to speak their language and to live according to their way.[99]. However, the events of August and then the introduction of the state of emergency had moved most of the common people to the side of the radicals. And the advent of a charismatic figure like Dudaev's encouraged those who had survived the deportation or raised in the memory of the genocide. They saw the general as the strong man who would protect them from Russian imperialism[100]. Independence, therefore, had different souls. And now that the die was cast, it was necessary to imagine which Chechnya should have emerged from this revolution.

Inventing a state out of the blue is no small feat. First of all, it was not clear where this "new Chechnya" began and where it ended. As we know, the country was part of a condominium with Ingushetia, and following the

---

[99] A Chechen resident of Grozny, with a degree in education, interviewed on the subject in 1994 stated: *My family was against full independence, and most intellectuals were of the same opinion. Many of us had received their awards in Russia. We had academic connections. We were against the radical nationalism and xenophobia that emerged under Dudaev.* Another, a journalist by profession: *I never supported independence. I thought it was not possible to build sovereignty on mere enthusiasm. I thought that there were no economic, social and political preconditions for an independent state to function.*

[100] A villager from Gikalo said in an interview: *In 1976 my family returned to Chechnya from Kazakhstan. Religion was persecuted, languages were persecuted, there was no TV program in Chechen language, the First Party Secretary was Russian, the Second Ingush. There was no work for us. The Ingush occupied the most lucrative positions, the Russians carried out the specialized jobs. And the Chechens had to sweat the seasonal jobs outside the Republic. The elite could not put together two words of Chechen and only pursued mercenary interests [...] When Dzhokhar [Dudaev, ed.] Arrived, everything changed. It was a magical moment. I can't remember this without crying. It was a star, an ideal, a meteor, which came to earth and crashed to the ground. [...] He was a romantic, a pure, a conscientious soul. For romantics it was everything [...].* Another young man named Khozh, who would later fight on the side of the separatists said: *For me Dzhokhar was an ideal. The first time I heard him at a gathering, when I listened to the elders, about the suffering they had been through, I knew he was right. He wanted freedom. He did not want the nineteenth century, the twentieth century, 1944, the great pogrom of the Chechen people, to be repeated.*

secession it was essential to draw precise borders, in order to avoid border accidents. Secondly, there were neither government structures nor the political tradition of an independent ruling class: Chechnya had not been a unitary state since 1200, and its self-awareness was acquired by fighting the Russians. Transforming an administrative apparatus that functioned roughly like one of our regions into an independent political machine was a real challenge. Especially if this administrative apparatus had also been abandoned by previous officials, and he was in total anarchy. In fact, since the August Putsch, all offices, commissions and departments had ceased to function, or had been occupied by armed militiamen. The new independent state would have to reactivate them from scratch, and to do so it would need a suitably qualified ruling class. In this regard, the lack of the new leadership was evident: the vast majority of the population was poorly educated, and among the educated Chechens there were few who were willing to collaborate with the separatists.

The anarchy in which public offices lived had already produced some rather serious emergencies, the first of which was the management of prisons and the fight against crime. Between October and November 1991 the prisons of the Republic had gone into turmoil. Many common criminals had managed to escape, sometimes by revolting and taking control of the prisons. Unable to cope with the situation, the authorities had let many detainees gain their freedom, mingling with the protesters and dispersing throughout Chechnya.

The other systemic emergency, which as we have seen had been Gorbachev's first concern as soon as it became clear that the USSR was collapsing, was the economic one: like the rest of Russia, Chechnya had been governed for sixty years according to the centralized system of production and distribution of services, and the collapse of the government had jammed the mechanism. To this was added the economic crisis that had already stagnated for some time in Chechnya - Ingushetia: in November 1991 40% of Chechens of working age did not have a job, and the economic collapse was closing the channel of seasonal jobs, thanks to the which many families supported. This mass of "militant unemployed" literally had nothing to survive, and the Declaration of Independence had given way to the looting of state property. It was not an organized process: it was rather a "side effect" of the revolution, in which the euphoria of the rebellion was accompanied by a "do-it-yourself privatization" of the assets and agricultural machinery of collective farms, state companies and of public shops. From the Kholhkoz, animals, agricultural products, tractors, tools and machines of all kinds began to disappear and reappeared in the fields of private families. Many farms were left without laborers and without assets, going down the drain, while the lack of qualified agronomists produced enormous damage to agricultural production[101].

---

[101] Journalist Timur Muzaev, one of the most attentive observers of the Chechen socio-political situation, reported in his periodic Political Monitoring the progressive dispossession of public property. Just to cite an example, in the northern districts of the country *The dissolution of the former economic structures has led to the seizure of cattle from collective farms [...] The information received on what is happening in the neighboring district of Naursk can, in our opinion, clarify the Big picture: Of the 153,000 sheep that were on state farms in 1990, only 49,000 remained by the end of the winter of 1992 - 1993, the number of pigs fell 8 times and that of livestock 3 times. [...] The population [...] proved unprepared to take care of the herds. The crop was grown on hundreds of hectares in the summer of 1992, but stray cattle almost completely destroyed it, trampling rice and corn ready for harvest. All the work people invested was destroyed in the bud. [...] There is a rapid looting of the agricultural park of collective farms. As a result, even where gasoline supplies arrive, field work is not carried out because the equipment is looted, and the kidnappers demand a ransom from local governments to return it. The collective farms "Chervlennaya", "Kavkaz" and "Vinogradny" were left without agricultural machinery. According to some experts, no wheat was sown*

If the problem of the looting of public property could have been solved as the state regained control of the situation, other problems, so to speak "systemic" in nature would have been far more difficult to overcome. These problems were the geographical position of Chechnya, the distance of alternative markets to the Russian one, the socialist economy and its dependence on oil. The first was unsolvable: Chechnya was wedged into the Russian Federation, it had no access to the sea or a navigable river. It was a sort of enclave, with a single international border, the one with Georgia, which, however, had no driveways all year round. The closest markets of a certain weight were that of Turkey, an emerging country but not yet the economic power we know today, and that of Iran, just out of a terrible war with Iraq and bowed by international sanctions. The Arab world, which the secessionists looked to, already possessed in large quantities the only resource that could be of interest to a country wishing to trade with Chechnya, oil. In any case, no foreign investor would have bet his money on a country which, as yet, was independent only in the minds of the Chechens, and had not received any international recognition. Therefore, at the end of 1991, an effective economic blockade by Russia would have brought the Chechen Republic to misery. The third problem, the socialist economy, seemed the simplest to solve on paper. The plan launched in Russia by Gajdar could also have been implemented in Chechnya, predictably producing the same effects. But the fact was that Dudaev and most of the separatists had no intention of following the free market model. Privatization, according to many of them

---

in Chechnya in 1992 [...] The economic difficulties are aggravated by the rampant crime on the one hand, by the institutional chaos of the authorities on the other.

(including Dudaev himself) would have opened the doors to a crowd of small profiteers who would have parceled out the national wealth to their full advantage, leaving the country in misery and poverty. This was partly acceptable: in fact, unlike Russia, the Chechen economy was almost exclusively concentrated around the production and refining of a single raw material, oil. Other potential economic drivers existed (agriculture, above all) but they needed large investments in order to become competitive and the state certainly did not possess this amount of resources. And so we come to the fourth problem: although in the 1970s the Chechen extractive industry had begun to enter into crisis, drastically reducing its production, the diversification of the industry had however focused on ancillary products for refining, making Chechnya one of the main Russian hydrocarbon processing poles. If Russia had closed its pipelines, the refineries of lubricants, fuel oil and gasoline would not have had enough raw material to process. As a result of the concentration of investments in the petrochemical sector, Chechnya was lagging behind in all other sectors. Catapulted out of the blue on the free market, local products would have been obsolete. The warehouses would be filled with goods that would not have been bought, because the market would have preferred their Western counterparts. The Chechen industrial system, like all the other ex-Soviet systems, was neither technologically nor culturally ready to compete with the European, American or Asian ones.

The new president

The conflicting sentiments of Chechen independentism all revolved around one person, Dzhokhar Dudaev. The Soviet air force ace who suddenly became leader of his people was an enigmatic and fascinating person. The journalist *Anatol Lieven* traces a critical but suggestive profile of him in his *Chechnya: the tombstone of Russian power*:

> I first met Dudayev in February 1992, and I must say that except for his physical courage, which was undoubted, my impression of him did not improve with time. [...] Dudayev was a smallish man with a well-organized, aquiline face, a neat pencil moustache, and dark, hooded eyes. He was trim, almost finicky in his dress as well as his manner and his speech. When he wore military uniform, it was always clean, pressed and ironed; if a suit and tie, the shirt was white and the tie was dark and always neatly tied at the collar - a most unusual thing for the post-Soviet Caucasus. [...] Dudayev had the cat's neatness and physical poise, the self-possession and self-satisfaction - so much so that I remember him as having had pointed ears, though this was not in fact the case. You could almost imagine him licking his suit to keep it clean, and grooming his moustache with his paws. Instead of gestures, he had a mirthless, artificial smile, which he flicked on and off by way of emphasis, sometimes accompanied by a theatrical, metallic laugh. But he did not have the cat's repose. [...]Another thing that struck me from the first was that this was a play-actor. His speech was exaggeratedly clipped, emphatic, martial and authoritarian. When speaking in public, he combined this with a heavy stress on the last syllables of words. Many aspects of Dudayev's behavior almost corresponded to a Western parody of a Third World tinpot dictator, a sub-Ghaddafi. [102].

The hopes of the secessionists and the fears of the moderates coagulated around this figure with certainly

---

[102] As is easy to understand from the tale, Lieven did not have much sympathy for Dudaev. The choice to quote him is not accidental: many authors have drawn pompous portraits of the General bordering on hagiography, especially after his death. This description, on the other hand, focuses on his image, describing a "character" capable at the same time of intimidating as well as causing discomfort and annoyance. An ambivalent characteristic common to almost all the characters who have traced a furrow in the history of their people.

very particular characters. Dudaev had conquered the streets with simple slogans, using a language capable of reaching even the least educated. *Homeland, freedom, resistance*: evocative words, capable of mobilizing the pure hearts of the romantics and the wounded ones of the victims[103]. But if mobilizing a square, especially while the system implodes, is all in all quite simple, taking over the reins of a newly born and already collapsing state is quite another thing. What Chechnya had in mind, then, this new leader to whom everyone looked with fear and hope?

Dudaev grew up in the Soviet Union. Trained at the Party school, his training did not go beyond that of a normal citizen of average culture. He had lived most of his life in the barracks and had studied neither economic theory nor political philosophy. His point of reference was the USSR, which had constituted his existential horizon throughout his life. He despised the neoliberalism that Yeltsin's economists liked so much, about which he said:

Capitalism is the slavery of wage labor. The Chechens will never have it: they were not and never will be slaves or mercenaries. For capitalism there is no future in the land of Allah. No matter how much socialism has been abused, we are close to it. And I'm not talking about the socialism they built here. I speak of what has been described by the best minds of humanity.

---

[103] An eighteen-year-old young man from Vedeno told in an interview: *When Dudaev came to power I was a student in a khyzhar [an Islamic school, ed.] Our teacher told us that Dudaev had been sent for us from heaven [...] and that his advent had been foretold in the ancient tradition. There were many gatherings at that time, and everyone was shouting "Allah Akhbar!". Then they started shouting "Dzhokhar! Dzhokhar!" Our teacher, who was the mullah of our school, also came to the rallies. [...] He also said that in a dream he had seen Dudaev descend from heaven on his wings. He told me: "with a leader like this we are invincible!"*

Dudaev dreamed of a reformed socialism[104], governed by capable young people who knew how to defend the weakest and give freedom of initiative to the most enterprising. He dreamed of a community of nations that did not crush pluralities under the heel of totalitarianism, but rather exalt their differences. He believed in a secular Chechnya, in which, however, the traditional Islamic element was alive and active, at the service of the poor and the marginalized. He wanted a country of which the words *Freedom*, *Honor* and *Duty* were the fundamental cornerstones. Basically, Dudaev had a point of view not very different from our social right movements. With this it cannot be said that Dudaev was a fascist. The word *fascism* made him shiver by representing for him, as for all citizens of the USSR, the archetype of absolute evil. But its political formula was certainly "national-popular": a secular state but not atheist, socialist but not collectivist, nationalist but not imperialist, authoritarian but not dictatorial and so on.[105].

---

[104] He himself, on several occasions, had called himself *socialist*. This orientation, as we will see, manifested itself mainly in the approach he held in the economic sphere, rather than in a real programmatic discourse. In his way of thinking, for him who had experienced nothing but that, Socialism represented that form of economy in which a benevolent state takes care of the needs of citizens, enabling them to fulfill themselves in an egalitarian society. He had an almost religious reverence for Leninist principles, which he believed to be fundamentally right. According to him, it was the Russian ruling class that abused Socialism, turning it into a totalitarian hell. Actualizing it, entrusting it to a young, honest and willing ruling class would have brought out its best. In this regard, the Minister of Economy of his government, Taimaz Abubakarov, wrote in his memoirs: *So [According to Dudaev, ed] the success or failure in the economy and in the social sphere were not due to political miscalculations, but exclusively to the quality of the staff. From time to time, Dudaev repeated to members of the government the tremendous promise to kick them out of work and replace them with twentysomethings, capable in his opinion of compensating for the lack of experience with the acumen and lack of those complexes that Soviet power had instilled.*

[105] Among other things, his political program read: *Internal politics: dismantle the management structures of the totalitarian regime of the CPSU,*

What would Dudaev's role have been in this egalitarian utopia? Essentially, that of the leader. He had a romantic vision of life, and he transposed this sensitivity of his into everything. He saw himself as a guide, a leader, a guarantor of the independence of his people, rather than a statesman.

In what context should this national-popular Chechnya fit in? Definitely outside of Russia. For Dudaev, the option of independence was not in question. It was the dogma of faith from which no political discourse could ignore. Russia, according to his point of view, was an invader who had imposed his law and his rule throughout the Caucasus, which prevented all the peoples who inhabited it from walking their path of

---

eliminating the negative consequences of the administration system of the colonial government of the republic. Exclusion from political life of social manifestations of racism, ethnic hatred, religious hostility. Prevention of violent actions against peoples, parties and movements.

Foreign policy: Strengthen the sovereign rights of a free, independent and democratic Chechen republic. Development of integration processes in the economy with Russia and other republics on the basis of mutually beneficial cooperation. Strengthen friendship, peace and good neighborliness with the peoples of neighboring republics. Establish neutrality, non-participation in military blocs, direct alliances with all countries, with the exception of states governed by anti-people regimes.

National policy: protection of the citizens of the Republic, regardless of their racial, national, religious, political order, on the basis of the International Declaration of Human Rights. Protection of the rights and freedoms of citizens in creative activities, entrepreneurship, the administration of religious beliefs, the organization of parties, movements, trade unions and other forms of social activity; Development of traditional cultures, language, literature, science and technology.

Economy: nationalization of public interest enterprises, monopolization of state structures of the economy and development of a mixed economy, creation of a republican fund in gold and currency, in order to create a convertible national currency. Full employment of the population.Social: State protection of the interests of the unemployed, disabled, pensioners, students, the poor. Income indexing of low-income categories. Control of the prices of bread and basic necessities from the state budget. Use of vouchers to ensure the well-being of the population. Compensation for damage caused by Soviet totalitarianism. Land distribution to rural residents. General amnesty for political criminals and for non-repeat offenders. Direct election of local administrators and use of the referendum as a form of participatory democracy.

freedom. Therefore, his Chechnya would never go back to being a peripheral province of Moscow. The same should have been for all other nations in the region. Dudaev believed that if the Chechen revolution remained an isolated event, sooner or later Russia would find a way to suffocate it. The example traced by the Chechens should have been followed by all the others: by the Ingush brothers, first of all, who still at the end of 1991 could not decide between staying inside Russia or reconstituting a Vaynakh Republic together with the Chechens, but also by the Dagestanis, by the Ossetians, Abkhazians, Kabardinos - Balkars, and all the other nations that made up the variegated Caucasian mosaic. Taken individually, these small homelands had no hope against the giants that surrounded them. A Caucasian Confederation made up of Azerbaijan, Armenia, Georgia, Dagestan, Chechnya, Ingushetia, North and South Ossetia, Kabardino - Balkaria, Circassia, Abkhazia and Adygea would have transformed that jumble of languages, religions and ethnic groups into a political reality for thirty millions of people, rich in natural resources, located on a strategic crossroads between Europe and Asia. An ambitious political project, which squinted at the Arab world and Turkey, and which aimed to shift the center of gravity of the Caucasus away from Russia. But that, on the other hand, presupposed being able to achieve a unity of purpose that the Caucasus, in all its history, had never experienced.

In what geopolitical context should this Caucasian confederation have been deployed? Tendentially, according to Dudaev, nowhere. The general was a supporter of non-alignment. He valued those leaders who had been able to maintain good relations with both the Soviet and Western blocs, without compromising their countries in dangerous alliances. He dreamed of a confederation that was strong in itself, that was not a pawn in any geopolitical game.

The provisional government

The new Chechen state had three main urgencies: the first was to keep the economy running. An executive instrument was needed that guaranteed the organization of work and the distribution of products, the payment of salaries and pensions, the functioning of hospitals, schools and services. The second necessity was to start making the governing bodies work. A President and a Parliament had been elected, but there were not all those intermediate structures that dealt with putting into practice the decisions that were taken from time to time. All the offices of the judicial sector were missing, and a good part of the executive one. Finally, there was an army to be armed to defend the newly won independence. What Dudaev and his people had achieved with the Declaration of Independence was not at all obvious, and although in Moscow they were all busy demolishing the USSR, sooner or later someone would return to lay their eyes on that small province that was being built. his business. In November 1991, a couple of armored brigades and the will to use them would have been enough to put an end to the experience of the Chechen Republic. Within Chechnya itself, numerous groups were taking up arms against the revolution: there were the Cossacks, who were afraid of ending up in the crosshairs of the Chechen nationalists and had armed themselves, the anti-Dudaevite opposition, which had formed its own. militia, and many criminal gangs raged out of control. It was necessary to frame the National Guard and put the local police back on track, in order to curb internal crime, consolidate the authority of the state and be ready to react to a Russian attack. Dudaev and the Parliaments immediately set to work.

Already on 2 November the Parliament met for the first time, electing Hussein Akhmadov as President, Bektimar Mezhidov and Magomed Gushakaev as Vice - Presidents. The commissions essential to the work of Parliament were also appointed: Yusup Soslambekov, the man who had led the assault on the Supreme Soviet, became chairman of the International Affairs commission. The Defense Commission was also appointed, to whose presidency the then Colonel of the Red Army Ibragim Suleimenov was appointed, the Justice and Public Order Commission, led by the lawyer Musa Edisultanov, while the Vice - President Gushakaev, who came from the sector of the construction, he also headed the Industry, Energy, Transport and Communications Commission. And then again the Agricultural Policy Commission, the Science Commission, the Education Commission and so on. Doctor Gleb Bunin, of Russian origin but who had served during the demonstrations for independence and had managed to get himself elected deputy, was placed at the head of the Health Commission.

During the first week of work, more than twenty resolutions were approved: the official languages of the state (Chechen and Russian) were established, the dissolution of all armed groups that were not part of the National Guard was decreed and a *National Security Service* was established to fight organized crime and put an end to the proliferation of arms in the republic[106]. To

---

[106] Regarding the decrees, laws and orders published on the site www.ichkeria.it Italian translations are available of those who somehow survived in official or journalistic form. The publication *The Five Thousand Days of Ichkeria*, currently under review, also contains the headings, as does the *Chronology* section of the site

guarantee the functioning of the state, the Parliament recognized all the laws in force in the Chechen territory as of November 1, 1991, with the exception of those that contradicted the Declaration of Independence. All assets and structures owned by the former Soviet government were also considered nationalized, and a mandatory oath to the republic was instituted for all employees of government structures.

To ensure the functioning of the economic system, a *Committee for the Operational Management of the Economy* (COFEC) was appointed, along the lines of what Gorbachev had done in Moscow. One of Dudaev's closest collaborators, *Yaragi Mamodaev*, was appointed to lead this "emergency executive". We never talked about him, even though he had been around for a while: a young director of public companies, he was one of the "new men" to come out of Perestrojka. He had practically nothing to do with socialism, but in Chechnya's independence he saw an excellent opportunity to make himself the "Chechen Gajdar". He joined the revolutionary front in the spring of '91, when he accompanied Yandarbiev to Tartu, where the President of the VDP would have tried to convince (successfully) Dudaev to take the field. At that juncture Mamodaev had guaranteed his full economic support, making his resources available to support the political activity of the new leader and even the sustenance of his family, if needed. In the aftermath of the Chechen Revolution, Dudaev and Mamodaev were very close.

There were similarities and differences between the two. Like Dudaev, Mamodaev was a successful young man. He was just 38 years old, he was a man of experience in the management of state companies and was appreciated by the Muslim clergy. Like the President,

above.

Mamodaev also wanted an independent Chechnya. However, what divided the two was the economic vision: for Mamodaev it was essential to introduce the free market, proceeding first of all with the privatization of non-essential goods and services. Dudaev, on the other hand, as we have seen, was a socialist, opposed to privatization or in any case hostile to the prevalence of the free market over state leadership.

Mamodaev's appointment was greeted with a certain skepticism both by the Vainakh Democratic Party, who wanted a more "political" figure to lead the executive, and by Parliament, which did not look favorably on Mamodaev due to the fact that he was born and grew up in the shadow of Soviet power and was in the odor of contacts with organized crime. In fact, it certainly cannot be said that the young entrepreneur was a seasoned politician, or a man of experience. Certainly the fact that he was one of the main financiers of Dudaev's electoral campaign and the solidity of the personal relationship linked the two had played an important role in his choice as President of COFEC. But it is likely that this was also guided by political assessments. First of all, a young entrepreneur could have attracted the interest of the Chechen bourgeois class, skeptical of the new leadership when not openly hostile. Secondly, the contacts that Mamodaev had in Russian industry and entrepreneurship, the legacy of his experience as an administrator of state-owned companies, could be useful in keeping important economic channels open in the event of a blockade by Russia.

COFEC was established with Decree number 3 of November 13, 1991. Mamodaev was supposed to keep the factories open and operate the offices. And above all, prepare Chechnya for the winter with sufficient food reserves[107]. The first urgency that had to be met was to pay salaries and pensions. The financial transfers needed to guarantee more or less regular payments still arrived from Russia, but these were not always sufficient to cover the expenses of the state. Lacking the resources to pay public employees, Mamodaev resorted to vouchers - petrol, used as alternative banknotes[108].

Another pressing problem to solve was the supply of the mountain populations, who were left without basic necessities. With winter just around the corner, it was essential to reach the villages and distribute what was necessary to avoid a famine. Mamodaev concluded supply agreements from the earliest days, obtaining the delivery of twenty-five thousand tons of sugar since November 1991[109]. Despite Mamodaev's successes,

---

[107] About the composition of this "economic cabinet" only fragmentary information is available, reported by Timur Muzaev in his Political Monitoring. We know that most of its members were entrepreneurs or company directors, hence the journalistic definition of the Cabinet of Entrepreneurs coined by the Chechen magazines. In addition to Mamodaev, Kh. R. Akaev, R. Bisultanov, R. Borshchigov, Hussein Akhmed Maraev, G. Musalimov, RS Elmurzaev and former Moscow strongman, candidate to replace Zavgaev, Professor Salambek Hadjiev. An in-depth examination of COFEC can be consulted on the *Governments* section of the site www.ichkeria.net.

[108] During the 4 months of the Committee's life, nearly 200,000 tons of gasoline and diesel were sold to the population as compensation for back wages, worth about 35 million dollars. This temporarily resolved the emergency - wages, but removed a large amount of resources from the state budget, considering that the value of the vouchers referred to the domestic market, which was 30 - 35% lower than export prices. This measure, initially used to solve temporary liquidity shortages, became a usual practice and then an official payment method from October 1992, so much so that these were used to guarantee the payment of a one-off payment of 25,000 rubles recognized by President Dudaev to the victims of communist political repression since 3 October 1992.

[109] To reporters who asked him how he would guarantee the supply of Chechnya for the winter he replied: *We do not want to isolate ourselves from anyone, neither politically nor economically, those who wish to exclude the Chechen Republic from Russia know that they risk cutting the country. entire region of the Caucasus linked through us. We are open to everyone, both domestic and foreign companies, to individual entrepreneurs, ready*

however, the economic emergency was far from resolved. Even if the order to close the borders had not yet arrived from Moscow, there was already a marked decline in the volume of imports of materials, equipment for companies, but also of foodstuffs such as fruit and vegetables. The young president of the Committee reassured the country, trusting in Chechnya's oil resources as an ideal bargaining chip for food-producing countries, and inviting foreign investors to visit the country. Perhaps he ignored the fact that the country's production capacity was drastically shrinking. Or maybe he knew, but he had nothing else to gamble on to pacify public opinion. The whole economic maneuver organized by Mamodaev was obviously based on the only strategic wealth that Chechnya possessed, namely oil and its processing products. Commercial agreements would be made with oil, the central state would be financed, even wages would be paid. And obviously, the trade balance rebalancing plan would be based on oil.

How to do it for all the other products? Since the Declaration of Independence, the country's borders had become a sieve through which goods of all kinds came and went practically unchecked. Mamodaev intended to lower taxes in order to attract foreign investment to the republic. From his point of view, this would have benefited the revival of the Chechen economy, if at the same time Dudaev had accepted a compromise with the free market. But the Chechen President did not seem to have ears for him: on the contrary, he publicly declared that the system of controlled prices would remain in force throughout the country, in support of the weaker groups. Neither Dudaev's nor Mamodaev's measures could work without the government placing a filter between the domestic and foreign markets: the lower

for any mutually beneficial cooperation.

purchase prices in the Chechen market would have invited investors to buy the controlled assets to resell them in Russia, with enormous profit margins entirely "financed" by the coffers of the central Chechen state. This mechanism would have brought the internal market to shortage, forcing the Chechens to resort to the black market, and in this context, as early as 10 December, COFEC imposed a block on exports for most agricultural products, raw materials, building materials and consumables. A special procedure was instituted for the export of petroleum and derivatives, while the population's access to gasoline supplies was limited by raising consumer prices, so as to discourage the purchase for resale by private individuals.

While Mamodaev tried to keep the ramshackle Chechen economy afloat, Dudaev and the Parliament dedicated themselves to the construction of the state and moved their contacts to obtain the recognition of the Republic by foreign governments. Dudaev appointed a provisional Cabinet of Ministers, pending a constituent assembly to give Chechnya a fundamental charter. Dudaev's Cabinet emerged as a political executive, in which the pre-eminent posts were entrusted to people of proven independence faith: the aforementioned Ugudov, a staunch nationalist, was appointed to the Ministry of Information. *Shamil Beno*, a Chechen of Jordanian origin known for his moderate positions was appointed Foreign Minister, while at the economy was called *Taimaz Abubakarov*, former minister of the Zavgaev's government considered a well-trained technician. *Sultan Albakov*, former employee of the Supreme Court of the Chechen – Ingush ASSR, became President of the Internal Security Service, an armed unit placed under the Ministry of the Interior, at the top of which was confirmed *Umals Alsultanov* (also former Minister of the

Interior of the Zavgaev's government) while *Elsa Sheripova*, member of the Executive Committee and very loyal of the President, was appointed to the Public Prosecutor's Office. *Aslambek Akbulatov*, a former lecturer at Leningrad State University, became Secretary of State[110].

The construction of the first executive and control bodies made it possible to reactivate the police, in order to put a stop to the wave of crime that was hitting the country. Months of demonstrations, assaults and riots had produced a widespread feeling of impunity, which had to be stopped at all costs. The actions of the criminals had become more and more striking, and began to include the kidnapping of characters in sight, in order to obtain a ransom or to wash personal conflicts in the blood.[111]. Criminals escaped from Naursk prison, who had initially mingled with the demonstrators (in part they had been "hidden" from us by the nationalists) marched openly in front of the Parliament building, demanding amnesty. In mid-December, the situation could be said to be out of control in many districts of the country, with newspapers daily publishing alarming articles about murders, robberies and kidnappings. It was urgent to put the Ministry of the Interior into operation as soon as possible, and to make the police officers operational

---

[110] In addition to these, *Mahmud Esambaev*, internationally renowned actor and dancer (appointed Minister of Culture) and *Dalhan Khozhaev*, historical researcher, appointed Minister of the Archives, made their appearance in the government team (of which only a few journalistic fragments have come down to us). The cards relating to the provisional government, as well as those relating to all the other ChRI governments found in this research, can be freely consulted in the *Nomenklatura* section of the website www.ichkeria.net

[111] On November 12, for example, just as Alsultanov declared to the press that the wave of violent crimes was running out of physiological peak due to the revolution, unidentified aggressors entered the Chechen State University - Inguscia, kidnapped the Rector and fatally wounded the Vice Rector.

again. But Dudaev's initiative rebounded against the protests of police officers, within whose body a "pro-ministerial" party and one opposed to Alsultanov's leadership were opposed. After a few weeks of hesitation, Dudaev directly took over the general leadership, assuming direct command. This decision-making attitude did not appeal to some members of Parliament, who criticized him for an exaggerated interventionism.

Some parliamentarians then felt dissatisfied with the presidential appointments. For his part, Dudaev contested the slowness with which Parliament discussed the state structure, asking the Constituent Assembly to hurry up to come up with a draft of the Constitution. Only a few weeks had passed since the declaration of independence and the first disagreements were already arising between the organisms born of the revolution. As the days passed, a *pro - presidential* and a *pro - parliamentary* party emerged. The tension between government and parliament was still shielded by the prestige enjoyed by Dudaev, and his popularity prevented, for the moment, a frond from occurring. Work then proceeded, focusing mainly on the reform of local administrations. On November 20, the new Mayor of Grozny was appointed, in the figure of the revolutionary leader Bislan Gantamirov. On the 26th was approved the bill *On local government*, in which was ordered the suppression of the Soviets and the constitution of elective councils lasting three years with direct election of the governor, to be held by the end of 1991. Finally, on December 25, Parliament appointed a commission of seven people who clearly defined and unequivocal the border that would have separated Chechnya from the newborn Republic of Ingushetia.

The Ingush problem was one of the main issues raised by Chechnya's independence and, as we shall see later, the negotiations for its resolution would have brought Dudaev one step closer to the war with Russia. The central focus of the political debate remained that of the lands ceded to North Ossetia during Stalin's dictatorship and never returned. The moderates wanted to keep Ingushetia in Russia, in exchange for Moscow's recognition of legitimate territorial claims. The radicals demanded independence because they did not believe that Russia would in any case support their demands or, if it did, it would be an instrumental support aimed at dividing the peoples of the Caucasus. Indeed, if the former legitimately feared that Dudaev would last shortly, even the radicals were right when they said that, among the Ossetians and the Ingush, the Russians would certainly favor the former, orthodox like them, to the detriment of the latter, Islamic and related to the Chechens. In any case, the acceleration of events imprinted with the Declaration of Independence had in fact passed the discussion.

Finding themselves alone, the Ingush were back in agitation, and already on November 9 they took to the streets, demanding that Moscow make the Law on the Rehabilitation of Oppressed Peoples effective and give Ingushetia the right to repossess the Prigorodny district. The demonstration soon became a permanent garrison, which lasted for weeks and weeks. Moderates and radicals were preparing the electoral campaign in view of a referendum, scheduled for November 30, in which the Ingush citizens would have had to express their desire to remain within the Chechen - Ingush Republic (which in the meantime, however, was already became something else) or whether to found an autonomous republic within the Russian Federation (with an authority also extended to the Prigorodny district)[112]. The referendum took place

[112] The question of the referendum was the following: *do you want the Ingushes to establish their autonomous republic within the RSFSR [The Russian Soviet Federative Socialist Republic. ed] with the return of the requisitioned lands and the capital on the right bank of the city of Vladikavkaz?* The radical nationalists of Niisho (the party led by Isa Kodzoev) contested the vote, arguing that, contrary to the good wishes of the moderates, it would only be a way to delay Russia's intervention in the arbitration with Ossetia, and that the only way to go was to join the independent Chechen republic in anti-Russian function. Kodzoev argued that only a Confederation of Peoples of the Caucasus could impartially manage the claims that all peoples boasted,

[113]Not everyone was in favor of a separate Ingushetia from Chechnya. Indeed, numerous local circles expressed themselves in the opposite way. The gathering of the elders of Ingushetia in the village of Surkhakhi, on December 26, 1991, issued an appeal like this: *In this difficult historical moment of a sharp turn in the destinies of all the peoples who have freed themselves from the totalitarian regime [...] the Ingush have found themselves in a period of uncertainty, powerlessness, illegality. All the hopes of the Ingush on the federal government and then on the Russian leadership have not produced results. Neither the law of the Supreme Soviet on the rehabilitation of the rights of oppressed peoples, nor the official statements of the Russian government, and above all of its President Boris Yeltsin on the solution of the Ingush problem, have led to nothing. [...] It is time for reasonable action to create a unitary Vaynakh state. [...] Beforeeverythingwe must defend the sovereignty of the republic, which the Chechens and the Ingush have bravely conquered [...] The Chechens and the Ingush are one people, and it is impossible to divide it into two parts [...] we were not divided when, after the Caucasus War, tens of thousands of families were forcibly deported to Turkey. We were not divided in 1944, when all were deported to the regions of Siberia and Kazakhstan [...] We were not divided when, last October, a state of emergency was imposed throughout the Chechen - Ingush territory. [...] We have only one faith, one language, one border. Nothing divides us, and together it is easier to solve everyone's problems. [...] Without solving this historically important task, no freedom is possible either in Chechnya or in Ingushetia.*

[114]Not even the Executive Committee, in truth, was a legitimate body: it was simply a political junta, an expression of the moderate pro-Russian movement. This was opposed by the People's Council, which emerged from the disputed Congress of the Ingushes, and an expression of Kodzoev's radical nationalism. In any case, the ruling of the elders gave a sort of political legitimacy to the Executive Committee, which immediately set to work by appointing an Operational Management Committee of the Economy, along the lines of what was done first by Gorbachev in Russia and then by Dudaev in Chechnya. and starting to prepare the elections of the following 5 January.

on November 30th. 75% of those entitled to vote went to the polls, ninety-two thousand people in all, and among these 97.4% expressed themselves in favor of secession from Chechnya, and the constitution of a federated republic with Russia.[113]. The party of moderates had taken over.

Suddenly Ingushetia found itself independent of Chechnya, and at the same time lacking any organization capable of handling this divorce. All central government structures, all offices, departments, ministries, had always resided in Grozny. Overnight, the Ingush found themselves without a state, without a leader, without an administration. The only authority, albeit not officially recognized, was the *Council of Elders*, immediately set to work to fill the void, appointing an Executive Committee, an expression of moderate nationalism, to call elections for January 5 and to appoint a government.[114].

Building a state

The plebiscite vote in the Ingush referendum on November 30 was determined by the fear that the tug-of-war between Dudaev and Yeltsin would lead to open war. For the moment the situation seemed to calm down, and the start of political negotiations between the two seemed imminent, but it was clear that if they did not reach a compromise solution, sooner or later the central government would have to face the separatists hard-nosed. Dudaev was well aware that if Chechnya did not agree to sign a federative agreement with Russia, Moscow would begin to push to re-establish constitutional prerogatives. For this reason, from the earliest days, the General set out to provide the new state with a regular army.

His idea was to build a small highly professionalized force, no more than 7,000 men. This would be organized into six departments: the National Guard would be the main fighting unit. The Border Guard should have guarded the borders of the republic, while the "internal troops" would have played the role of militia at the disposal of the Ministry of the Interior. The Special Forces would be the army's specialty departments, and among these the Presidential Guard was soon established, in charge of defending the President, his family and government structures. *Movlad Dzhabrailov*, Dudaev's personal karate master, was appointed under his command. The labor service and the reserve would constitute the mass that could be mobilized in case of war.

All citizens aged 18 to 26 were called to arms, for a year and a half military service for non-graduates, one year for educated citizens[115]. The Soviet army had formed good non-commissioned officers to whom to entrust the training of the troops, and a few good officers to command the large units. In addition to Dudaev, who was the Chechen with the highest military rank ever, there were three colonels available: *Viksan Shakhabov*, air force officer and former fellow soldier of Dudaev and *Musa Merzhuyev*, colonel of the anti-aircraft defense, both available, and *Aslan Maskhadov*, Colonel of Artillery, who was still on duty, but who could have

---

[115] With a specific decree of 24 December 1991 (*Law on the defense of the Republic*) all citizens aged 18 to 26 were called to arms for a year and a half military service for non-graduates, one year for citizens educated. The volunteer units that had formed the National Guard were essentially left to fend for themselves. Many returned to their homes, or entered the "official" departments in the process of being constituted. Others followed the only remaining platoon commander, Shamil Basayev, and quartered in a sports complex on the outskirts of Grozny, where he continued to conduct their training flanked by another early volunteer, Umalt Dashayev.

resigned from the Red Army from mid-1992. In addition to this, weapons, ammunition, logistics equipment, spare parts for vehicles, and a lots of other utilities. At the moment, however, there was very little available: a few hundred firearms, many of which, moreover, they had been distributed in the confused days of the state of emergency and were now in the hands of those who had taken them. It seems that the warehouse that the separatists had taken over the KGB headquarters had also been looted, and the weapons distributed among the militia groups who had taken into custody of the building[116].

Around Chechnya there were Soviet military warehouses full of uniforms, tents, logistics material but also light and heavy weapons, anti-tank weapons, anti-aircraft weapons. And even armored vehicles, tanks, vehicles for the transport of troops. At the military base of Khankala, on the outskirts of Grozny, there were even fighter-bombers: reserves capable of fully arming Dudaev's army, if he could get his hands on it. Not being able to seize all that goodness yet, for the moment the

---

[116]In an interview released towards the end of 1991, the Vice - President of the Chechen National Security Service, Khataev, stated about the seizure of the KGB arsenal: *I don't think it happened spontaneously. Let's ask the question: who needed it, who was interested? The KGB had very heavy compromise material on the leaders of the mafia clans, who had now penetrated the power structures at various levels. [...] in my opinion, the mafia groups were one of the parties most interested in the barbaric looting of the KGB building [...]* . A different account of the disappearance of the weapons comes to us from the memoirs of Zelimkhan Yandarbiev: *[...] the properties and archives were looted by those who were placed there for their protection and conservation, that is, mainly by the gang of Bislan Gantamirov . Weapons suffered the same fate. Unfortunately, contrary to our warnings about his reputation [...] in the short period from 19 August to the elections, Gantamirov managed to curry favor with the President [...] at that time the thefts of the KGB building took place.* By the time Yandarbiev wrote his memoirs, relations with Bislan Gantemirov had seriously deteriorated, and an exaggeration on the part of the author cannot be excluded. However, it is undeniable that in the period immediately following the collapse of the Chechen-Ingush ASSR the building was looted, and most of the weapons "disappeared."

President limited himself to freezing all the armaments and bases on Chechen soil, prohibiting their transport outside the borders. If the Russians wanted *to get their toys back*, they would have to leave some of them as a pledge. Negotiations regarding the outcome of the Soviet armaments were undertaken already in the aftermath of the Declaration of Independence. In December 1991, the Russian Defense Minister, *Pavel Grachev*, had a meeting with Dudaev on the matter. The Chechen President promised to *facilitate the withdrawal in every way* on condition that *a part of the weapons and military installations* remained *in Chechen hands*. According to informal reports, the General made a proposal to keep 50% of the armaments and materials for himself.

If the problem of the functioning and defense of the state were urgent, no less urgent was that of international recognition. The Chechen Republic was a self-proclaimed state, devoid of any official support from abroad. Dudaev wished to deal with Yeltsin as an equal, but for this to happen, Chechnya would have to be recognized by the world community as an independent state. This recognition, however, was difficult to obtain. The world perceived the Chechen one as a problem within Russia, and even the states that had just gained independence from the USSR did not go beyond generic declarations of solidarity. Thus, a week after the Declaration of Independence, no foreign head of state had shown up. Only *Nursultan Nazarbayev*, President of Kazakhstan, he had had a telephone conversation with Dudaev, however, limiting himself to a generic manifestation of friendship[117]. While waiting to be able to start a round of official visits abroad, Dudaev tried to

---

[117]Nazarbayev at that juncture did not promise anything politically important: he limited himself to guaranteeing assistance to the numerous Chechens who still lived in his republic, in accordance with the relations built between the two peoples during Ardakhar.

get noticed in the international press. Its first appearance in European newspapers was on 7 December 1991. On that occasion, a statement from the General appeared in the columns of German newspapers in which it was said that the Chechen Republic would be willing to give political asylum to the now decayed President of the German Democratic Republic, *Erich Honecker*. He was about to be put on trial in Germany. Dudaev's initiative was unsuccessful, and finally Honecker exiled himself to Santiago de Chile, where he died in 1994. The stunt was more publicity than anything else, but it allowed Dudaev to make himself known for the first time in the world. A month later, when it was now clear that the USSR would dissolve and the Commonwealth of Independent States would rise in its place, Dudaev and the Parliament issued a declaration in which Chechnya would be willing to join the new union on a level of legal equality with the other ex - Soviet states. At the same time, it declared its neutrality with respect to any military alliance that could force the country to resort to war as a means of resolving international disputes.[118].

The hope was to establish as many diplomatic relations as possible, forcing Russia to open negotiations for the recognition of the country. For the time being, however, the international initiatives of the Grozny government remained a dead letter: no recognition came by 1991, and by the end of the year the Chechen

---

[118]The text of the declaration read: *We declare our willingness to join any regional Commonwealth or expression of the entire former Soviet Union on equal terms, and our determination to promote integration processes based on them. [...] The Chechen Republic will not participate in any military alliance and agreement of an aggressive nature, but reserves the right to use all means recognized by international law to protect its sovereignty and territorial integrity. [...] The Republic will not resort to the use of force or the threat of its use against other states. [...] calls on all states and republics of the former Union to recognize the sovereignty of the Chechen Republic [...] declares to recognize the state sovereignty of all republics in accordance with the norms of international law.*

Republic was still a de facto independent state. Time was running out, and sooner or later negotiations would have to be opened with Moscow. On a couple of occasions, the Russian government had already tried to meet Dudaev: the first time *Galina Starovoitova*, Yeltsin's personal advisor, had tried on 18 November. On that occasion Dudaev had discharged Starovoitova by saying that any decision concerning the negotiations would have to be agreed with Parliament. A second time, the Vice-President of the Russian Supreme Soviet, *Yuri Yarov*, tried. Again Dudaev postponed the decision to Parliament, although he declared that no negotiations could take place before the recognition of full independence by Moscow.

In light of the failure of the policy of international recognition, and of the deadlock in negotiating relations with Russia, one thing seemed increasingly evident: that Chechnya could not have survived for long if its gesture had not been received and emulated by all *small oppressed homelands* of the North Caucasus. Dudaev strongly believed in an independent Caucasus, and wanted Chechen independence to trigger a chain reaction that would force Moscow to negotiate. In this sense he had passionately supported Georgian nationalism, and had made a personal alliance with *Zviad Gamsakhurdia*, the first leader of independent Georgia. Of the same opinion, in various capacities, were many other political thinkers of the Caucasus, who since 1989 had set up a political platform that would carry forward the idea of a Confederation of Peoples of the Caucasus. Their main reference was to the Republic of the Mountain, established in 1918 in the aftermath of the Bolshevik Revolution[119].

---

[119]In an interview with the Turkish daily *Zaman*, Dudaev stated:
My plan is for the creation of a union of the countries of the Caucasus directed

For Dudaev, independence was only the first step in a domino effect, which would lead all the peoples of the Caucasus to free themselves, and then unite in a confederation of sovereign states. The cornerstone of this "Caucasian revolution" would have been Chechnya, which had initiated this process and which seemed to have the credentials to guide it[120].

Dudaev's geopolitical thinking, however, was not hegemonic. His intention was not to "conquer the Caucasus", but to propose a genuinely anti-imperialist and essentially anti-Russian project. This vision of his, naïve perhaps, certainly unattainable, did not take into account in fact that among the 19 ethnic groups that inhabited the Caucasus, many did not consider coexistence within the borders of the Russian Federation at all a problem. Indeed, the main sponsors of the Confederation of the Caucasus Mountain Peoples, who as we will see were the Abkhazians, were pressing precisely to remain under the umbrella of Moscow. Thus, while the Chechen general made friends with the Georgian Gamsakhurdia, Abkhazia (which as we have seen was an autonomous region of Georgia itself) rebelled and proclaimed secession.

But let's go in order. Between 1 and 2 November 1991 the Assembly of the Caucasus Mountain Peoples held a

against Russian imperialism, which means a united Caucasus. Our main goal is to achieve independence and liberation by acting together with the other republics of the Caucasus that have been oppressed by Russia over the course of three hundred years.

[120]The belief that he was a sort of "Fidel Castro of the Caucasus" was interpreted as extremism by many Russian political scientists - In particular Sergei Roi, deputy editor of the newspaper Moskva, coined the term Chechen Nazism, using these words: *The ideology of the Dudaev regime rests on two pillars: Islam and a Chechen version of Nazism, not separatism or simple nationalism, but an extremely aggressive and expansionist version, which manifests itself for example in the plans for a "Great Chechnya" that extends from the Caspian Sea to the Black Sea, and in Dudaev's insistence that Chechens are ethnically the central nation of the Caucasus.*

very popular congress in Sukhumi, the capital of Abkhazia, during which the *Confederation of the Caucasus Mountain Peoples* was formally established, self-proclaimed legitimate heir of the homonymous republic established. in 1918. The first document produced by the Confederation was a Declaration of Alliance with which all the representatives expressed their solidarity in the desire to establish an autonomous political entity[121].

The presence of a large Chechen representation, as well as the esteem that Dudaev and the separatists enjoyed among the peoples of the Caucasus, made themselves felt when the political bodies of the Confederation were appointed. In fact, a Caucasian Parliament and an Executive Committee were set up to follow up on its deliberations. Yusup Soslambekov was elected president of the Parliament, who at that time also held the position of President of the International Affairs Commission of the Chechen Parliament. The Confederation immediately found itself having to face some serious problems: first of all not all nationalities were represented there: none in the stocks of Turkish origin (Balkans, Karakay, Nogai and Calmuks) had responded to the invitation, while the Ingush had joined but they had not participated. Secondly, the entities that had joined the Confederation were not real republics, but political movements that did not enjoy state legitimacy. The only state that existed at that time, even if only in fact, was the Chechen Republic. Thirdly, the position that the Confederation should have taken vis-à-vis Russia was not clear. Finally, each people had territorial claims

---

[121] The text of the Declaration read: The participating peoples declare that they intend to act in a spirit of brotherhood, friendship and cooperation, with the aim of developing and strengthening political, socio-economic and cultural ties among the Caucasus Highlanders, following the principles of state sovereignty, cooperation, mutual support and non-interference in the internal affairs of the republics they represent.

on the neighboring people, and this made it very difficult to find a political understanding. Complicating the already complex geopolitical framework in which Chechnya was trying to defend its independence were the conflicts that were unleashed in the South Caucasus. the only state that existed at that time, even if only in fact, was the Chechen Republic. Thirdly, the position that the Confederation should have taken vis-à-vis Russia was not clear. Finally, each people had territorial claims on the neighboring people, and this made it very difficult to find a political understanding. Complicating the already complex geopolitical framework in which Chechnya was trying to defend its independence were the conflicts that were unleashed in the South Caucasus. the only state that existed at that time, even if only in fact, was the Chechen Republic. Thirdly, the position that the Confederation should have taken with regard to Russia was not clear. Finally, each people had territorial claims on the neighboring people, and this made it very difficult to find a political understanding. Complicating the already complex geopolitical framework in which Chechnya was trying to defend its independence were the conflicts that were unleashed in the South Caucasus.

Political tensions in the Caucasus

As we have seen, the federated republics of Georgia, Armenia and Azerbaijan had taken advantage of the collapse of the USSR which, without caring too much about the complex ethnic situation within their borders, had declared the independence of all their districts, even those inhabited by populations other than their own. In particular, there were three autonomous regions in which the sovereignty of the newborn republics was openly contested: they were the "Georgians" *Abkhazia* and *South*

Ossetia and the "Azerbaijani" *Nagorno - Karabakh*. In all three there had been riots and violence, which had immediately spoiled relations between the three independent republics and, within these, between the ethnic majorities and minorities that inhabited the autonomous provinces. The inter-ethnic conflicts intersected with the frictions between the majority and opposition political forces. This explosive mixture was always on the verge of exploding, and the parties involved, mostly led by improvised leadership and pickers, poured fuel on the fire. As long as the Soviet Union had guaranteed order, alternating peace talks with the deployment of the army, the situation remained more or less under control. But with the progressive withdrawal of the Red Army, this diaphragm had disappeared, and within a few months the whole region was inflamed.

The first open conflict broke out in Georgia between Zviad Gamsakhurdia and his opposition. The latter, elected head of the then Supreme Soviet in 1990, had initially held a policy of openness to democracy and multi-partyism. This approach had put him to grips with the claims of ethnic minorities, who complained of poor representation in parliament and equally poor cultural and linguistic recognition. Following the August Putsch, the President, who had maintained a line hostile to the coup leaders but opposed to any form of armed insurrection, was accused, as had happened to Zavgaev in Chechnya, of not having firmly opposed the coup. Meanwhile, his heated hostility towards Moscow had taken the form of a veritable paranoia, which had isolated him from the more moderate fringes of his majority. The semi-dictatorial approach he developed as a result of this, his refusal to recognize the rights of ethnic minorities, branded as supporters of Russian imperialism, and in general the climate of creeping civil war that reigned in the country prevented the government to be recognized by the great world powers. On 2 September 1991, the friction between the majority and the opposition resulted in a large street demonstration that the government severely repressed, causing numerous injuries. As a result, the Georgian army broke up into multiple factions, some loyal to Gamsakhurdia, others hostile to the president. The capital Tbilisi became the scene of widespread unrest, during which the first deaths began to occur. Gamsakhurdia continued to oppose any opposition demands, refusing to call new elections or to resign. Numerous politicians from major parties hostile to his government were arrested on suspicion of plotting a coup, while the news organizations that flanked them were shut down. The latent clash between the fringes of the National Guard, divided between loyalists and opposition followers, led to a military coup on December 20, 1991, during which government opponents occupied Tbilisi and besieged the Georgian president in government neighborhoods up to early January 1992, when he managed to flee first to Azerbaijan, then to Armenia.

The fall of Gamsakhurdia further complicated the already difficult geopolitical framework in which the Chechen government found itself operating. Georgia, in fact, was the only country beyond Russia to share an international border with Chechnya, and a possible blockade of movements on that side too would have isolated the country from any land contact. It was essential that at least that corridor remained open, and that through this Dudaev was able to find sufficient contacts to ensure freedom of maneuver. So Dudaev decided to invite the now fallen Georgian President to stay in Chechnya together with his most faithful dignitaries. Gamsakhurdia would have arrived in Grozny in the first days of January, where the Chechen President would have settled him by hosting him as a personal friend, while the other was preparing his revenge.

The cultural renaissance

While in the palaces of power Dudaev, Mamodaev and the Parliament busied themselves to set up the new independent state and make what remained of the old republic work, the Chechens experienced an unprecedented cultural freedom. Finally, after almost a century of repression, the Islamic centers could freely teach religious precepts. Furthermore, traditional culture was experiencing a real revival. The population experienced an awakening of conscience that pervaded everyone, from young students to the elderly veterans of the exodus. And one of the most interesting political - cultural initiatives of the independence leadership took place towards the elderly: the rebirth of the *Mekh - Khel.*

This was the ancient Council of Elders, an institution that had its origins in the Chechen tribal system and that had spanned the centuries before being wiped out by communism. In ancient times it was precisely the Mekh - Khel who administered relations between people and families, who was the custodian of common history. One of the main points of Yandarbiev's Vaynakh Democratic Party was its reconstitution as a body of the state. Dudaev saw it more as a kind of "sponsor" that helped to give the impression that Chechnya was regaining its identity. The first meeting of the Mekh - Khel took place shortly before the elections, on 21 October. Each village sent three of its elders to represent. At its guide was placed (or placed) Said Magomed Adizov, a rather agitated elder,[122].

The traditional network of Chechen clans, the Teip, also experienced a new liveliness. On November 22, 1991, under the patronage of Dudaev himself, the first Teip Congress was held in Grozny, during which the frayed Chechen social structure, crumbled following the deportation and then the tumultuous return home, tried to regroup. The animators of the project had in mind to update the Teip network to the modern social and economic system. They even came to propose the creation of a sort of Cooperative Credit of the Teip, a "bank of the clans" that would grant small loans to families and businesses, but the project failed to take off due to low subscriptions.[123].

If the re - institutionalization of the Teip immediately appeared more as a publicity stunt than anything else, the true cultural force of the Chechen people, Islam, returned to the fore with genuineness. Centuries of Russian oppression and seventy years of Soviet obscurantism had increased the Chechens' desire to manifest their beliefs with renewed vigor. Thus, when

---

[122] Institutionalized by the Parliament on 24 December 1991 in the *Law on the Activities of the Parliament of the Chechen Republic*, the Mekh - Khel was given authority over moral control and the supervision of institutional activities. This recognition, however, was revoked after just two months (February 1992) due to the arrogant behavior of some of its main exponents, against which many citizens complained, as well as the claim of its President, Adizov, to directly influence the activities of the Parliament.

[123] Over the months many other congresses were to be held, even if behind these there was often not only the desire to rebuild the traditional network of social relations, but the ambition of politicians who tried to constitute their electoral containers. In fact, the reconstituted Teip system caused more confusion than anything else. From territorial disputes with other TEIPs, to electoral disputes, these meetings ended up creating mostly discord and rancor. In some cases it even came to plan the constitution of military regiments based on belonging to a specific Teip. Such a measure would have turned Chechnya into a battlefield in which blood feuds and small local potentates would have taken the country hostage more than, in fact, was already happening.

Dudaev declared the independence of the state, he did so by holding the Koran in his hands, an attitude that in a secularized Western state would have been considered grave and dangerous, and which instead, in the mentality of the Chechens, sounded profoundly necessary and right. It was not long before the Islamic sentiments of the Chechen population showed themselves in the legislative initiatives of the parliament. Not even a month after the start of the legislature, in fact, three laws of clear Islamic inspiration were approved. The first was the one that prohibited the carrying out of autopsies on corpses (with the exception of those expressly requested by the judicial authorities). The second prohibited men from practicing the profession of gynecologist. The third, finally, instituted Friday as a day of celebration, reintroducing working Sunday. Three provisions which in themselves could not qualify Chechen legislation as "confessional", but which introduced juridical precedents not in line with the corpus of a secularized state. The second prohibited men from practicing the profession of gynecologist. The third, finally, instituted Friday as a day of celebration, reintroducing working Sunday. Three provisions which in themselves could not qualify Chechen legislation as "confessional", but which introduced juridical precedents not in line with the corpus of a secularized state.

The opposition is reorganizing

While the nationalists gave birth to their independent state, the moderate opposition and the remnants of the old republic sought a new political center of gravity around which to reorganize. The Chechen revolution had deprived Soviet officials of the apparatus on which their power was based: in vain had Zavgaev pleaded his cause in the offices of the Russian Supreme Soviet. After losing his seat and his seat, all he had to do was take the lead of the "dethroned" and rebuild his basis of consensus from scratch. On November 25, according to the TASS news agency, officials deposed by the Executive Committee spoke on state TV condemning the elections as *illegal* and *rigged*. As proof of what has been stated, they bore the testimony of some citizens residing in the northern districts of Upper Terek and Naursk, who complained that they did not participate in the elections. These were the two territories most densely inhabited by Russians and Cossacks, who had already taken little part in the revolution themselves. Furthermore, Upper Terek was Zavgaev's homeland, and his ouster from power had robbed many of his associates who inhabited that region from wages and senior positions. The district of Naursk, then, had experienced the worst side of the revolution, having to witness the mass evasion of the detention center that was located there and the consequent soaring crime. There is no doubt that the north of the country was the least affected by the claims of the nationalists.

Indeed, the first manifestation of open hostility towards the nascent Dudaev government was held in Upper Terek. On December 5, just a month after the Declaration of Independence, representatives of some twenty-five villages declared that they did not recognize Dudaev as their president, nor the newly elected parliament as legitimate. The protesters complained that the election of the organs of the Republic had taken place without taking into account the opinions of the residents and practically without their participation and claimed the right to hold a confirmatory referendum in which all citizens could participate. Finally, the demonstrators organized themselves into a movement: "teams" were formed made up of local young people, who could be mobilized as needed in an armed militia.

It did not take long before the dissent manifested on December 5 gave way to a real branch: following the law passed by the parliament on the election of local administrative offices, *Umar Avturkhanov*, already an official of the *MVD* (the militia under the orders of the Soviet Interior Ministry), was elected Governor in the District of Upper Terek. He was a man from the Soviet apparatus and capable of attracting to himself the hopes of former party officials who were suddenly without a point of reference. He was also appreciated in Russian circles, having been part of the establishment, and liked by the military, being a former militia officer. Avturkhanov immediately disowned Dudaev. His gesture of open rebellion earned him the closeness not only of the Russians and the Cossacks, but also of the moderate opposition which had boycotted the elections of 27 October. For the time being, however, the composite reassemblement of opponents to Dudaev was little known, and even less supported by ordinary people.

The end of the year saw the launch of a measure that further increased the already strong popularity of the President: on December 28th he recognized by decree full ownership of the public housing apartments assigned to large families, single mothers, chronically ill patients and disabled people, as well as workers in the cultural, artistic, health and education sectors[124].

The 1991 balance

Although only 60 days had passed since the Declaration of Independence, a brief assessment could already be made. The separatists had achieved a series of goals: first of all they had achieved the de facto

---

[124] This was Dudaev's only large-scale privatization measure, although it did not bring any benefit to the state coffers.

independence of the country. The Soviet army had not intervened to quell the revolution. Dudaev's leadership was popular, appreciated by most Chechens, the clergy and a part of the bourgeoisie. Parliament had taken office and was working enthusiastically. Mamodaev's interim government seemed to be keeping the situation under control, at least ensuring that basic needs were met. Chechnya was equipping itself with a rudimentary government apparatus and a regular army, and Moscow for the moment did not yet seem willing to engage in a head-on confrontation.

However, many problems remained unsolved. First, the country's independence was not a legal reality. No government had officially recognized Chechnya, no embassy had been opened in Grozny, and no Chechen embassy had been opened in any foreign country. Domestically, Chechnya was still in chaos. Hundreds of firearms had been distributed during the revolution, and very few of them had returned to government arsenals. Some had gone to the popular opposition militia that was being organized in the north of the country. The government was not yet in control of the territory, and was barely able to assert itself only around Grozny. Crime was rampant. The borders of the republic were porous and the rule of law was struggling to be restored. L' the country's economy, already fragile in itself, was in danger of collapse, and the government did not have a clear position on which choices to make. The absence of an organized legislative system and an executive recognized by all political forces made the political situation precarious. The relations between the President and the Parliament, then, were not the best. Initially hailed as the guide who would protect the Republic, Dudaev was beginning to be seen by some MPs as an authoritarian leader. In some cases the deputies most critical of him had openly opposed certain of his appointments and did not tolerate his egotism. This friction between executive and legislative power, which in a consolidated democracy would have been seen as a normal dialectical moment,

On December 31, in his first year-end speech, Dudaev stated:

"Dear fellow citizens! The year that has just ended represented a turning point in our Republic. Together, we have experienced one of the most significant events of the last century and a half in the history of our people: the peaceful revolution of the people. "The backbone of the imperialist and totalitarian regime, the diabolical legacy of an atheist monster, is broken. The Chechen Republic has unequivocally declared its commitment to freedom, universal human values and an unwavering will to complete independence. But there is no true freedom without faith in the Most High! And we must return to the path that our Creator chose for us! We have great things to do, and great difficulties to overcome. But we have a virtuous goal, so we will be successful. The confidence in this is given to me by the spirit of the people, by their will, by their character. There is no barrier that everyone's will cannot overcome. We will win, we have no other choice! I am sure that the free Chechen republic is the first stone thrown in the foundation of the future state of all the Vaynakhs, a free and united Caucasus. Our fathers fought for this, their pains and sufferings are ours. I am pleased to be able to say, addressing you today: Citizens of the Chechen Republic! This is our achievement. We must protect it, regardless of our nationality, because we are all citizens of a free state! " I am sure that the free Chechen republic is the first stone thrown in the foundation of the future state of all the Vaynakhs, a free and united Caucasus. Our fathers fought for this, their pains and sufferings are ours. I am pleased to be able to say, addressing you today: Citizens of the Chechen Republic! This is our achievement. We must protect it, regardless of our nationality, because we are all citizens of a free state! " I am sure that the free Chechen republic is the first stone thrown in the foundation of the future state of all the Vaynakhs, a free and

united Caucasus. Our fathers fought for this, their pains and sufferings are ours. I am pleased to be able to say, addressing you today: Citizens of the Chechen Republic! This is our achievement. We must protect it, regardless of our nationality, because we are all citizens of a free state!"

In Dudaev's words there were the triumphalism of the leader, the solemnity of the head of state, but also and above all the invitation to the Chechens to find a common denominator that would keep them united against the centrifugal forces that could have torn the state apart. And that common element, for Dudaev, could only be Islam, a belief shared by the vast majority of the population.

CHAPTER 5

THE REPUBLIC

"With the will of Allah the people of the Chechen Republic, expressing the aspiration of the Chechen nation, guided by the ideas of humanism and with the aim of creating an equitable society, proceeding from high responsibility towards the present and future generations of our compatriots, respecting all the rights and interests of all nations and peoples, by proclaiming the Chechen Republic an independent and sovereign state and recognizing itself the same rights as all the others in the community of nations, accepts the this Constitution and considers it from now on as the main law of society and of the State ".

Preamble of the Constitution of the Chechen Republic of Ichkeria

The big sale

On January 1, 1992, the USSR broke up. Two hundred and ninety million people suddenly ceased to be Soviet citizens. Few were in a position to understand what transformations their world was undergoing. The majority continued to try to survive the economic crisis, hoping that the reform plan launched by Yeltsin would bring the Western well being that perestroika televisions had shown them. On January 2, the decree of price liberalization came into force, the first step towards a market economy. Until then these had been set by the government through economic planning. From that day on, however, the law of supply and demand began to determine the value of goods. The measure immediately generated an economic earthquake: products whose cost was kept artificially low skyrocketed while others were blown away by the competition. As a consequence of the ever diminishing appreciation of the ruble on international markets, the currency suffered a very strong inflation.

The Russian economists were well aware of what would happen, but they considered it the price necessary to ferry the Soviet system into the free market. Gajdar in particular thought that the increase in prices would not exceed the threshold of 300%, and that within a few months it would fall below 10%, and then return to the normal dynamics of cyclical growth and decline typical of the Western system. However, contrary to what he had predicted[125], inflation continued to gallop from week to

---

[125] An example of this is what was declared in an interview by the financier Jeffrey Sachs: *When we embarked on the reforms we felt like doctors called to the bedside of a sick person. But when we put the patient on the operating table and opened it, we realized that its anatomical structure and its organs were of a very particular type, which we had never encountered in medical schools.*

week, month to month, without stopping[126], while the industrial system was facing a dramatic crisis: in the course of 1992 alone, production decreased by 20%. At the same time, production costs increased, forcing companies to raise prices and further limiting the purchasing power of consumers. In short, a devastating spiral was triggered in which poverty and inflation were self-sustaining. The reduced circulation of capital broke down the revenues of the state, forcing it to reduce expenses. The lack of liquidity prevented companies from investing, or from purchasing raw materials and components necessary for production. Wages began to be paid late, then through coupons, finally through the same products as the factories where the workers worked. Inflation reached such levels that the state mint was unable to meet the continuous demand for cash, wich began to run low: barter began to spread as an alternative to an overvalued and not easy to find currency.

Within a few months the factories began to close, and the Russians returned to experience a phenomenon they had not known for decades: unemployment. Hundreds of thousands of people found themselves unemployed, and within a few months the thousands became millions.

---

[126]The theoretical model on which he and his collaborators were based was very optimistic. Gajdar overestimated the competitiveness of Soviet production, the capacity of the young Russian business class and the resilience of the economy to the speculative aggression of Western financiers. During the first quarter, prices increased on average by 800%, in some cases they rose twenty or thirty times compared to the Soviet period. Just to give a few examples, the Salt went from 9 kopecks (hundredths of a ruble) to 9 rubles, a hundredfold increase. Matches increased by 250 times. In general, prices fluctuated in the order of 20 to 30 times for most essential goods and services. Wages, on the other hand, limited themselves to doubling, so that the power of purchase of Russian citizens was reduced to almost zero. The volume of purchases on the market decreased dramatically, preventing the economy from disposing of production and jamming the production chain.

In an attempt to prevent even the country's main wealth, oil, from becoming unavailable to ordinary people, the government excluded raw materials from price liberalization. But in doing so he placed a very precious commodity at controlled prices on a free and internationalized market. The result was that those few Russians who had the opportunity began to buy it in large quantities on the domestic market and then resell it at higher prices abroad. On this business many entrepreneurs founded billionaire economic successes, buying oil on the Russian market at very low prices and reselling it with increases of 30, 40, 50% on foreign markets. Thus the first "oligarchs" were born, who became enormously rich on the shoulders of the public budget. If the central state had used these capital gains to boost economic growth, it might have reversed the course that was leading Russia to economic collapse. Instead, by not doing so, it gave birth to the class of the so-called *New Rich* or *New Russians*, who became immensely powerful without doing anything but speculating on the price of oil. The accumulated capital was promptly moved to foreign current accounts or used in the purchase of luxurious properties in Europe, America and Asia, to prevent inflation from eroding them. Thus, while the government was forced to use the proceeds from the sale of oil to support the lower social classes, increasingly poor and unemployed, a handful of speculators became excessively rich.

Those responsible for this brutal social transformation of the country were not only the members of the Russian government. An important role was also played by all those Western *experts* who were hired as *advisers*. Characters accustomed to enriching themselves on speculation, who had cut their teeth in much more hostile environments compared to which Russia, still lacking an adequate legal system to regulate the capitalist economy, seemed like a playground. The financiers of *Goldman Sachs*, of the *International Monetary Fund*, the agents of the great Western and Asian investment banks hit the former Soviet Union as the conquistadors had hit the Indians. The countries that emerged from the planned economy all suffered the same fate: the loans generously given by the The West made their economies dependent on a permanent, unquenchable debt capable of conditioning their internal and foreign policies. The former USSR experienced the so-called *debt slavery*: countries such as Ukraine, Moldova or Russia itself agreed to enter into commitments that were defined in journalistic terms as *mouthfuls of oxygen*, whose interests soon ended up consuming all the deficits of budget, forcing governments to raise taxes to pay the installments due.

The second pillar of the "liberal revolution" of Gajdar and associates, as we have seen, was privatization. Privatizing in itself is not difficult in a mature capitalist system. In the former USSR, on the other hand, it was a completely different story, because private property did not exist, and there were not even the rules of law necessary to regulate the infinite variables that exist in the exchange of property and in private economic initiative in general. The USSR was a socialist state, and the problem of regulating the private economy had never been raised. However, the neoliberals approached privatization with the same blind optimism with which they had approached price liberalization. Gajdar assigned the project to *Anatolij Cubajs,* economist and professor at the Leningrad University, a staunch supporter of *shock therapy*. As he stated in an interview, he intended *[...] To build capitalism in Russia, and to do it in a few years of frontal attack, thus creating production norms that had taken the rest of the world centuries [...]*. Cubajs devised a "horizontal" privatization system: wanting to ensure that all citizens have the same opportunities to become owners of businesses and services, he calculated the value of all public property at 1,260,500 billion rubles in 1991. Divided by the 148,700,000 inhabitants of the country, public wealth amounted to 8,367 rubles for each Russian, 10,000 to make a round figure. Cubajs then proposed to distribute to each Russian a voucher of that face value, anonymous and freely salable. In this way each citizen, from the company manager to the worker, would have had the same opportunity to own part of the privatized companies. According to the models developed by Cubajs, with the progress of privatization these vouchers would have seen their value increase. However, there were numerous unknowns, or at least numerous risky details in this operation: first of all, the vouchers quantified wealth, but did not carry the burden of foreign debt that weighed on this wealth. The value of the vouchers was nominal, and inflation was rampant. With the current depreciation rate, holding those pieces of paper meant seeing their value depreciate day by day. This awareness prompted millions of citizens to get rid of it as soon as possible, to save what little money they could make immediately. Millions of vouchers were placed on the market simultaneously, causing an immediate depreciation. The directors of many public companies, having sniffed out the deal, set up personal investment funds with which they bought up these securities, buying them at ridiculously low costs, and quickly finding themselves owners of the company they had managed as public officials. Organized crime found in vouchers the system of laundering billions of dirty rubles, buying companies and entering "clean" industrial salons, raking vouchers from workers, housewives, pensioners who ran to get rid of them to fill a shopping cart or buy a television[127].

To favor a quick privatization of the large state-owned companies, Gajdar transformed them into a joint-stock company, giving the property partly to workers and partly to financial investors. Again, most of the shares, given free to the workers, were quickly rounded up for a few rubles by financial speculators, who secured control of the state industry. Gigantic businesses such as the *Uralmas* heavy machinery factory, still one of the largest in the country today, were bought for the price of an apartment in London[128]. *Zil*, an automobile factory in which 103,000 workers were employed, was sold for less than five million dollars. The privatization war bulletin is long and dramatic, but suffice it to cite another example: the country's leading mining company, *Norilsk Nickel*, was bought for $ 170 million against a reported turnover of $ 3 billion.

The advent of this new "ruling class" disinterested in the fate of the companies it had bought, but eager to make the most of it, produced a real industrial disaster[129].

---

[127] Over time it became clear that the *voucherization* of the state was a colossal scam, as Gajdar himself admitted in his memoir, declaring: *The distributed voucher has only a social - psychological meaning [...] only an elite could quickly become aware of the possibilities offered to it by privatization. [...]* .

[128] Kacha Bendukidze, who bought the industrial complex, said in an interview: *For us privatization was a godsend. It allowed us to step up and buy whatever we wanted from the government on favorable terms [...] We took a large chunk of Russian industrial capacity, even though we were unable to buy even one square meter of real estate in Moscow. It was easier to get hold of Uralmas than a single warehouse in Moscow [...] We bought that plant for a thousandth of its real value [...]. Of course, if someone offered us a billion dollars for Uralmas we would say yes [...] In my past life I was a biologist and a communist. Today I am a businessman and a liberal.*

[129] Between 1992 and 1995 the gross domestic product contracted by 60%, industrial production by 58%, oil production by 42%, agricultural production by 35%. Steel production contracted by 40%, automobile production by 61%, that of tractors by 90%. Combine production in 1995 was just 6% of that in 1992.

The collapse of industrial production produced millions of unemployed, and the consumption of the population contracted dramatically. Purchases dropped between 30 and 40%, and with them the average life expectancy, which experienced an unprecedented regression: a year after the start of privatization, this had dropped by 4 years for men and by 8 years for women. The social consequences did not take long to manifest themselves in all their gravity: an exemplary indicator of the living conditions of a society is the rate of abandonment of children. In Russia in 1993, two million were estimated, one hundred and fifty thousand in the capital Moscow alone. This army of starving teenagers would have poured into the suburbs of the big cities, often joining the ranks of the organized underworld.

The economic blockade

The long premise that we have made perhaps allows us to better understand why the Russian leadership began to take seriously the Chechen problem only at the beginning of 1992. With all the reorganization work to be done to rebuild the state and the economy from scratch, with everyone those centers of power to be occupied, with *all that good things* to be privatized, the situation in Chechnya appeared to be a third level problem. In Moscow it was thought that after all, Dudaev's revolution was nothing more than an upheaval, a resurgence, a reaction to the political vacuum, which would break down as the new institutions began to function again. So, when the waters had calmed down a little and Yeltsin had a chance to focus again on that rebellious little republic, he did so with the tranquility of someone expecting a slow and gradual lowering of tones, a return to normal after a few months of agitation. The Russian leader was convinced that Dudaev and his men were just a band of adventurers, and he would continue to think so for a long time to come. He also underestimated the character of the Chechens and was convinced that it would be enough to "remove the alimony" from the General to force him to flee chased by the elderly left without pensions. An economic siege lasting a few months, at most a year, would have been enough, and then the economic growth generated by liberal reforms in Russia would have convinced even the most grim nationalists to return to the fold. The Russian leader was convinced that Dudaev and his men were just a band of adventurers, and he would continue to think so for a long time to come. He also underestimated the character of the Chechens, and was convinced that it would be enough to "remove the alimony" from the General to force him to flee chased by the elderly left without pensions. An economic siege lasting a few months, at most a year, would have been enough, and then the economic growth generated by liberal reforms in Russia would have convinced even the most grim nationalists to return to the fold. The Russian leader was convinced that Dudaev and his men were just a band of adventurers, and he would continue to think so for a long time to come. He also underestimated the character of the Chechens, and was convinced that it would be enough to "remove the alimony" from the General to force him to flee chased by the elderly left without pensions. An economic siege lasting a few months, at most a year, would have been enough, and then the economic growth generated by liberal reforms in Russia would have convinced even the most grim nationalists to return to the sheepfold.

Thus on January 29, 1992, Russia imposed an economic blockade on Chechnya. By order of Yeltsin not only all subsidies from the central government stopped, but also the payments of state salaries and pensions were frozen. The donations remained in force only in the northern districts of the country, inhabited by the Cossacks and in that of Upper Terek, in which the governor Umar Avturkhanov openly contested the secessionists. This would get the message across that rebelling against Dudaev was worth the money. The possibility of a closure of the internal borders by Moscow and a stop of transfers by the federal treasury was already the subject of debate in Grozny, and its news was not a great surprise for the separatists. For his part, Dudaev had prevented her, ordering the blocking of any transfer from the country to Moscow. However, the problem was serious, because Chechnya was preparing to face the blockade without yet having had international recognition, without Russia itself considering it an independent state, without a real government in office, and without this government had embarked on a serious path of economic reform. With respect to the latter issue, as we have seen, there was a strong dissonance between the views of the President, who was essentially a socialist, and those of the head of the provisional government, Mamodaev, of liberal orientation. Regarding the economic question, the Chechen leadership urgently had to ask itself the problem of avoiding the encirclement: for the moment it was only a transfer block, but there it was to be expected that soon there would be a real embargo. Even before that, the socialist system had to be transformed into something different, which would remove the risk of insolvency from the state coffers and restore dynamism to the productive system.

The central issue was obviously "what" and "how" should have been privatized. Dudaev was pressing to leave the economic direction in the hands of the state, opposing any privatization of state service or industry[130] while Mamodaev argued the need to *privatize all that can be privatized* to leave public finances the oxygen necessary to function efficiently[131]. Meanwhile, the ordinary management of the economy was still entrusted to the Mamodaev Committee and to Dudaev's personal initiative. These from January 1992 decided to directly take control over the export of petroleum products. Dudaev feared that speculators would get rich behind the government, so he decreed that every single export should require its explicit authorization. This generated a first strong disagreement with Mamodaev, since black gold was the resource - the cornerstone on which the latter intended to base his economic policy. The counterpart, for Mamodaev, was the authorization for

---

[130] A consequence of Dudaev's socialist sentiment was economic interventionism in favor of the vulnerable. Dudaev's first intervention in economic policy was the creation of a Price Committee to oversee tariff control. *The price cannot be spontaneous, it should be adequate to people's possibilities* he repeated. For this reason Dudaev decreed that the bread be sold at the symbolic figure of 1 ruble per kilo. The state would take over the expense. Within 12 months the public budget could no longer bear such a welfare mechanism, which among other things generated very strong speculation (the Chechens took bread at a ruble a kilo and went to resell it abroad, or on the black market at higher prices).

[131] Dudaev agreed to only four privatization measures, according to Taymaz Abubakarov, his Minister of Economy, in his memoir, *The Dudaev's Regime*: the first was the decree by which he donated state-owned apartments to some categories of citizens we talked about at the end of the previous chapter. The other three were works begun in Grozny in the Soviet period and never completed: a large warehouse on Lenin Street, a covered basement and a hotel on Chechov Street. The supermarket was sold in 1992 for 150 million rubles. The proceeds were invested in the purchase of consumer goods for the population. The operation ultimately failed, because due to the banking blockade imposed by Moscow the acquiring company, which had pledged to finish the work within two years, failed to find sufficient funds. The covered basement was always bought for the same price by the Moscow Credo Bank, which intended to build a garage park there. The hotel complex was instead sold in 1993 for the sum of 350,000 dollars. The proceeds from these last two sales went to finance the renovation of public buildings.

the liberalization of prices for consumer goods and non-essential services, advocated by the president of COFEC since November 1991. Dudaev demanded that basic necessities remain controlled by the state, but he authorized the liberalization of all the others from January 4, 1992. The result was the same as we have seen happen in Russia. Within a week, most of the supplies had run out, and the store shelves were empty[132]. This happened because producers, seeing prices skyrocket, preferred to keep inventories steady, waiting for yet another rise rather than discarding the goods.[133]. Workers and consumers began to agitate from mid-January, demanding a lowering of prices or a rise in wages[134]. Squads of citizens began to patrol the markets, attempting to force traders to keep prices low. On

[132]Consumer prices began to rise dramatically: already on January 5, 24 hours after the issuance of the decree, pasta had risen six times in price, milk threefold, oil, sugar and meat had skyrocketed, and it was already difficult to find them on the market. A note from the TASS news agency on January 6 reported that *All products, except baked goods [calmed by law, ed.] Have increased threefold, and those manufactured have doubled. However, the shelves remain half-empty. [...] The price of gasoline has risen 3 times. In the Grozny labor collectives, especially in the construction sector, workers are threatening to strike if they do not see their wages increased in line with rising prices. [...]*.

[133]The smuggling of controlled but practically absent products became endemic. Bread, flour, medicines were sold on street corners, or in makeshift flea markets. A sack of flour, which the state guaranteed at 1 ruble per kilo, was sold for 15 rubles on the street. The dizzying rise in prices then generated a shortage of banknotes, and the use of bartering became the norm. On January 10, a week after the decree, prices continued to soar. By now, 250 rubles were needed to buy a chicken, the equivalent of 250 kilos of "calmed" bread. For a kilo of sausages it took 64 rubles, but the shelves were emptying within half an hour of opening the shops.

[134]The first strike took place on January 15, 1992. Workers at the Grozny Avtospetsoburodovanie car plant got into a state of agitation, demanding a fivefold salary increase. The factory management immediately denied the willingness to meet the workers' requests, having to deal with an increase in the prices of the components that were already bleeding the company budget. Teachers also took to the streets on the same day, demanding an increase in wages.

January 15, 1992, the central market was literally occupied: groups of insurgents imposed "social" prices for the whole day, but the following day they began to rise again. In an attempt to calm people down, COFEC introduced a ration card for sugar, oil and butter. Parliament intervened on January 18, passing a law that severely punished smuggling and illegal foreign trade. The practice of hiding goods in warehouses by speculating on rising prices was also prohibited. The Mayor of Grozny, Gantamirov, tried to do his part by setting up a special "social security" office to raise funds for the weakest sections of the population.

By mid-February, the economic situation was practically out of control. The COFEC insisted on the principle of rationing, inserting an increasing number of goods in the ration card. The cost of this controlled system weighed entirely on the already exhausted state coffers, and was financed through the import of products exchanged for oil and its derivatives, of which the state continued to hold a monopoly. But from early March it was clear that the state finances could not hold up any longer: the insolvency crisis was expected by the end of the month, coinciding with the payment of state salaries. The state of unrest spread to many high categories of workers in the following days. On March 26, the firefighters went on strike, interrupting the fire protection and security service[135]. Dudaev made a big

---

[135] According to reports from the TASS news agency, public salaries, especially those of policemen, had been "frozen" since January, waiting for the necessary liquidity to pay them. On March 16, the agency reported: *For the third day the teachers of many schools in Chechnya are on strike [...] the main request of teachers is to increase their salary several times and to ensure payment. Teachers, as well as employees from many other sectors, unfortunately were not paid for the third month due to the severe shortage of cash in the republic. Today it became known that in an attempt to get out of the crisis and avoid its repetition, the Cabinet of Ministers of the Chechen Republic has decided to organize auctions and exchanges for the sale of its petroleum products. In order to enhance the commercial activity in the*

statement with Moscow, urgently calling for a liquidity injection, and threatening to block oil supplies if this didn't happen. The economic blockade ordered by Yeltsin, in fact, did not include the stop to the supply of crude oil to Chechen refineries, where the plants processed strategic raw materials such as aircraft lubricants. Yeltsin had not been able to interrupt this flow, since these plants were present only in Chechnya, and the Russian industry could not make up for the lack of these products. Behind this state of necessity there was obviously also the intention to use the crude oil valve as an instrument of pressure to be loosened and tightened if necessary, if it was possible to open a serious negotiating table.

Giving an order to the country

One of the causes of the chaos that paralyzed the republic was the absence of a constitutional system that guaranteed the regular functioning of the state. There was a President, there was a Parliament, but there was no scaffolding on which these bodies could work in concert with each other, according to very specific rules, which governed the dialectic between the legislative, executive and judicial powers. The lack of an official government and the delay in the promulgation of the Constitution increased the friction between Parliament and the

---

territory of Chechnya, the income tax has also been abolished. " The next day, the bulletin of the same agency read: "The unplanned holidays started today in many schools in Grozny. The teachers are on strike. The demands are not only economic: a triple increase in salary with a further increase of 90%. A week earlier, the Deputy Prime Minister of the Republic, Taymaz Abubakarov, had managed to stop the strike by promising teachers to meet their conditions. But apparently he failed to do so. In Grozny, not only teachers have been paid for several months, but also law enforcement officials, doctors and a number of other segments of the population. Postal orders are not issued, no bank deposits are opened. [...]

President: already in the first days of January Yusup Soslambekov, one of the protagonists of the Chechen Revolution, had threatened to form an opposition group if Dudaev had not proposed a government team to the assembly in a short time. Dudaev, for his part, he did not intend to limit his personal power, so on January 16 he declared that he would keep the role of Prime Minister for himself, concentrating in his figure both the highest authority of the Republic and the top of the executive power. Parliament had no intention of allowing such behavior, and in an attempt to restore a democratic counterweight to Dudaev's assumption of full power, it instituted the post of Deputy Prime Minister. In any case, Dudaev proceeded to form a government team to be formalized as soon as the Constituent Assembly had passed a fundamental charter.

He intended to set up a government in which even the moderate forces, which were cut off from the revolution, could at least partially recognize themselves. For this reason he tried to include personalities from the past administration, and invited elements of the moderate opposition. The first name was the illustrious presidential candidate of the now dissolved Supreme Soviet, Salambek Hadijev. However, he refused: Hadjiev knew that Dudaev would not allow him to carry out those liberal policies that would have been necessary to restart the disastrous economic machine of the republic. Moreover, since the time of the assault on the Soviet, he had developed an open hostility towards the General and his *military methods*[136]. With the hope of including Hadijev

---

[136] In an interview years later, Hadijev stated: *I told him that I would not take part in this [government project] because he had the typical statist view of things. He was a typical army man: strength, order and submission! [...] I said that we should assure the people that we were heading for independence and that he should first deal with the economy step by step, but not the way he wanted, keeping everything within the state sector [...] but he had an old way of thinking, that everything had to be in the hands of the Division commander. I*

faded, Dudaev turned to another exponent of the economic department, Taymaz Abubakarov. He had been briefly at work in the Zavgaev government, too little to be identified with the past regime and in any case enough to represent its continuity. Abubakarov accepted, marking a first political success for the General. A second point Dudaev scored by obtaining the support of *Usman Imaev* at Justice. Imaev had been an official of the Soviet Foreign Ministry, then he had joined the Ministry of Justice of the Chechen-Ingush RSSA, and had headed the State Privatization Committee until August 1991. After the August Putsch he held the role of the Ministry of Social Welfare. He was therefore a multifaceted character, with a respectable curriculum, even if very young and unwelcome in Parliament.

While Dudaev carried out the negotiations for the constitution of the government, the legislative assembly worked on the constitution. The model used as a reference was that of the Estonian Constitution, partly because of the friendship and contacts that the Chechen nationalists had with the small Baltic country, partly because Estonia was very similar to Chechnya in size and population. The draft of the Constitution was ready by the end of January[137]. Parliament configured the Republic as a parliamentary regime. The assembly that emerged from the November elections should have been the fulcrum of the whole system, and would have had very extensive powers, such as that of approving the list of ministers proposed by the President, the appointment of the President of the Constitutional Court, of the Supreme Court, of the Attorney General, the Investigative Committee and the National Defense

---

told him this was unrealistic.
[137] A translated and commented version of the Constitution passed in 1992 is available on the website www.ichkeria.net in the *Constitution* section.

Service, the Governor of the National Bank, the National Health Service, all the ambassadors. He would have had the power to call referendums, declare war and declare a state of emergency, approve the budget and declare the president's impeachment if he abused his position. The President of the Republic was thought of as the guarantor of state unit and the commander-in-chief of the armed forces. Every citizen could have been elected President, by direct and anonymous vote. The President was granted the power of veto over the laws of Parliament, but a qualified parliamentary majority could have prevented his intervention in the legislative process. The transmission belt between the central power and the territory would have been the local governments, directly elected by the citizens. In general, the principles that inspired the Chechen Constitution were those of Western countries[138]. The Chechen state should have been democratic and founded on multi-partyism. Freedom of speech, of the press and of conscience were guaranteed[139]. According to the dictates of the Constitution, Chechnya should have been a secular country. But ignoring the strong Islamic tradition of the people would have alienated that founding charter from the people it intended to rule. For this reason, the Constitutional Commission decided to establish Islam as the state religion, while recognizing freedom of worship to all citizens of the republic.[140].

---

[138] As the then President of Parliament, Hussein Akhmadov recalled: *In the first Constitution there was no mention of traditional institutions, and religion was given very little emphasis. The whole commission had the constitutions of the United States and European countries on its desk. We produced many implementing decrees. We were oriented towards the democratic European model.*

[139] Article 7 in this regard stated: *The mass media are free from censorship. [...] The monopoly of communication by state bodies, public associations, political parties, groups or individuals is not allowed. [...].*

[140] Article 43 stated: *Freedom of conscience is guaranteed. Citizens of the Chechen Republic have the right to profess any religion or not to profess any, to*

While waiting for the definitive version of the Constitution to be voted on by Parliament and promulgated, legislative activity continued incessantly. On January 8, the commission charged with identifying and proposing an effective border between the Chechen Republic and the nascent Republic of Ingushetia presented the final report, in which it recommended the re - establishment of the borders prior to the constitution of the Chechen - Ingush Republic in 1934. The parliament hastened to approve the proposal. This act was contested by many Ingush associations, because in the course of the seventy years following the unification most of the eastern areas of Chechnya had been populated by Ingush, as in the case of the districts of *Malgobek* and *Sunzha*. Bringing the borders back to those of 1934 would have in fact "annexed" numerous Ingush villages to the power of the Chechens, who had no longer lived in those urban centers for decades. But Ingushetia still did not even have a President or a Parliament that could plead its cause, and in any case everyone was focused on the claims against Ossetia, regarding the Prigorodny District. The protests of the local committees, which from January 12 took to the streets, sometimes armed, to protest against the measure, did not make Parliament retrace its steps. To those who objected to the decision to annex the districts of Malgobek and Sunzha, Parliament replied that the measure was aimed at avoiding that, with the signing of a federative pact between Ingushetia and Russia, these districts were annexed to Moscow.

Another legislative intervention of some importance was that relating to the constitution of a Chechen nationality and an obligation for all State officials to

celebrate religious ceremonies and to conduct any other religious activity that does not contradict the law. [...].

acquire it in order to continue to operate in their offices. On February 17, this procedure was made mandatory by law, by affixing a specific stamp to the old Soviet passport. A mandate was given to prepare the draft of an identity card and a passport bearing the logo of the Chechen Republic, in order to progressively replace those of the USSR. The official documents of the new republic would have been written in the Latin alphabet, rather than in the traditional Cyrillic script, considered a colonial legacy.

While Dudaev and Parliament worked to give order to the country, diplomacy began to work to build a diplomatic bridge with Moscow, which would lead to the easing of the economic blockade and open a negotiating channel for the stabilization of relations between the two countries. A window for negotiations seemed to open between January and February 1992. At that time, Moscow was taking up the question of ethnic minorities and autonomous republics, left without a precise constitutional connection with the Russian center. Putting order in the system of relations within the new Russian Federation was anything but easy: the "new Russia" was made up of as many as 92 legal entities: there were the autonomous districts, the Oblasts, the Kray, the Autonomous Republics, the metropolitan cities, a soup of different institutions, endowed with different autonomy from the central government, each of which tried to gain something from the renegotiation of relations with Moscow. Yeltsin had hitherto been busy consolidating his power base by eliminating Gorbachev's last supporters. Then he had to deal with running the economic machine and starting liberal reforms. Now that these two priorities seemed to be resolved, all the sheep had to be brought back to the fold. If this was rather easy compared to federated subjects inhabited mainly by

Russians, it was much less so than those in which non-Russian peoples represented the majority. From the end of 1991 all the federated subjects were involved in an extensive debate on the signing of a series of agreements, then collected in the collective term of "Federative Treaty", in which the areas of competence and supremacy of the federal bodies over local ones would be re-discussed. The signing of the *Federal Treaty* was scheduled for March 31, 1992. Only two republics refused to agree on that date to sign the new federal agreement: Tatarstan and, obviously, Chechnya. Tatarstan, a country rich in oil and raw materials, demanded a long and exhausting "head-to-head" negotiation, which would only end in 1994 after long and delicate meetings. Chechnya asked for the same thing, but adding to the preconditions that it was considered an independent republic. For the moment, Yeltsin made the best of a bad situation, and agreed to meet the Chechen representatives in Sochi, on the Black Sea, to start negotiations.

The talks began a few days before Parliament adopted the Constitution, and on the Chechen side they were led by Yandarbiev. They continued until March 14: on that date Russia and Chechnya seemed to find an encouraging starting point for the resolution of their relations. In fact, a document was signed in which a course of meetings was opened during which the question of the independence of Chechnya, the definition of the political and legal form of relations between the two countries, and the creation of an economic and military system would be examined. common. The process was supposed to lead to the signing of a treaty between the two countries. Yandarbiev returned to Chechnya convinced that he had scored a good blow, having received explicit guarantees on the recognition of the republic by

Moscow. The Russian ambassadors had the same impression, having confirmed the Chechen side's willingness to sign a treaty. It was evident, however, that neither of them had a clear opinion of the other, as the events of two weeks later would make clear.

The coup d'état of March 31st

As we have seen, while Dudaev consolidated his power and the state independent Chechen was beginning to take shape, opposition to the separatists gathered around the figure of Umar Avturkhanov, a former official of the Ministry of the Interior, recently elected Governor of the Upper Terek District and openly hostile to the new government. Both moderate nationalists and members of the old Soviet ruling class gathered close to him. There were about thirty notables, among which the aforementioned Hadjiev, who had snubbed Dudaev's invitation to be his deputy, the now apparently marginalized Zavgaev and the leader of Daimokhk, Lecha Umkhaev, stood out. The Movement had the manifest support of Moscow, which intended to use the opposition as a lock pick to undermine the Dudaevite front. As March 31 approaches, the date on which all the federated subjects should have signed the new Federative Treaty, the opposition began to show its willingness to intervene so that Chechnya would interrupt its secessionist path. On March 6, while the Sochi negotiations were underway, Avturkhanov issued a communiqué in which he appealed to all citizens of the Chechen republic, urging them not to recognize either Dudaev or Parliament. On the same day, the governor declared a State of Emergency in Upper Terek and activated a Headquarters, from which he distributed weapons to the population and mobilized the Union for the *Defense of Citizens of the Chechen - Ingush Republic*, a voluntary anti-Dudaevite and pro-Russian militia . As reported by its own representatives, 50 million rubles came from Moscow to finance the activities of dissidents, while small arms flowed from the nearby Russian military base of Modzok. The opposition also gave itself a name: *Movement for the Restoration of the Constitutional Order in the Chechen - Ingush Republic.*

On March 17, a first leaflet signed by members of the movement began to circulate in Grozny. It called for the resignation of Dudaev, accused of being the cause of the dramatic situation in which the country was plunging. In the following days, armed detachments of the Union for the Defense of Citizens took up positions in the districts of Sunzha, Achkoy - Martan, Shali and Grozny. Dudaev was trying to avoid a direct confrontation with these armed formations, partly because he hoped to bring their leaders back to a political alliance with his government, partly because he was not sure that his National Guard would be able to resist a well coordinated attack[141]. The weakness of the regular troops was clear from the opposition, and Avturkhanov was convinced that a well-orchestrated assault on Grozny would be enough to bring down the General. So the leaders of the Movement

---

[141] At that time it was made up of a few hundred volunteers, few and in constant conflict with each other: one side supported Gantemirov, another Basayev. In February 1992, the frictions between the two teams had reached their peak when it was discovered that the weapons of the main military warehouse in Chechen hands, the one found inside the KGB building following the assault on the building, were almost all disappeared. Basayev accused Gantemirov (who had custody of them) of stealing them to arm his "faction". Gantemirov denied any allegations but offered no plausible explanation for their disappearance. If we exclude these forces, Dudaev was left with a small nucleus of fighters, whom he had framed in the Presidential Guard, whose task was to defend his person, his family members and major government buildings. But there were about thirty scarce people, too few to be able to resist a direct attack by an organized army.

for the Restoration of the Constitutional Order organized their coup d'état. On the evening of March 30, the coup leaders gathered in a house in Grozny, near Kirov Park, not far from the TV station, and organized an *Emergency Committee*. On the morning of March 31, around 7:00 am an armed commando entered the state TV and disarmed the few guards who guarded the building. Armed patrols occupied the main road axis of Grozny, the one that from the north - west of the city reaches the southern suburbs. No department of the National Guard intervened. Still at 9.30, more than two hours after the blitz, no loyalist forces had reacted to the attack, while a large crowd of civilians, mostly opposition supporters, had gathered in Kirov Park, chanting supportive slogans. to the Emergency Committee. In the meantime, a second detachment of coup leaders had reached the vanguard that had launched the attack: now the rebels numbered between one hundred and one hundred and fifty armed men. The units dependent on the Ministry of the Interior, recalled by Dudaev to intervene, remained closed in their quarters by explicit order of the Minister, who declared that he would not allow the participation of his units, pledging only to guarantee *as far as possible the maintenance of the public order*. With this attitude, the Ministry of the Interior was in fact going over to the side of the insurgents. Everything was ready for the arrival of the leaders of the Emergency Committee and the overthrow of Dudaev.

But no one showed up. What happened to the leaders of the revolt? They simply got into a fight, split up the Russian funds, and went back to where they came from. It had happened that during the night the members of the Emergency Committee had faced each other to decide who should be the leader of that heterogeneous and contradictory bunch of post - communists and anti -

Dudaevites. It turned out that everyone wanted to be President, but that no one was going to lead the military operations. After a heated altercation, the leadership of the coup was abandoned to its fate. Thus, at 11 am on March 31, despite the rebels having taken control of the square, there was no one able to order the continuation of operations. Left without a direction, the coup turned into a farce. The loyalist forces, who arrived near the state TV only around 11, found themselves facing a hundred militiamen without a chain of command, surrounded by a cordon of disarmed and disoriented demonstrators.

At about noon the sentence of the coup d'etat came from the Parliament in plenary session. Akhmadov voted for the introduction of the State of Emergency throughout the country, declaring the actions produced by the Emergency Committee *a coup attempt*. When the rumor began to circulate that the rebels were financed and armed by the Kremlin, a popular reaction was unleashed: a crowd of people gathered in front of the Presidential Palace, and even supporters of the coup, knowing that it was orchestrated by Moscow, they changed sides and joined the loyalists. The silence of the members of the Emergency Committee did the rest, and at 18:35 a triumphant Dudaev, now back in control of the situation, addressed the citizens, inviting them to rise up in defense of the sacred right of the people to freedom, to independence and national dignity, against the reactionary circles of Russia and their local puppets. Within hours, a crowd of loyalists gathered around the state TV, the last building still in the hands of the coup leaders, while the units of the National Guard prepared to break into it. At 19:20, the ultimatums expired, the assault began.

The shooting lasted a few minutes, after which the National Guard managed to penetrate the TV station, displacing the rebels and capturing a dozen of them. About fifteen people died. Those who had not already left took advantage of the throng to sneak out of Grozny, while the rebel units that had not been hired by the National Guard retreated from the city to their departure bases. At 10 in the evening, the coup d'état could officially be said to have failed, and the TV resumed broadcasting on the government channel. Yandarbiev spoke to the country, accusing the coup leaders of being a destructive force in the pay of Russia. In the following days the VDP and the other loyalist movements organized a large street demonstration in support of independence, in which thousands of people participated[142].

Avturkhanov and the other rebels withdrew to Upper Terek and, trying to save face, declared that March 31 was only a "demonstration action" and not a coup. Whatever the purpose of the attack, the result was to mobilize the streets in support of Dudaev, making him even more master of the political scene.

The capture of the arsenals

---

[142]The Government and the Parliament issued a general appeal in which it was said: *We, representatives of all the villages and districts of the Chechen Republic, gathered in a demonstration of many thousands on 1 and 2 April 1992, express our support for the elected Parliament. and to the President of the Chechen Republic, we express our anger against the perpetrators of the raid on the public broadcaster and the attempted coup by the reactionary forces of the so-called opposition, agents of the Russian Empire. We strongly urge Parliament, the President of the Council of Ministers to take emergency measures to curb the anti-constitutional actions of the opposition forces and rampant crime. In order to stabilize the situation, we propose to introduce the death penalty in public for serious crimes against the state, as well as for crimes against the life of the citizens of our republic. [...] We urge the citizens of the republic to be vigilant, not to succumb to panic [...].*

The failure of the March 31 coup made it clear for the second time that the bugbear of a Russian invasion was capable of bringing public opinion back together on Dudaev's side. Just as it had happened in November of the previous year, when Yeltsin's emergency decree had favored the General's seizure of power, the news of Moscow's support for the coup had been enough to restore his initiative. For his part, Dudaev could be satisfied. Despite the serious situation in which the country found itself, he had managed to take advantage of a critical situation. But he too had learned something: that revolutions are not made without weapons. This time there was very little missing: if the coup leaders had not sabotaged themselves, his government would have ended even before it was born[143].

From the first days of April Dudaev began to ask with increasing insistence for the withdrawal of federal units. Thus, the question of armaments was once again brought to the table. The Russian Defense Minister, Pavel Grachev, had already started consultations with Dudaev at the end of 1991, negotiating for the withdrawal of war materials. This time he sent his plenipotentiary, General Ochirov. Dudaev proposed to him the same terms of the agreement he had with Grachev: half each, and all happy.

---

[143]Until then the numerous federal bases, mostly located near Grozny, had remained under the control of the Russian military even if, on the sly, the Chechens had stolen some firearms by stealing them from warehouses or buying them since the beginning of the year, by corrupt officers. In particular, the "attacks" to which the Russian army seemed not to resist were multiplying. On 7 February, the facilities of the 93rd Radiotechnical Regiment were attacked, and 43 crates of ammunition and 160 firearms were stolen. On the same day, Chechen fighters attacked the base of the 382nd Air Training Regiment, looting 436 automatic weapons and 265 pistols, as well as a large quantity of cartridges. The next day, two complexes of the 173rd Military District training center were attacked. All without any victims, which denounces a certain connivance between the Russians stationed in the bases and the separatists.

The issue of the withdrawal of the federal army was not just a political one. In Chechnya still in May 1992 there were hundreds of Russian soldiers and officers, which the political and military escalation had put in a state of serious insecurity[144]. On February 7, a band of dozens of armed men managed to penetrate a military base of the 566th Infantry Regiment, which it had demobilized just a couple of days earlier. The attackers entered the warehouse using open flames as torches, and within minutes the warehouse was blown up. Through the gates opened by the detonations, hundreds of civilians and conscripts of the National Guard poured into the base, barely held in check by their superior officer, *Iles Arsanukaev*. The human tide of looters swept over everything he could find, until it reached the depot of anti-personnel mines. Some inattentive triggered one, setting off a second chain reaction. In the end, there were

---

[144]The Russian photographer Yuri Pirogov recounts in this regard: *On January 5, around 7 pm, the doorbell of Major Zaochkin's apartment rang. When he opened the door, two Chechens, who were standing on the landing, attacked the officer and started beating him, asking for money and weapons. The attackers also beat his wife, who came following the screams. Both the Major and his wife fainted from being beaten. The thieves robbed the apartment and fled. On January 7, two unknown men entered a guard post, guarded by Sergeant Petruha. They hit him with numerous blows to the head and fled. [...] In February, the attacks on military camps became even more dramatic. On February 1, in the area of Assinovskaya station, strangers armed with machine guns captured and destroyed a communications center, seizing about 100 firearms and other military equipment. On February 4, a regimental seat of the Ministry of the Interior was attacked. More than three thousand firearms, 184,000 ammunition, as well as all the regimental supplies and supplies were stolen. The same fate befell the air defense radio center on February 6. On February 8, the 1st and 15th military camps were attacked. All weapons, ammunition, uniforms and supplies were seized from the warehouses [...] The officers who resisted [...] were taken hostage. The body of Captain Vashchenko [who opposed one of these attacks, ed] was found in a swamp on the outskirts of Grozny two months later. He had gunshot wounds and traces of beatings. [...] from the second half of February, the situation worsened further. On January 8, Major Vladimir Chagan, on duty at a base in the* suburbs of Grozny, was attacked and killed by "anonymous bandits".

several dozen dead and wounded. It was clear that this situation, in wich no one was actually responsible for weapons with enormous destructive potential, had to ends as soon as possible.

On June 6, Dudaev demanded the general and complete withdrawal of all troops of the Russian Federation within 24 hours of the ultimatum. The local Russian commanders took the ball, loaded their trucks with everything they had on hand and left overnight, leaving their bases full of weapons unattended. The "50 and 50" agreement was not even considered. The Russians just crammed their vehicles with what they found there and then and left the warehouses to themselves. Even the most sophisticated weapons, such as anti-aircraft installations and missile launchers, remained in the hands of the Dudaevites. Within a few weeks, 260 warplanes, 90 tanks and armored vehicles, 44 armored vehicles fell under the control of the National Guard. And again: 942 military vehicles, 139 pieces of artillery, 89 anti-tank devices, almost forty thousand firearms including submachine guns, heavy machine guns, rifles and pistols, 27 anti-aircraft devices, as well as a gigantic quantity of ammunition. The regular units were not the only ones to take possession of the weapons. In the chaos in which the country was pouring, the withdrawal of the Russian military opened the doors to real mass looting. Civilians eager to grab valuables to resell on the black market, criminal gangs, adventurers of all kinds poured into Russian bases at night, challenging fences and minefields to get their hands on all that goodness.

With all that material at his disposal, however, Dudaev was finally able to arm a real army. The General started with heavy vehicles, forming an armored regiment. This would have secured the regime from any "Sunday coup".

The means and infrastructures were not lacking: the loot of almost a hundred vehicles including tanks and other armored vehicles, on paper, would have been sufficient to constitute an independent unit from the powerful impact force. On paper, we said, because on closer inspection those vehicles were not that great: the backbone of the new armored unit would have been 38 T-72 tanks, most of which, however, were reduced to scrap. Another 11 T - 72 and 1 T - 62 were unable to move, and could function, at the limit, as fixed artillery positions.

Exporting the revolution

One of the main effects of the Chechen revolution had been to give a new reason for living to a generation of young people who until then had known nothing but poverty and unemployment. Living in Chechnya in 1992 meant having within reach every possible stimulus towards a life devoted to combat: the dream of every young idealist, in every part of the world. In Islamic and nationalist Chechnya, the ideals were independence and faith. In this sense, the figure of the aforementioned Shamil Basayev is exemplary. Coming from a family of Vedeno, the "capital" of mountain Chechnya, raised in mediocrity, sometimes of expedients, lived on the margins of the Soviet Union, in the Chechen revolution he had found the centering of his existence, and in Islamic militancy his inspiring belief.

We had left him grappling with Gantamirov, who had resold most of the armaments looted from the KGB warehouse in Grozny during the Revolution. Between the end of 1991 and the beginning of 1992, the clash between Basayev and Gantamirov saw a temporary victory for the second, who managed to get himself appointed by Dudaev Mayor of Grozny, thus being able to arm his own personal militia, the so-called *Municipal Police of Grozny*. It was not a department of auxiliaries, but a real fire group equipped with weapons of war. Basayev, who remained on the fringes of power in his barracks on the outskirts of Grozny, in command of his platoon of young soldiers, tried to regain ground by "exporting the revolution" outside the Chechen borders. In him there is no it was only the belief that without an "uncontrolled fire" in the Caucasus there would be no future for his country. Above all, there was the desire to establish himself as a man dedicated to combat, to the permanent revolution, a sort of "Che Guevara" of the Caucasus. His first chance was the conflict in Nagorno - Karabakh. We have already mentioned this in previous chapters: Armenians against Azeris intent on ethnic cleansing one another. At the end of December 1991, with the dissolution of the USSR, the "buffer" represented by the regular forces of Moscow disappeared, and within a few months the whole region was inflamed. The Armenians who inhabited those lands, formally annexed to the Republic of Azerbaijan took up arms, and so did the Azeris.

Basayev arrived in Azerbaijan in May 1992, together with the first Chechen volunteers who came to support the Muslim "Azerbaijani brothers" against Armenian Christians. He fought under the command of an exploration department, which distinguished itself on numerous occasions. But the progressive bogging down of the conflict, and the distrust shown by the Azeris towards the combative Chechen volunteer units, whose deeds threatened to put the regular army units in a bad light, convinced Basayev to return home. Also because, on the horizon, a much more "popular" conflict was looming, that of Abkhazia.

Here the resistance of the "little" Abkhazians against the "big" Georgians was an inspiration for all the peoples of the Caucasus who felt oppressed. When Zviad Gamsakhurdia was elected President of Georgia in October 1990, the Abkhazians also elected a nationalist, *Vladislav Ardzimba*, as their president. As in the case of Ossetia, the catalyst had been that of the referendum on the State of the Union in March 1991. The Abkhazians had voted in favor of the preservation of the Soviet Union, while the Georgians had declared independence on 9 April 1991. In response, the Abkhazians had declared secession from Georgia and their willingness to remain in the USSR. The Abkhazian Parliament, however, was attended by a strong Georgian component that opposed the ratification, while the Georgian Council of State considered the declaration null and void.

The situation continued in a state of crisis until August 1992, when the Georgian army invaded Abkhazia. The improvised Abkhaz National Guard failed to oppose, and the government withdrew from the capital Shukhumi to Gudauta in the north of the country, along with a small army of volunteers. The Georgian invasion caused the peoples of the Caucasus to rise up. The Confederation of Peoples of the Caucasus, which we saw already being activated in 1991 in support of the Chechen revolution, reacted promptly, sending the first volunteers as early as August 15, 1992 under the command of Colonel *Sultan Sosnaliev*. Civil society mobilized by holding demonstrations in the main cities of the North Caucasus. These were the recruiting center for numerous armed groups, which began to flock to Abkhazia. On August 17, the Confederation Parliament met in extraordinary session in Grozny, and established a solidarity platform for Abkhazia, denouncing the Georgian action. From 21 August the President of the

Confederation, *Shanibov*, ordered the general mobilization of volunteers and the arrest of Georgian citizens as prisoners of war.

As hundreds of armed volunteers crossed the border into Abkhazia, the Russian government turned away, leaving a corridor open to volunteers. After all, a Georgia in chaos was a Georgia more easily conditioned, and after the political reversals of the previous two years, the Moscow leadership intended to gradually regain control of its suburbs. In this sense, support for armed movements that kept newly independent countries such as Georgia in chaos helped to de-legitimize the new ruling classes that emerged from the collapse of the USSR, and justified the more or less direct intervention of the Kremlin in the management of their affairs. That is why the Russians at that juncture supported the military preparation of a group of Chechen secessionists, when in theory they should have disarmed them. In that great chaos that was the Caucasus at that moment, yesterday's enemy could be today's ally, only to return to being an enemy when his collaboration was no longer needed. This was the case with the Chechens in Abkhazia. The federal government had decided to support the separatists in order to limit the authority of independent Georgia, stripping it of its autonomous republics and bringing as many provinces as possible under the umbrella of Moscow. But this game was dangerous: by supplying Chechen volunteers with weapons and training, they were creating a small army of veterans much more difficult to put on the run than the garbage National Guard who was defending Dudaev and his government at the time[145].

---

[145]In this regard, the words of the then Georgian president Eduard Shevardnadze sound emblematic: *Take the example of Abkhazia. Thousands of Chechens fought there and went through the school of a terrible war. They realized that war is a method of political pressure. Who was*

The heterogeneous voluntary formation that operated on several occasions in Abkhazia saw the participation of some of the most convinced supporters of Chechen nationalism. They went to fight *Isa Arsemikov*, deputy in the Chechen Parliament, Vice - President of the Confederation of Peoples of the Caucasus and Chechen representative in that organization, *Khamzat Khankarov*, early activist of the Popular Front and volunteer of the National Guard, and of course Shamil Basayev, who in Abkhazia he would have gained leadership of the fighting units. The volunteers who answered the call of the Confederation gathered in *Nalchik*, in the Republic of Kabardino-Balkaria, and from there they reached Grozny, where they were framed and supplied. On August 19, a first group of 240 militiamen headed for Abkhazia, led by Basayev. The volunteers crossed Ingushetia, North Ossetia and Kabardino - Balkaria almost without encountering resistance from the federal authorities. By August 21, the unit, renamed *First International Brigade*, reached the front line, while a second detachment of about 170 volunteers was formed in Grozny. Within a few days, the *Second International Brigade* was also on its way to Gudauta. Leading it was an energetic commander, *Ruslan Gelayev*, whom we will hear a lot about in the next chapters[146]. The two groups joined the small vanguard which had already taken position on

---

behind them? Let's take a look. Is it possible that only Dudaev has kept such a number of people? A fighting group operating for three or four months, supplied with weapons and ammunition, which alternates with another group and so on, for a total of 6 - 7,000 people. Probably the number of Chechen volunteers did not reach the figure quoted by Shevardnadze, but surely the Abkhazian experience allowed the creation of units of veterans trained in urban combat and hardened by house-to-house battles.

[146] This time, however, the column of volunteers was hindered more by the federal units, so much so that on more than one occasion Gelayev literally had to storm the checkpoints, kidnapping the Russian military to clear the way.

the front line, under the command of Sosnaliev. He had organized a headquarters and was leading a first effective resistance, so much so that he earned the title of Minister of Defense of the small secessionist republic.

The situation seemed desperate, because the separatists and the international brigades had to defend themselves from an army that on paper was preponderant in men and means, which already controlled most of the territory, including its capital, and which had forced the separatists into two pockets: the coastal one, whose military and political center was *Gudauta*, compressed between the rivers *Bzyb* and *Gumista*, and the mountainous one, corresponding to the district of *Tkvarcheli*. The bulk of the independence forces concentrated on the first, since it was the only one that included a city of a certain strategic value and because refugees from other districts of the country had gathered there. Basayev was appointed Deputy - Minister of Defense by Sosnaliev, and he began to prepare a counter-offensive that would free one of the two open fronts around Gudauta, thus allowing the small independence army to avoid a two-sided attack. On 1 October Basayev went on the attack, trying to break through the siege on the north western side of Gudauta, towards the town of Gagra. Volunteers made extensive use of heavy weapons, which were certainly supplied by Russia (tanks, armored transport vehicles, even combat helicopters were employed). The Georgian defense forces were taken by surprise, quickly losing most of the war equipment. The resupply of the now encircled Georgian contingents was impossible, because a Russian "pacekeeping" fleet, moored off the city, it prevented any docking of military transport vehicles. The bulk of the remaining defenders were evacuated, while a small contingent covered their escape barricaded in the railway and police stations. When even this last defense collapsed, the separatists supported by the international brigades swept into the district, occupying Gagra and the surrounding countryside and chasing Georgian civilians and soldiers to the border with Russia: the few who survived were repatriated by the Russians by sea or by airplane. For all the others it was the beginning of hell: a real anti - Georgian pogrom broke out, during which violence and murders were recorded.

Once that front was stabilized, the secessionist army was able to face the Georgians on only one front, the southern one, still being able to count on the direct or indirect support of Russia. Besayev managed to reach the mountain district of Tkvarcheli by helicopter. Meanwhile, his partner Gelayev had returned to Chechnya, being replaced by another good fighter, *Umalt Dashayev*.

The war between Ossetians and Ingush

As the civil war raged in Azerbaijan and Georgia, the situation also became complicated on the western borders of Chechnya. We have already mentioned the crisis in South Ossetia, also a separatist Georgian province which was in fact under siege by the Tbilisi militias since the end of 1991. During 1992, a wave of Ossetian refugees had crossed the mountains and it had spilled over into *North Ossetia,* an autonomous federated republic with Russia, bordering its southern twin through the *Roki Pass.* If the southern Ossetians had their flaws with the Georgians, the northern ones, as we have seen, had to contend with the claims of neighboring Ingushetia, wich had detached itself from Chechnya in the hope of being given control over the Prigorodny District. In June 1992, Russia officially recognized the birth of the *Autonomous Republic of Ingushetia* as a subject of the Federation. The law, however, did not establish the boundaries of this entity, and imposed a moratorium on the thorny issue of Prigorodny until 1995: in this way the Kremlin chose not to settle territorial issues, increasing uncertainty and favoring an escalation of violence[147]. In early 1992, armed groups organized themselves into the *Ingush National Guard*, following the example of the Chechens.

The detonator that set off the conflict was the killing of an Ingush girl on October 20, 1992. The girl was hit by a military vehicle belonging to the Ossetian militias near Prigorodny, and in the following days another five Ingush were killed. On 24 October, a mourning demonstration was held by the Ingush community, during which the demonstrators proclaimed the annexation of the Prigorodny district[148]. On the same day in Ingushetia the National Movement approved a resolution in which it defined the Ossetian actions as genocide and accused the Moscow government of not having taken any measures in defense of the population. Consequently, self-defense groups were established under the authority of the local police. The violence

---

[147]. The Ingush leadership reacted with disdain to the recognition law: *The National Assembly of Ingush [...] expresses deep indignation at the anti - Ingush and anti - Chechen policy of the aforementioned legislative act. This law [...] pursues the aim of consolidating the Ingush lands in Ossetia [...] which in turn makes it possible to continue the genocide of the Ingush people. [...]*.

[148] The claim quoted: *All these provocations have been carefully prepared and carried out with the aim of pushing the Ingush people into an armed conflict with the Ossetians, in order to prevent a peaceful solution of the problem. [...] In North Ossetia the inhabitants of Ingush nationality are deprived of any civil rights; they are being fired en masse from their jobs, registration and the buying and selling of houses are prohibited, a state of emergency has been introduced and a curfew has been introduced in villages inhabited by the Ingush, transport routes have been cut off and freedom of movement has been restricted. [...] The decision was taken to organize extraordinary sessions in all the Prigorodny District Councils to discuss the modalities of detachment from North Ossetia and its annexation to Ingushetia.*

mounted, not a day passed without a victim being counted on one side or the other. The Ossetian government demanded the disarmament of the Ingush militias, threatening military intervention. Finally, in the night between 30 and 31 October, civil war broke out. Armed volunteers from Ingushetia entered Ossetia, captured a military base and took 111 Ossetian soldiers hostage. The guerrillas reached the outskirts of Vladikavkaz, where they were stopped by the regular army, while the federal troops remained inactive in their bases. The next day Ossetian civilians began to crowd the public offices demanding that they be distributed weapons to defend themselves. In the meantime, the Ossetian National Guard and the voluntary popular militia began to occupy the villages and to take hostage all the Ingushes they found. Only then did the federal government move, sending Deputy Prime Minister *Chiza*, the chairman of the emergency committee *Sojgu* and Colonel *Gennadi Filatov* to resolve the issue. It was the latter who spoke on state TV, declaring:

Today at 12:45 military aircrafts landed, with an armed force that will be deployed in the territory of Ossetia. Russia has not forgotten its faithful sons, the Ossetians, who have served it loyally for many years. Already today these soldiers, together with the departments of the Ministry of the Interior of the Russian Federation, will begin military actions against the aggressor.

From the tone of the statement there was no doubt which side Moscow would support. On November 2, the Kremlin instituted a state of emergency, and the following day the army drove the Ingush guerrillas out of Prigorodny, and then began advancing into their territories. The clashes continued until November 5 and resulted in around 500 deaths and between 30 and 60,000 refugees. These took with them many Ossetian hostages, who imprisoned in the basements of the houses where they had found refuge, in inhumane conditions. By contrast, 200 Ingush hostages were never found, and the Prigorodny district was virtually emptied of all their presence. The Ossetians destroyed about 3000 houses[149].

The conflict ignited the passion of Chechen public opinion. The events had shown that the Kremlin was not only unable to implement the Law on the Rehabilitation of Oppressed Peoples, but during the violent phase of the conflict it had maintained a position clearly on the side of the Ossetians[150]. Furthermore, the military

---

[149] A witness of the events recounted: *In the village where I lived, the tanks arrived and started shooting at the houses. So we ran out, and we saw that on our gate, at the bottom right, there was a white cross, freshly painted. And so did all the houses where the Ingush lived. We ran off to a farm, down the road, because we knew there was a basement. When we arrived we saw that there were already other people hiding. We stayed there for three days, the women and children below, the men, armed, above. Everyone said: in a while the Chechens will arrive, to help us, to save us. The Chechens did not come, but everyone was hoping for it. After three days, two Ossetian soldiers arrived. They said they would escort us to the border with Ingushetia and from there we would go on alone. They gave us two trucks, people started to get in, but as soon as we got out on the road, more military vehicles arrived. They beat the men, took away their weapons, instead of taking us to Ingushetia they transported us to Sunzha, and there another nightmare began. They held us hostage for 3 weeks They only fed us after 3 days. We were more than 200, all hungry ... The last day they divided the males, on one side those who were over 18 years old. On the other, the little ones, children and women; they took us to the border with Ingushetia We were happy [...] But at the border the Ingush told them "we have no one to exchange them with". They had taken us hostage to exchange us with Ossetian hostages taken by the Ingush. But the Ingush had no hostages to exchange us with. Then they transported us to Beslan, to a gym near the airport. The next day they swapped us with seven Ossetians. My father, on the other hand, only released him after three months, and he never told us what happened to him during his imprisonment.*

[150]. The Executive Committee of the Chechen National Congress stated: *The government of the Chechen Republic had repeatedly raised the question of the need for a just solution to the Ingush problem. However, the official circles of Russia invariably failed the efforts undertaken by the Chechen side. Unfortunately, some representatives of the political movement within Ingushetia itself, continuing to place hope in the "big brother", Russia, had led the Ingush problem into a dead end with their reckless actions. [...] The Parliament and the President of the Chechen Republic have clearly and*

occupation of Ingushetia opened a real political crisis. As a shared border between Chechnya and Ingushetia had not yet been defined, there was a risk that federal "peacekeeping" forces would end up more or less voluntarily trespassing into Chechnya, with predictable, unpleasant consequences. After a few days, faced with the prospect that the Russian government would extend the declaration of the State of Emergency also to the provinces of Malgobek and Sunzha, which the Chechen government considered part of its sovereign territory, the parliament of the Chechen republic declared:

If the Russian government pursues this policy, the Parliament of the Chechen Republic, in accordance with the norms of international law, will regard these attempts as an armed aggression against the independent Chechen state. All responsibility for the consequences of such a step will rest with the government of the Russian Federation.

The first Russian - Chechen crisis

This sudden escalation wrecked the negotiations that began in January of that year in Sochi. Despite the Russian skirmishes and the failed coup of March 31, in fact, the two sides had reopened negotiations at the end of May, with a diplomatic mission to Moscow led by Yandarbiev. At first, the Russian delegation had disavowed the agreements made in Sochi in mid-March, before the opposition coup, proposing to Yandarbiev to cancel the negotiations and start over. The Chechens had opposed it, and after a diplomatic stalemate of a few days a compromise was reached: Russia would have considered the Sochi document as a starting point on

---

unequivocally declared their policy of non-intervention in the internal affairs of the Russian Federation.

which to reopen a negotiating table. The press had closely followed the progress of the negotiations. Musa Temishev, writer on the newspaper *Ichkeria*, wrote:

> *I said, I say and I will say that we Chechens must be together with Russia. I repeat: "together", but not "inside". There is an essential difference in this. I am for an economic, cultural, monetary and military space with Russia. I am in favor of Chechnya being an organic part of the Russian Commonwealth. I repeat, a Commonwealth. A Commonwealth exists only among peers.*

Temishev's thought was very common. Most independent Chechens did not necessarily mean a state of cold war, closed borders, isolation from Moscow. Dudaev himself had stated that he wanted a common economic and military space with Russia, and even the Minister of Information, the arsonist Ugudov, declared that he wanted to establish a common financial and defense space. The negotiations restarted in June were abruptly interrupted in early September, when some maneuvers by the federal army in neighboring Dagestan raised fears of an armed intervention in Chechnya.[151]. After the summer, and after the "incident" in Dagestan in early September, Russian Vice President Rutskoi had held meetings with Soslambekov. At that juncture it had been decided to set up a Chechen representative office in Moscow and a federal one in Grozny, and Rutskoi had also promised to temporarily ease the economic, financial and air blockade in place for almost a year. On September 25, a further meeting was held in *Chishki*, on the outskirts of Grozny, this time between *Yurii Yarov*,

---

[151]The local populations, mostly Chechens and misers, had poured into the streets blocking the federal columns and ending up taking two officers hostage. By the afternoon of 7 September the two battalions had been withdrawn towards the interior.

Vice-President of the Russian Supreme Soviet, and Bektimar Mezhidov, Vice-President of the Chechen Parliament. The Russian delegation recognized the March and May agreements as a concrete basis for negotiating positions between the two countries.

The Ossetian-Ingush crisis and the occupation of Ingushetia by the federal army blew up all the work done up to that point. From November 10, federal troops entered Ingushetia and, as feared by the Chechen parliament, the army also occupied the districts of Malgobek and Sunzha. Dudaev responded by declaring a state of emergency and threatening retaliation if the Russians continued to occupy them. The invaders were given until the morning of the 11th to retreat. Had they not done so, the Chechens would have *risen to war*. The Confederation of Peoples of the Caucasus gave Dudaev a hand. The Chechen and Russian troops came face to face on the unmarked border between the two republics, aiming at their guns. If the war had broken out then, this could have inflamed the whole Caucasus. The political situation in many republics was fragile, and with the civil war in Abkhazia, the civil war in South Ossetia, the civil war in North Ossetia and Ingushetia, the war between Azeri and Armenians in Nagorno - Karabakh, independent Chechnya, the outbreak of another conflict could have caused the whole region to rise up.

The skirmishes continued for a few days until on 12 November a Russian delegation led by Russian Deputy Prime Minister *Sergey Shakhrai*, an Ingush in the retinue of *General Aushev*, the informal leader of Ingushetia, and a Chechen led by Vice - Premier Yaragi Mamodaev, defined the terms of the disengagement of the Russian and Chechen forces, establishing as a "provisional" border that of 1934 claimed by Chechnya. The next day, however, the federal troops did not withdraw: they remained in their posts, occupying the positions they should have vacated. Panic immediately spread to Chechnya. While Dudaev publicly accused Russia of treason, Parliament Speaker Akhmadov addressed the international community for help against an impending Russian invasion of Chechnya. For a few days the events of November 1991 seemed to repeat themselves: crowds of people surrounded the Presidential Palace, demanding the distribution of weapons to defend the independence of the country. Dudaev proclaimed the partial mobilization of the army. Parliament appointed a team of negotiators who reopened a negotiating table with Shakhrai, managing to start talks on November 13th. Meanwhile, both the Chechen and Russian armies were massing against each other.

The situation was at the limit when, in the late morning of the 13th, the requests of the Russian delegation were presented to the Chechen side: they asked for the withdrawal of the armed formations on the *Samashki/Achkhoi-Martan* line for two days, in order to create a buffer that it avoided the infiltration of armed volunteers into Ingushetia and allowed the federal units to withdraw. The line proposed by Shakhrai was a few kilometers back from the present front line and seemed to be a bearable compromise to bring the crisis to a happy conclusion. But for Dudaev any concessions to Russia were unacceptable. Therefore, disavowing the results of the negotiation, which he said was carried out by a delegation not authorized by the President, he returned to the attack, taking it out first with the Ossetians, to whom he promised reprisals for their behavior (which he said had caused the Russian military intervention and the consequent crisis) then directly with Russia, threatening general mobilization if this did not withdraw its troops beyond the borders of Ingushetia. To complicate the situation, an incident occurred in the village of Sernovodsk, where federal troops came into contact with a crowd of Chechen civilians and illegals. The crowd prevented the Russian column from proceeding, and it peacefully returned to its positions. But in the eyes of the Chechens, the news was even more evident proof of the Russian will to invade their country.

As had happened in November 1991 and then in March 1992, public opinion gathered, firm against any pressure from Russia.[152]. Dudaev for his part introduced martial law in the districts of Sunzha and Achkhoi-Martan. Hussein Akhmadov, who meanwhile was desperately trying to reopen negotiations and avoid a war, flew to Moscow to meet with representatives of the Russian government. It is not known what arguments he used with Yarov, the fact is that the next day Yeltsin himself publicly declared that he would in no case authorize military action against Chechnya. From 15 November, diplomatic channels reopened in Nazran, the provisional capital of Ingushetia. By late morning the agreement was reached and the units of both armies were preparing to retreat, when the umpteenth "stop" came: according to reports, a Chechen unit had taken prisoners some Russian soldiers along the front line. The situation quickly turned hot again, and Shakhrai first ordered some members of the Chechen delegation to be held as hostages until the Russian military was released. It was not possible to understand who had caused that chaos just now that the crisis seemed to be over. Then it was

---

[152]. The same Daimokhk movement, the one led by Lecha Umkhaev who had abandoned Congress and condemned the assault on the Supreme Soviet in September 1991, issued a note in which it declared itself *categorically opposed to the resolution of the internal problems of Chechnya by Russia or by any other state "and threatened:"* In case of intervention "the statement quoted" we will be the first defenders of our homeland.

known. And it was not good news, because apparently the author of the blitz was Dudaev himself.

Mamodaev, who in addition to having risked arrest and risked a blow to the head, went on a rampage, lashing out at the General, who eventually admitted to having been involved in a confrontation with an advanced Russian patrol and having her unarmed to ensure the safety of the presidential staff. Shakhrai threatened not to withdraw the troops and not to return the hostages if the confiscated weapons were not returned to the federal soldiers. The following day the weapons were returned, and a new delegation led by Mamodaev, and this time expressly authorized by Dudaev, went to Nazran to formalize the end of the negotiations and the definitive withdrawal. This time there were no incidents, and by the next morning the armed forces withdrew from the theater of operations. The crisis was over, Chechnya was safe. But the relations between Mamodaev and Dudaev, and between them and the Parliament, were irremediably compromised[153].

Dudaev against everyone

The crisis of November '92 shattered relations between Dudaev and the other offices of the state. Chechnya had been one step away from going to war with Russia. Parliament and Deputy Prime Minister Mamodaev had done everything to carry out the negotiations necessary to resolve the emergency, Dudaev

---

[153]Interviewed on the subject years later, Mamodaev said: *We were there to make war with Russia in November 1992, after the incident in the village of Assinovskaya, where Dudaev arrogantly disarmed eight Russian soldiers and threatened to shoot them on the spot. Dudaev knew that I, as Vice - Premier, and other representatives, had signed an agreement. [...] Dudaev instead rushed along the border with the exhortation: "Come on children of Chechnya, let's go to war with the Russians!". The Russian military were terrified, Dudaev's men kept their rifles pointed at their heads.*

had taken the path of direct confrontation, assuming a warlike attitude, projected towards an escalation of the confrontation, convinced that at the in the end, the Russian authorities would not have had the courage to unleash their army against the Chechen people. On the President's side there was experience: the so-called Chechen Revolution had been successful precisely thanks to the obstinacy with which Dudaev had opposed any compromise solution. On the other hand, a year later, the situation was quite different: first of all, the USSR was no longer there. Secondly, the internal situation in Chechnya had changed: almost a year of economic and financial blockade were leading the country to poverty, and many were wanting an end to the tug-of-war with Moscow. The majority of the deputies of Parliament, in particular, seemed to be well disposed to a negotiation solution that would keep Chechnya in a "light union" with Russia, perhaps sacrificing independence tout - court for the benefit of a large autonomy[154].

The issue of independence was fundamental, but it was not the only one on which Parliament and the President disagreed. First, there was the question of the representativeness of the state. According to Akhmadov, the Parliament, as it came out of the elections of 27 October, was not sufficiently representative to be able to claim full political authority. In fact, it was made up exclusively of Chechens and in his opinion a supplementary election was necessary to extend the representation also to the Russian, Cossack and Ingush components. The proposal was also supported by Deputy Prime Minister Mamodaev. He too argued that

---

[154] In this capacity Akhmadov, the President of Parliament declared: "*We ourselves have strong horizontal links with Russia and the rest of the world. We are ready to pursue a coordinated policy on finance, defense, information and conclude other necessary contracts and agreements. But we strongly reject political centralism.*"

the forces of Russian and Cossack entrepreneurship should be represented and stimulated in any way to contribute to the well-being of the country, and that a failure to recognize the representation of ethnic minorities inhabiting Chechnya would have prevented any recognition of an "ethnocentric" state by the international community. For Dudaev, on the other hand, the Chechen state had to be led by the Chechens, so the question of an enlargement of representation on an ethnic basis was out of the question. Furthermore, the President feared that the entry of non-Chechen elements into the state bodies would favor the penetration of Russian influence into the country's politics.

Another hotly debated issue was the economic one. Leaving aside the already discussed issue of liberalization, there was the question of the "economic sphere" in which the new country should have positioned itself. Akhmadov argued the need to maintain a common budget with that of Moscow, and to remain in the ruble zone. Dudaev, on the other hand, argued the need to break free from it, to establish its own currency and its own independent budget. Finally, it was not yet clear how this independent Chechnya should have been called: Dudaev wanted to rename it *Chechen Republic of Ichkeria*, thus emphasizing the "mountainous" nature of Chechnya.[155]. Parliament was opposed to this choice which revealed a clear ultranationalist positioning.

A rift was emerging between the two main powers of the state to which two "parties" referred: the "Presidential" one, in favor of extending the powers of

---

[155] Ichkeria is a region located in the southwest of present-day Chechnya, the ancestral seat of the oldest Chechen Teip. According to the authors of the idea of a *Republic of Ichkeria*, the independent state should have discarded the "colonial" legacy of the word "Chechnya" in favor of a more indigenous term, such as the one that identified the epicenter of Chechen ethnogenesis, the Ichkeria precisely.

the President, and the "Parliamentary" one, which instead wanted to further limit them in compliance with the Constitution. Within the same Parliament these two currents began to count: out of forty-one deputies, twelve were openly Dudaevites, fifteen supported Akhmadov, the others oscillated from one position to another.

The main battlefield, as in any clash at the top systems, was that of appointments. The first confrontation took place when Dudaev, instead of appointing a Prime Minister, had assumed both the positions of Head of State and Head of Government. This accumulation of offices had been stigmatized by Parliament, which at first contested the action, then had to surrender to the evidence and suspended the controversy. On July 2, 1992, however, a substantial group of parliamentarians had reopened the application, contesting the establishment by the President of government services parallel to those established by parliament, such as the National Security Service and the Investigative Group, effectively duplicating two equivalent institutions appointed by the Parliament. The group of parliamentary opponents also contested the appointment of Yaragi Mamodaev as Deputy Prime Minister, complaining about the lack of confidence that the President should have asked for before the appointment. Due to these numerous violations of constitutional dictates, the opposition group demanded Dudaev's resignation from the office of Prime Minister, and the restoration of constitutional prerogatives.[156].Locally, Dudaev also

---

[156]Sometimes the superimposition of government bodies to equivalent structures of parliamentary appointment occurred through a "constitutional trick". In an attempt to limit parliamentary "interference" in the appointments, Dudaev and Mamodaev began to create "State Committees", which had the functions of a ministry but were not formally ministries, so they were not subject to parliamentary approval. Thus the Ministry of Justice became the

dismantled the old Soviet system and replaced it with a system of prefectures. This contradicted Article 73 of the Constitution, which stipulated that regional governors should be elected, not appointed. Parliament responded by holding regular local governor elections. The result was a diarchy in which the elect challenged the nominated and vice versa.

At the end of 1992 the conflict between the executive and the legislative powers became so acute that two powers actually governed in Chechnya: a parliamentary one, adhering to the constitution, and a presidential one, loyal to Dudaev. Within the institutions, the pro - Dudaev and pro - Akhmadov parties sabotaged each other, paralyzing the state. In an appeal in May 1993, thePresident of the Investigative Committee of the Republic, Khasanov, wrote to Yusup Soslambekov:

Since the establishment of the Investigative Committee, various power structures of the Republic, including law enforcement agencies, have hindered the Committee's activity [...] the leadership of the investigative authorities has evidence of a number of people who have been arrested [...] placed in the preliminary detention facilities of the Ministry of the Interior and then released [...] There are situations in which officers of the city police on duty release guilty while ignoring the sentences for arrest, thus complicating the crime situation and eliminating the principle of certainty of punishment [...][157]

Committee for National Reform, while the Ministry of Economy became the Committee for the Management of the National Economy, the Cabinet of Entrepreneurs replaced the Ministry of Productive Activities etc. At the top of these newly established bodies, with powers equivalent to those of a Ministry, were men loyal to Dudaev.

[157] In another appeal, this time from the Deputy Director of the National Security Service to the President of Parliament, we read: *Staff of the National Security Service detained 18 wagons of petroleum products at the Gudermes station [...] to check the legality of the above contract appointed we requested the cargo documents, which were not delivered to us on the basis of an oral order from Interior Minister Albakov. [...] I ask you to intervene and*

The same situation was observed in the legislative sector of the state: Dudaev vetoed the resolutions of the Parliament, and the Parliament did not vote on the enforceability of Dudaev's decrees. Just to cite a few examples: Parliament established the National Security Service, appointing a certain *Abdurakhmanovich* as Director. Dudaev wanted one of his own and, by his own decree, established the National Security Service under the President of the Republic, and appointed *Salman Hasimikov* as President. Then the Parliament intervened, which abolished the Dudaev decree. But Dudaev did not give up, and on April 8 he vetoed the parliamentary decree. Thus it came to the point that there were two National Security Services, competing with each other, one loyal to Parliament, the other to Dudaev.

At the end of 1992, while the Public Prosecutor's Office, the Investigative Committee, the National Security Service, the Tax Police, the Governor of the National Bank and the mayors of Grozny and Gudermes sided with the Parliament, the Government, the Attorney General, the Committee on Legal Reform and Committee on National Economy Management were with Dudaev. Between these two camps were the Constitutional Court and the National Congress, which remained neutral with respect to the diatribe. Over time, Mamodaev joined the fight between the two-party system. In an interview released in November 1992, he stated:

Fully and consciously, the President stops everything that can lift the Republic and make it a democratic state of law. It resists all regulations, accounting and control systems. [....] Of the approximately one thousand orders and resolutions of the

carry out a parliamentary investigation into this fact.

Cabinet of Ministers, 900 are paralyzed by the President's veto and counter-decrees [...].

The 1992 balance

In mid-October 1992 Dudaev gave an interview to ITAR - TASS in which he took stock of the first year of his government. The interviewer first asked the General how he assessed the road taken by Chechnya in that year of government. Dudaev replied:

The journey has been huge. [...] Not only have we withstood all the tests, but we have managed [...] to maintain relative stability in the social and economic sphere. [...] To the best of our abilities, we protect citizens from sharp increases in energy prices. We support the disabled, the elderly, large families. We are preparing to carry out real privatization, and not the feared "looting.

Regarding the risk of the Chechen ethnocentric state provoking actions of ethnic hatred, the General replied:

Representatives of nationalities live in the Chechen Republic. And today we practically see no differences between Chechens, Russians, Georgians. We do not divide people on a national and religious basis. All the citizens of Chechnya are one.

When the reporter raised the opposition's point of view, diametrically opposed to that of the President, he replied:

I look at things objectively. And I don't understand who you call "opposition". Those who secretly carry weapons, drugs and bloodlust? I say that there is no platform for a political opposition with a clear agenda. To my great chagrin.

The interviewer then made explicit reference to the crisis in relations with parliament, to which Dudaev countered:

The parliament, the highest legislative body of the Chechen Republic [...] tries to occupy the functions of the executive and even the judiciary. I consider them ... growing pains. We have to tolerate these mistakes. After all, we have lived through so many decades in which the party and the soviet usurped all kinds of power: legislative, executive, judicial, administrative, whatever. It is necessary to get sick, like childhood diseases. We will strive for a clear separation of powers. At that point the friction between the state structures will decrease.

The journalist then turned to the question of negotiations with Russia, citing the concern of the people and some politicians about the harshness of the Chechen government's approach towards Russia. Dudaev replied:

I'd like to see our relationships improve. But there is a fierce struggle for power in the Russian leadership now. In this fight someone is trying to play the Chechen card. There is no need for a war here [...] Others need this war to divert people's attention from social and economic problems [...].

From his point of view, the Chechen revolution had been a substantial success. According to him, the Chechen state had been able to withstand the collapse of Soviet structures, even in the economic field, and had managed to guarantee the survival of the weakest sections of the population. The opposition simply did not exist, and the friction with Parliament was "growing pains", a necessary stage of maturation that would eventually reach its epilogue. The risk of a war with Russia was generated by the appetites of Moscow's riotous ruling class, which would have been willing to even wage war to seize power.

In Dudaev's words there was certainly the optimism that is required of a Head of State, of a political leader who finds himself at the center of the hopes and fears of an entire people. The real situation in the country, in reality, was much worse than that described by its President. The blockade imposed by Moscow was bringing Chechnya to the brink. The inconsistency of Dudaev's policy and his stubbornness to pursue a statist system without the necessary resources to support it had brought finances to collapse, forcing the government to use fuel coupons as a bill to pay salaries.[158]. The blockade also prevented the much-desired foreign investors from arriving in Chechnya. The only significant "investment" that came from abroad in all of 1992 was that deriving from the divestment of the monetary reserve of the Estonian Republic, which exiting the ruble zone discarded its reserves by sending a few tons of overvalued rubles to Grozny.

Those who came en masse, however, taking advantage of the porosity of the borders and rampant illegality, were the criminals and the corrupt. The most striking example was that of oil. More than the extraction per se, which in Chechnya was no longer a leading sector and which in the years of independence decreased almost to zero, the country was an important refining center for petroleum products. Despite the blockade imposed by Moscow, the Russian government continued to allow the

---

[158] To allege only the economic blockade as the cause of the country's catastrophic situation would be excessive, as well as false, since the "siege" was systematically circumvented, especially on the Dagestan border, and smuggling was always tolerated, if not directly favored, by federal officials who guarded those borders. If we talk about oil, then, throughout 1992, Russian pipelines continued to pump crude oil to Chechen refineries, which in turn continued to export gasoline and fuel oils to Russia and abroad. In this way the government was able at least for the whole year to pay, albeit in fits and starts, salaries and pensions for an estimated value of 2.5 billion rubles.

pumping of crude oil into the pipelines to the Grozny refineries, which could process about 23 million tons (for an estimated profit of 300/400 million dollars in 1993 alone).[159]. But not even this blatant circumvention of the embargo allowed the state to function properly, also because a large part of these profits often ended up in the hands of unscrupulous officials. The population benefited little or nothing of these resources, which mostly ended up in the hands of a few adventurers.

Even with respect to the issue of the relationship with ethnic minorities, the scenario described by Dudaev was emphasized with respect to the reality of the facts. The entire political program of the revolutionaries was centered on the Chechen nation. This position was dangerous in a population of more than 30 ethnic minorities. From their point of view, however, the ethnocratic solution was the only one that could have saved the Chechens from Russia. The result was a system based on strong ethnic discrimination against non - Chechens[160].

---

[159] According to Yusup Soslambekov, Chechen refineries produced in 1992 alone four million tons of diesel, 1.6 million tons of gasoline, 125,500 tons of kerosene and 36,600 tons of industrial lubricant, for an estimated profit of about 130 million dollars.

[160]. As we can read from one of the reports by the aforementioned Timur Muzaev on one of his periodic political monitoring: *[speaking of the Russians, ed.] Today they can hardly be seen in government, in commerce, in the police and in other key positions. [...] This is demonstrated, for example, by the fact that four representatives of Chechen nationality were elected deputies in the four districts in the local authority elections in February 1992. [...] From the list of 82 cooperatives active in the region (as of 19 October 1992) [...] there are only 2-3 surnames of representatives of non-Chechen nationality. [...] Subjected to various types of oppression in the economic sector, as well as robberies and other acts of violence, the Cossacks enjoy no protection from the police. [...] A few years ago, about one third of the region's population was Cossack. Today, due to mass migration, only in Shelkovskaya there is still a rather high percentage of Cossacks (25%), in some villages [...] there are no more than 5 - 7 families left. In the period between July 1991 and July 1992 alone, 278 Cossack families left [...] It can be said that the relationship between Cossacks and Chechens has reached a critical threshold beyond which a situation close to a state of civil war is possible.*

The situation of the Cossacks was particularly explosive. Tendentially pro-Russian, always in friction with the Chechens, with the advent of the economic crisis they began to form a separate body, far from republican institutions and largely hostile, sometimes dedicated to banditry[161]. They felt protected by a series of decrees that Yeltsin, in the course of his electoral campaigns, had issued with the intention of rehabilitating them as a "military class", that is, to restore them to the status they had in the time of the Tsar. A strong revanchism followed which, inevitably, clashed with the rising nationalism of other nationalities, who saw in them nothing more than the spearhead of Moscow's power.[162]. One of Dudaev's first measures was to exclude Russians and Cossacks from paying social pensions. When asked why he had decided to leave Cossacks and Russians without pensions, Dudaev angrily replied: *Why don't they ask the Russian authorities instead of asking Dudaev? Dudaev himself does not receive a pension for thirty years of service in the armed forces!* For the Chechen president, the Russians living in his republic were not his problem, but a problem of the Russian Federation. This lack of interest in minorities, when not open hostility, led many of them to emigrate. In 1992 alone, 50,000 Russians left the republic, following the 20,000 who had left the previous

---

[161] As the specialist Sergei Arutyunov noted. *Perhaps the heaviest blow to Russian-Chechen relations was the explosion of Cossack banditry. These were gangs that already in 1991-1992 carried out roadblocks, attacked and robbed non-Cossacks, threatened armed women and children and did all this with substantial impunity.*

[162] This event, reported by the Moskovskie Novosti newspaper on August 5, 1994, explains the situation: *On August 5 a pogrom was carried out in the Chechen farms of the village of Galyuganovskaya [...] the Cossacks arrived accompanied by people in military uniform. They beat everyone they met on their way, put people on the wall, robbed them and tore the earrings from girls and women. Viskhan Pashaev, a 17-year-old boy, was killed with two gunshots to the head. The Cossacks tried to kidnap a woman's daughter, and only a miracle made it possible for her to obtain her release by begging. The Cossacks were screaming loudly that they would only submit to Yeltsin.*

year. By 1995, the emigrants would have been 250,000. For those who stayed, conditions certainly did not become more favorable. The Russians became the perfect target for crime. Those who openly opposed this climate went underground. It was not a real persecution, but a feeling of general impunity in which the minorities were the most exposed, and the Russian one in particular.[163].

The chaos of the institutions and the economic blockade were transforming Chechnya into a paradise of lawlessness, the economic center of which was the Grozny bazaar. It was a place where practically anything could be bought. There you could find luxury products, electronic appliances, exotic fruits, carpets, firearms and weapons of war[164]. It was mainly supplied by Grozny

---

[163] In a collective letter sent to the Moscow government by Russian residents shortly before the outbreak of the war, we read: *They took away the Saturday party and imposed the Friday one [...] at school it has been compulsory to speak Chechen [...] for two years we do not receive our wages or pensions. We constantly hear invitations to leave and return to Russia. But we are in Russia!"* the letter continues with the list of sixteen people who are declared killed by Chechens. And then again: *"The Chechens break into the houses, beat everyone, ask for money and gold that we never had. They tie the elderly to their chairs [...] after having robbed them.*

[164] In his memoirs, the journalist Anatol Lieven, who visited Chechnya at the end of 1992, says: *Compared to the great bazaars of the past, this was perhaps nothing extraordinary: no architectural grandeur, no spices or exotic carpets, just a typical street of offices and apartment buildings lined with crudely built stalls, in a sea of mud and waste. The amount of items for sale was huge, but the range was not very wide. Most were standard goods from the Caucasus and South Russia: large piles of local fruit and vegetables, smoked sausages and chickens, fruit sauces and pickled carrots. And a mass of important cheap goods, mainly from the Middle East, Turkish beer and jeans, perfumes, soft toys from Pakistan, a ' A virtually endless supply of cheap men's aftershave and dubious-looking alcohol and spirits, including a terrifying Scotch Whiskey named "Black Willie". At night the street lamps were off, the bazaar was lit by piles of burnt trash. [...] The market was so big because under Dudaev the Grozny airport functioned as a free access port in Russia, without customs or border guards. For some reason, Russia did not take steps to close the airport until November 1994, while the corruption of the army and the police allowed, upon payment of "unofficial taxes", the free flow of goods into Russia. and from this to the Grozny Bazaar. [...]. On Via Rosa Luxembourg [...] there was the only entirely public arms market in the territory of Former Soviet*

Airport, which was renamed *Sheikh Mansur Airport* in honor of the Chechen national hero. In theory, there was an air blockade on Chechnya, but this was violated with impunity at least 100/150 times a month[165]. The smuggling was so pervasive that almost one in two Chechens were apparently involved in various capacities. Obviously there were not only consumer goods, but also and above all illegal goods in the black market wallet. Particularly in the arms sector, Chechnya was both a crossroads and a direct buyer. As for drugs, they were traded more through Chechnya than inside Chechnya. The illegal trade in oil stolen from pipelines then became endemic and a source of livelihood for many families.

The situation of widespread illegality was also fueled by the prison system which went down the drain, the amnesty promoted by Dudaev to increase the ranks of his National Guard, the escape of prisoners from the Grozny Preliminary Detention facility and the Naursk penal colony. Crime was also increasing significantly because of this, with 9984 cases recorded in 1992, corresponding to a 68% increase over the previous year.[166].

Union. *On this sidewalk, next to the main post office, everything was on display: from simple grenades to sophisticated sniper rifles, all of Soviet origin, most from Russian army arsenals, many of them intended to kill Russian soldiers. . They were simply lying on the tables in the street: if it had rained, they would have been covered with plastic bags.*

[165]Historians *Gall* and *De Waal* have described the illegal import - export system, based on the so-called "shuttle - tours": A group of individuals set up a "tourist company" and rented a plane, often from Ukraine or Azerbaijan. The "shuttles" then took care of acting as small transports, flying continuously to and from Grozny airport. To get around the blocking of flights, each "company" paid up to $ 20,000 a month to airport officials. The generated market volume, essentially tax-free, allowed traders to sell their goods at a 20 - 30% discount on average Russian prices.

[166]The total number of crimes considered "serious" increased by 94.6% compared to 1991 (2341 against 1203), and the number of murders increased by 80.6% (242 against 134), rapes by 34% (63 against 46) but above all the thefts due to poverty increased dramatically, which recorded a + 234.3% (2434 against 727) the

Continuing on the analysis of Dudaev's speech, let's move on to what the president did not mention, starting with Justice. From an institutional point of view, the judicial system had remained substantially unchanged compared to the Soviet era, and only between July and November 1992 did the Parliament start its reorganization.[167]. The functions of the Ministry of Justice were carried out by the National Committee for Legal Reform, an office directly dependent on the President of the Republic. Starting from January 13, 1992, however, the need to finance the justice sector, after Moscow had stopped payments, led to the presidential decree *On the order of financing of the Legal Reform Committee*, agencies and institutions under its jurisdiction, people's courts of the Chechen republic in which it was established that the judicial structure would

---

burglaries even went up by 275.4% (214 against 57). Still drawing on the memoirs of Anatol Lieven, we report his experience with the "police forces" of independent Chechnya: "The train stopped in Grozny, five hours later, shortly after 4 in the morning. Everything was dark. A gunshot was heard from afar. The handful of other people who had gone out with me disappeared into the night. I, as a good member of the British middle class in unfamiliar territory, are going to find a policeman; or rather, a group of heavily armed Chechen policemen and their friends, who refused even to look at the passport I offered them out of hospitality, shared their meager breakfast with me and accompanied me, through curfew, to a kind of hotel, the Kavkaz. The police captain proudly emphasized the egalitarianism of the Chechens: "From the millionaire to the train driver, the important thing is to be a Chechen, we have very strict rules on how we behave with each other. You will see for yourself that we never shoot each other. But against our enemies we will fight to the death. [...] The more I knew them, plus the Chechens seemed to me a people who had rejected not only much of the Soviet version of modernization and the modern state - with all its works and all its empty promises - but modernization in general. In this they reminded me in some way of the Afghan Mujahideen, but much more disciplined, organized and supportive. [...]. "

[167] The reader who wants to deepen the question of the judicial system in the Chechen Republic of Ichkeria can consult the deepening *From Tribunals to Islamic Courts* available on the website www.ichkeria.net in the *Insights* section.

have to support itself with the proceeds deriving from the registration fees, including materials and salaries. The lack of funds and low and insecure wages produced a widespread phenomenon of corruption. This had already exploded even before Dudaev gave his pickaxe blow to justice with the aforementioned decree, so much so that a decree of 8 January the Parliament called on the judicial authorities to prosecute citizens who refused to recognize the rule of law and they tried to influence the work of the courts. But even this decree was devoid of practical enforceability and remained little more than a declaration[168].

In his interview, then, Dudaev did not refer to health and education, two other very delicate sectors that in 1992 had ceased to function. Teachers and doctors had not received their salaries for months, and the support of those who carried out their work voluntarily fell to the private initiative of the parents of the students or the relatives of the sick. Healthcare was collapsing, and there were no funds or supply channels to supply the already insufficient hospitals, so much so that between the end of 1991 and the beginning of 1992, diseases considered eradicated such as cholera reappeared in Chechnya. In the infrastructure sector, the country was not doing better. The lack of material was accompanied by the crisis in the services provided by a state that had ceased to provide them: there was a lack of constant supplies of drinking water, electricity and gas for heating. There was no longer a financial center that paid wages and pensions. Even the most basic services, especially for cities, such as the garbage collection service had gradually stopped working. In Grozny, mountains of garbage began to

---

[168] In 1992 barely 12% of the crimes recorded in the republic were subject to trial, and only 327 of the 1204 offenders were sentenced to prison.

accumulate, dirt and urban decay began to add to poverty[169].

While the so-called "big projects" had all been frozen in anticipation of better budget seasons, city governments, deprived of central government funding, were unable to pay for services, which began to be provided intermittently.

Finally, the welfare state. On this issue Dudaev had spent many words and implemented numerous initiatives, aimed at ensuring the ownership of social housing for the weaker sections of the population, guaranteeing them calm prices, public subsidies, even compensation (rather symbolic for the truth) for reparation. for the deportation of '44. In reality, most of his decrees remained on paper, because there were no resources to support his welfare. In these situations, the General brought out some of his worst "outings": he went so far as to accuse pensioners of wanting to discredit him as bought from Russian pensions, and as such traitors to a normal social system in which children are parental welfare. On the problem of the crisis in the educational system and the fact that Chechen girls remained at home to do housework, when asked about the question, he answered that it is normal for a woman

---

[169] Anatol Lieven recalls: *Between January 1992, when I visited Grozny for the first time, and November 1994, the increase in degradation was extremely marked, as well as the progressive collapse of most municipal services, since Dudaev's government has stopped funding them. The streets fell apart, huge piles of trash piled up, the telephone system broke down - a taste of the end of modernity as we have known it. [...] But this was not simply a collapse into barbarism. Because if on the one hand the works of the Soviet state were decaying, on the other Grozny under Dudaev was characterized by a commercial vitality unmatched in any other area of provincial Russia. And if much of this activity was criminal, it was organized crime, fashioned and regulated by tradition, and not mere banditry, albeit in the context of a privately armed population, capable of making the wildest dreams of the National Rifle Association meaningless. The potholed roads were home to a splendid assortment of Western luxury cars, and since potholes suffered badly, and were driven with little respect for their sensitive Western tools, the business of repairing them was one of the biggest. of the city.*

to reach third grade. *We have given you freedom, now you have to build a life for yourself!* he used to say. Maybe he didn't really think so, but certainly the effect of certain statements was not flattering. More likely, Dudaev seemed unable to cope with the vertical collapse that the Chechen state was undergoing from all points of view.

According to what Dudaev described in his speech, the parliamentary branch was a simple hiccup. The extra-parliamentary one, on the other hand, was made up of criminal terrorists. Yet, in reality, an entire district of the country, Upper Terek, was beyond the control of the government. Of course, after the coup of March 1992, opposition exponents also worked with weapons and intrigues: on June 30 of that year a commando disabled the state TV by undermining the building, and in the summer an attempt was organized. of murder with a car bomb from which Dudaev miraculously escaped unharmed. However, there was also a political opposition that perhaps it would have been worthwhile to involve in the debate, such as that of the Daimokhk movement, who did not hesitate to take the side of Dudaev when it seemed that Russia wanted to invade the country in November 1992. Returning to the opposition born in Parliament, this was now increasingly openly critical of Dudaev's actions. At the basis of this friction there was not only the question of the relations between the powers of the state, but also the perspective to which the independence experience had to turn. For many of the parliamentarians, Yusup Soslambekov first and foremost, independence had to be the bargaining chip with which to negotiate with Russia from a position of strength, obtaining greater concessions at the signing of a new Federative Pact. This "instrumental" vision of independence was totally rejected by Dudaev. For him independence was not a negotiable value.

Towards the end of 1992 it became clear to everyone that Dudaev was unwilling to compromise with the parliamentary majority, and what he believed to be a "constructive opposition" began to become a dangerous thorn in his side. The defections from the loyalist front also involved Dudaev's own government team. In the summer of 1992, the Foreign Minister, Shamil Beno, resigned in controversy with the General. For Beno, who thought roughly like Akhmadov and Soslambekov, the question of independence should not have become a political trap for Chechnya, which had not yet been recognized by anyone, despite the efforts made by Beno's successor, *Shamsuddin Youssef*.[170]

Finally, the Council of Elders deserves a note, which, as we have seen, was established at the beginning of 1992, and which in the course of its first year of life had found a way to remain unpleasant to the majority of the population. Gradually, and encouraged by Dudaev, the head of the Mekh - Khel, Adizov began to demand the political recognition of his Assembly. He even went so far as to carry out what today we would call a "flash - mob" in parliament in favor of his candidate for the Ministry of Health[171]. Over time it became clear that

---

[170] In the second half of 1992, Dudaev, the separatist government had launched the political campaign for the recognition of Chechen independence with renewed vigor. the President had sent Vice Premier Mamodaev on a business trip that took him to Japan. Dudaev himself, accompanied by the new Foreign Minister Shamsuddin Youssef, had visited Turkey, Jordan, Syria, Northern Cyprus and Bosnia Herzegovina between September and October, before crossing the ocean and reaching the United States. Here he was received by the Democratic presidential candidate, Bill Clinton, and by the Secretary of the United Nations, Boutros, Ghali, before concluding his "Grand Tour" in England. Almost always warmly welcomed, however, he was unable to wrest anything more than a few declarations of friendship from the Middle Eastern and Western chancelleries. At the end of 1992, no government had yet opened an official representation in Grozny, nor authorized the opening of a Chechen diplomatic office.

Azidov was using the Mekhk - Khel as a political platform to take power, or to shore up Dudaev's.[172]. The presence of the Council of Elders, initially hailed as a sign of the vitality of civil society, became progressively pervasive, until it became unbearable. The pro-government newspaper Ichkeria of 6 August 1992 read:

Something strange has happened to a significant portion of our elders. There is a feeling that they are obsessed with something. Day and night they sneak into the offices of the authorities. They look for ways to get some sort of position, wherever they can ... you see, during the revolution they were standing at the rallies, for that now they need to be rewarded, and if that doesn't happen, they organize self-styled "Mekh - Khel" or "Islamic centers"[...].

The members of the council claimed the right to intervene not only in moral or family matters, but also in disputes concerning trade, business, work.[173]. Again on *Ichkeria* we read:

---

[171]As Hussein Akhmadov reported in an interview, *The Mekh - Khel received legitimacy at a public demonstration during the August Putsch. Its president Adizov was a very resolute, courageous, quick and talkative elder. Taking the leadership of the Mekh - Khel, he tried to dictate his conditions. For example, he wanted Baron Kindarov to be appointed Minister of Health. Baron was a doctor, who organized tents and medical support during the protests during the revolution. Thus Adizov was shouting everywhere that only Kindarov could be the Minister of Health. One day Adizov with a group of elders entered the parliament demanding the appointment of Kindarov. Then he threatened: "The Mekh - Khel has expelled Imam Shamil, he will do it with you too!" My Deputy, Bek Mezhidov, told him to leave.*

[172]Also Akhmadov, regarding the relationship between Adizov and Dudaev, said: *Adizov tried to revive the Chechen traditions in his interests. It was very difficult to stop this elder. He attacked all authorities except Dudaev. Dudaev was the hero of the nation. He was a martyr, who had taken off his shoulder pads as a General, sacrificing his career on the altar of independence. Adizov organized congresses, asked to limit the powers of parliament, demanded my resignation, organized protests under my window. I didn't like that man [...].*

[173]In another article, Ichkeria reported the situation in the village of Pervomajskaya, a few kilometers northwest of Grozny, in which

The Mekhk - Khel has been a sacred institution for all Chechens since ancient times. Its tasks are to settle issues of war and peace, support local traditions, reconcile blood feuds, but certainly not among these are the control of warehouses and supplies, traffic police interventions, resignations and the appointment of authorities. .[174]

The claim to have a prominent political role, combined with the pervasiveness of its presence and excessively nationalist rhetoric led the Mekhk - Khel to be completely discredited, reduced to a mere propaganda facade of the Dudaev regime. In 1994, no one would have put up with this group of grudging old men. Adizov's political role quickly waned, and with the onset of the First Chechen War he vanished altogether.

---

the elders had intervened against the director of the local Kolkhoz, and when he had refused to comply with their indications they were came first to physical threats, then to assaults.

[174]In the same article, dated 24 May 1992, the story of the vice president of the Mekhk - Khel, Hussein Bisultanov, was retraced, who as a simple worker, relying on his position, had managed to earn the position of supervisor of the laboratory of the factory in which he worked. . Due to the poor quality of his work, Bisultanov was persuaded by his own colleagues, as well as by the factory manager, to retire. The Mekhk-Khel, who came to the rescue of his vice president, protested to the point of forcing the director of the factory to resign, and the factory itself to hand over one of its warehouses to Bisultanov as a personal enterprise. The position of the Mekhk - Khel was condemned by the workers of the plant themselves, who sided against Bisultanov (accused, among other things, of having been a convinced communist until the Cheche Revolution) by signing a protest note.

CHAPTER 6

THE REGIME

"The methods chosen by Dudaev to achieve independence were contrary to common sense. Instead of being guided by the norms of international law, from the first days of his activity he chose a confessional path in establishing relations with the Russian Federation. At the same time, a significant part of Parliament considered a priority to establish relations with the Russian Federation based on peaceful and political relations. [...] A group of parliamentarians demanded that the Presidency of the Chechen Republic abandon the populist methods of government, that it would constitute, as in all civilized countries, the law enforcements [...] I was forced to hold a speech on republican television in early January 1992: immediately establish a Cabinet of Ministers, take control of the armed forces, to ensure the safety of the citizens of the republic and their property [...]. Furthermore, I reserved the right to go to the president's opposition, even though I remained a staunch supporter of the need to gain independence and build a new Chechnya. This position was dictated by the fact that I began to understand that Dudaev was using the idea of independence only as a tool to achieve his goals.".

Yusup Soslambekov - "Chechnya, a view from the inside"

The January negotiations

At the beginning of 1993 the process triggered by Perestroika and continued with the collapse of the USSR could be considered complete. In every former Soviet republic communism had been overwhelmed and the one-party regime had been replaced by democratic systems. These were young, unstable governments, in which the authoritarianism of the leaders who had created them was opposed to the parliamentary institutions. Just as was happening in Chechnya, where the overflowing figure of General Dudaev was barely contained by Parliament, institutional conflicts also broke out in Belarus, Georgia, Armenia, Azerbaijan and Russia itself. The results were of two types: where the parliamentary current won, Western-style democracies were established. Where, on the other hand, the national-popular leaders won, republics with a strong presidential vocation or semi-dictatorial regimes were born. Both in Russia and in Chechnya the evolution of the conflict would have led to the same epilogue.

In Chechnya, Dudaev found himself increasingly isolated. Its supporters, for the most part members of the presidential entourage and nationalists of the VDP, were entrenched in defense of radical positions, in contrast with the willingness to compromise of moderate nationalists. A growing extra-parliamentary opposition, then, refused to participate in political life. In Russia the situation was not very different: the policies of the Gaidar government were in full swing and presented the Russians with a very high bill. During 1992, the country's GDP had collapsed by 14.5%, and the estimates for 1993 gave no hope for the better. The economic crisis had left half of the population in bankrupt. All sectors of public spending had been cut, starting with social benefits, the health system, and obviously the army, reduced to the shadow of itself. The shock therapy was costing Yeltsin a noticeable decline in support and had by now turned him away from the support of the President of Supreme Soviet, the aforementioned Chechen politician Ruslan Khasbulatov. The latter, initially close to the positions of the president, especially in the confused days of the August Putsch, had aligned himself with social democratic positions, critical of Gaidar's liberalism. Around him the majority of the deputies of the Soviet had adhered to currents, movements and parties in favor of a moderation of government policies. initially close to the positions of the president, especially in the confused days of the August Putsch, he had aligned himself with social democratic positions, critical of Gaidar's liberalism. Around him the majority of the deputies of the Congress had adhered to currents, movements and parties in favor of a moderation of government policies.

The road to a "liberal counter-revolution" seemed open, and first of all passed from the abrogation of the emergency powers that Yeltsin had requested and obtained to implement his "tears and blood" maneuver, which would naturally expire by the end of 1992. The President asked for its extension, but this request clashed with the intentions of most of the deputies hostile to the Gaidar government and with those of Khasbulatov, who wanted to revoke those powers as soon as possible. Therefore, Yeltsin's request ran into the refusal of the Congress which, indeed, on December 9, 1992, distrusted Gaidar from the leadership of the executive. Like what was happening in Chechnya, also in Russia the presidential power, proponent of a radical policy, clashed with the parliamentary one, intent on defending the constitutional order.

Yeltsin's reaction was not long in coming, and on December 10 the President gave an angry speech, accusing the Supreme Soviet of wanting to sabotage the reforms and bring Russia back to the Soviet era. Finally, he proposed a popular referendum on citizens' trust in the President, the government and the Parliament[175]. After two days of mutual broadcasts, Khasbulatov and Yeltsin reached a compromise whereby the President would agree to subject his work to a popular vote of confidence and would make a change of the guard in the executive, in exchange for the extension of almost all emergency powers until the day of the referendum, to be held in April 1993. There and then the agreement seemed to hold: Elstin fired Gaidar and replaced him with *Viktor Chernomyrdin*, eclectic and politically fickle, president of the main company producer of oil and natural gas in Russia and one of the most important on the planet, *Gazprom*.

Mired as he was in the crisis with Parliament, Yeltsin had neither the time nor the opportunity to deal with Chechnya. For this reason he let his plenipotentiary *Sergei Shakhrai*, who had already represented him in the numerous meetings with the separatist delegations in 1992, deal with carrying out the negotiations with the counterpart, with the only imperative not to let the small Caucasian republic succeed in obtaining recognition as an independent state. Shakhrai had three options to choose from: supporting the extra-parliamentary opposition and fostering an armed rebellion in the republic, opening a round of negotiations with Dudaev, or trying to

---

[175]Describing the purpose of the referendum at a press conference, Yeltsin proposed his question: What course do the citizens of Russia take? The course of the President, a course of transformation, or the course of Congress, of the Supreme Soviet and its President, a course aimed at bending reforms and ultimately towards aggravating the crisis?

circumvent him by taking away the support of his own parliament. The third solution seemed to him the most effective, because it weakened the main obstacle to the reintegration of Chechnya (Dudaev in fact) without "getting his hands dirty" with undercover operations. There was always time to arm some rebels to send them to kill the Chechen president. On the other hand, it was possible to divide the independence front only now that relations between the general and the representatives of the Parliament of Grozny were compromised. Thus, throughout the month of December, Shakhrai worked to keep close to both Mamodaev and the most energic of the Chechen deputies, Soslambekov, now hostile to the President.

Shakhrai, Mamodaev and Soslambekov met first in Vladikavkaz, then in Moscow, preparing a draft Federal Treaty that would see Chechnya join it as an independent state. The first result of this renewed understanding was Shakhrai's promise to loosen the economic blockade and start paying pensions and subsidies to Chechen citizens again, as soon as the draft Treaty was approved in Grozny. It seemed that after so much bitterness a common ground of negotiation had been reached. But as it had always been until then, the hopes of the Chechen negotiators ran into Dudaev's stubborn refusal, who did not intend to adhere to any federative treaty, of any nature, under any conditions. For the time being, however, the consultations went on. After all, it was not so important for Shakhrai to reach an agreement immediately, as to isolate Dudaev as much as possible. On January 6, 1993 Mamodaev declared that he had presented a draft treaty between Russia and Chechnya, and that he had discussed it broadly with the Russian Deputy Minister for Nationalities *Ramzan Abdulatipov*. The document, which was to be discussed in the following days, would have resulted in the transfer of numerous powers by the Chechen state to the Russian Federation. As was to be expected, Dudaev replied with a categorical "No". Shkahrai and Soslambekov agreed to continue negotiations on the basis of the federative "between equals" principle, hoping that the parliamentary faction would be able to get the better of Dudaev, and the divorce Russian - Chechen managed to compose himself.

As soon as the Russian delegation arrived in the Chechen capital it was immediately clear to everyone in what difficult climate the negotiations would take place. The airport was militarized, and the diplomatic procession was guarded by heavily armed Dudaevites until they arrived at the Parliament building, where talks were to be held. On reaching their destination, the Russian delegation began negotiations with the Chechen one, made up of the President of Parliament, Akhmadov, Vice-President Mezhidov, the President of the Foreign Affairs Commission, Soslambekov and the Chechnya representative in Moscow, *Sherip Yusupov*. Within minutes, a detachment of the Presidential Guard reached the Parliament building in combat gear. It seemed that Dudaev was determined to stop the negotiations at any cost, arresting all present if necessary. Akhmadov and Soslambekov mobilized anyone who could help them, including relatives and friends. The intervention of parliamentarians and civilians, who crowded in front of the building and prevented the special forces from intervening, allowed the talks to continue.

The fact itself remained however very serious, and indicative of the climate of mutual suspicion that now hovered between the President and Parliament. The two delegations eventually signed a preparation protocol for a treaty on mutual delegation and division of powers. The protocol gave the Chechens the victory of a recognition of their republic as a subject of law. Likewise, it guaranteed the Russians the prospect of a treaty that would keep Chechnya within the political space of Russia. On this basis, Chechnya could have ceded portions of its sovereignty to the Russian Federation not as a lower-level entity, but as an equal entity that voluntarily joined a federation of sovereign republics. From a legal point of view, the difference was actually important: the entry of Chechnya was recognized as voluntary, and not as a constraint due to the application of the principle of supremacy. On a practical level (which was what interested Dudaev most) however, it meant the return of Chechnya to Russia, the loss of independence and the recognition of Moscow's political primacy. On January 19, the Chechen press published the draft of the treaty, angering Dudaev. He repudiated the protocol, declaring that no agreement could be reached before the country was recognized as an independent republic, infuriating Soslambekov and Akhmadov in turn.

Frustrated by Dudaev's attitude, Soslambekov declared that if the general opposed the negotiations, Parliament would hold a popular referendum, forcing the President to sign the federative treaty. He declared to the press: *We are building a state not for the President and not for the Parliament, but for the entire people of the republic, its future generations!* The third delegate of Parliament, Vice - President Bektimar Mezhidov, also railed against the President, accusing him of not wanting to find a common language. Dudaev replied through his Information Minister, Ugudov, who stated: *While, on the whole, the government supports the conduct of Russian - Chechen negotiations, does not agree with a series of formulas in the protocol signed by the Russian delegation and the representatives of the Chechen parliament on 14 January.* Yandarbiev echoed him, arguing that the tenor of the signed document lowered the level of the negotiations as it had been set up between March and May 1992. Soslambekov then attempted to rectify the disputed points, drafting a draft treaty under which Chechnya would joined the Russian Federation by an independent entity.

Abkhazia on fire

While in Russia and Chechnya the institutions fought for control of the state, inter-ethnic conflicts flared up in the rest of the Caucasus. The clash between Abkhazians and Georgians, which seemed to have come to a standstill in the autumn of 1992 with the reconquest of Gagra by the separatist militias, re-exploded with violence in December 1992. The Abkhaz militias, supported by the aviation and the federal artillery, began a heavy bombardment on Georgian positions on the outskirts of the capital Sukhumi, still in the hands of the Tbilisi government. It was the prelude to a full-scale attack. On the morning of March 16, the separatists set out to conquer the city. Losses on both sides were huge, but the attackers failed to break the Georgian defenses.

To be able to undermine the Georgian defensive device, the separatists devised a bypass maneuver that allowed them to swoop down on the city from the north, through the mountain villages of *Akhalsheni*, *Guma* and *Shroma*. The road that connected the three small towns, inhabited mainly by Georgians, led directly into the city center from the north, allowing the separatist units to avoid the ford of the Gumista River, along which the Georgian trenches ran, and to have to conquer house by house the western quarter of the city, consisting mainly of tall Soviet-era buildings. The Georgians were not prepared to face such an action, and the garrison set up to defend the villages was quickly overwhelmed. After passing the three inhabited centers, the separatist militias prepared to strike down on the city, when near the village of *Kamani*, the last guard post before Sukhumi, they found a fierce detachment of the Georgian National Guard waiting for them. The battle raged for two hours before the defenders, decimated and out of ammunition, left the village. Meanwhile, Russian-backed secessionist units landed east of Sukhumi, completing its encirclement and beginning the siege of the capital. The conquest of the villages to the north was followed by the usual script of ethnic cleansing that had been seen in Gagra: in the two days that followed the conquest, the militiamen indulged in looting, rape and murder, in particular in the village of Kamani, whose population was almost entirely exterminated[176].

After two weeks of fighting, a ceasefire was reached on July 28, and while Russia and Georgia began political talks. The Georgian leader, Eduard Shevardnadze was forced to accept the de facto independence of Abkhazia, and the open conflict subsided. At that point the presence of the International Brigades of the Confederation was no longer necessary, and over the following weeks most of the volunteers returned from the theater of operations.

The contribution of the Caucasian foreign fighters to the Georgian - Abkhaz war was important: hundreds of them died on the field, and many others were injured. The numerous Chechen volunteers who had participated in the campaign returned home not only as winners, but

---

[176]Kamani village was mostly populated by Georgians. Upon their arrival in the village, the separatists attacked the population with the clear intention of exterminating it. Between 9 and 11 July 1993 all the remaining inhabitants were captured, tortured and brutally killed. The violence did not spare the nuns and prelates of the local Orthodox monastery, who were also killed with cruel ferocity.

above all as veterans. The house-to-house battles and skirmishes on the steep mountain paths of Abkhazia had been an ideal training ground to form the backbone of the separatist armed force, and to bring out the first field commanders from that amalgam of militiamen. Among them they distinguished theirselves Shamil Basayev (who came to cover the role of Deputy Minister of Defense) Ruslan Gelayev (commander of the II International Brigade), Umalt Dashayev, Turpal - Ali Atgeriev, Khamzat Khankarov, Isa Arsemikov.

The constitutional reform

If in Abkhazia the main separatist military leaders were making their bones, in Chechnya the confrontation between the institutions was more heated than ever. Here the bitterness between the parliamentary party, in favor of a compromise agreement with the Russian Federation and the limitation of the powers of the Head of State and the presidential one, aligned on radical positions and firm in the defense of Dudaev's semi-dictatorial prerogatives, had reached the escalation. The "battle of appointments" for the control of institutions and the system of cross vetoes was paralyzing both legislative and executive activity, exposing the Chechen Republic to the serious risk of collapsing on itself, to the great satisfaction of the federal authorities.
At the beginning of 1993 Dudaev tried to get out of the political siege in which he found himself by exploiting the instrument of the constitutional amendment: considering it essential to guarantee the nascent Chechen state governability at any cost, the President gave a mandate to the Secretary of State, Aslanbek Akbulatov, to prepare a series of amendments to the Constitution, so that it was corrected towards a decisive

presidentialism. The result was a project that provided for the constitution of a bicameral system: the Parliament would become the *House of Representatives*, composed of 41 deputies elected in the territorial districts. The other chamber would be called the Council of the State Chamber and would have been made up of 14 members representing scientific - cultural organizations and representatives of ethnic and religious minorities. The President of this chamber would be the Secretary of State, with the title of Vice - President. The Constitutional Court would be abolished, and its functions would be transferred to the *Supreme Court*. Finally, *Sharia courts* would be established, with the task of acting as "Peace Officers" in civil and family matters[177]. The great novelty would have been the shift of the axis of power towards the President, with the introduction of a republic in which the leader would have had full authority to train and fire the members of the executive, from the Prime Minister to the holders of the various departments, without, the approval of Parliament.

The proposal aroused a hive of controversy. The federation of trade unions of Chechnya formulated on February 12 a formal request for resignation from the President, guilty of having *completely ruined the economy of the republic*. He was echoed by the parliamentary opposition, who accused the President of abusing his power. Soslambekov's parliamentary group, Bako, accused the

---

[177]The project to establish religious courts to administer civil justice in matters of a customary nature was the first project actually aimed at diverting the state towards confessionalism. From Dudaev's point of view, the provision was certainly aimed at acquiring the consensus of the religious, removing them from the parliamentary field. It is possible that the President's aim was to make Sharia courts mere "peace officers", limiting the intervention of religious law to minor issues. As we will see later, the initiative was instead vigorously resumed by his successor, Zelimkhan Yandarbiev, and extended to the point of supplanting the secular judiciary itself, laying the foundations for the establishment of an Islamic state.

President of *attempting to usurp power in Chechnya and to be preparing a coup d'etat* by introducing amendments to the Constitution proposed by Dudaev, which *actually produce a presidential government in the Republic, and nowhere. case can be accepted.* On 23 February the forces of the parliamentary party gathered in plenary session, in which they condemned *the methods of force* with which Dudaev wanted to *obtain a change of power through new presidential elections.* For his part, Dudaev summoned the heads of the local administrations of the mountain villages on February 15. During the meeting, local officials agreed on the need to organize a series of meetings with citizens to discuss the proposal for a presidential republic. On February 17, *Daymokh*, *Marsho*, *Civil Accord* and *Slavic Congress* accused Dudaev that he was leading the country to catastrophe. According to their exponents *The incompetence of the authorities in domestic and foreign policy can lead to the isolation of the Republic from the outside world, and as a result of provocative attacks and extremist statements by President Dudaev and the inconsistency of Parliament, the Republic may be deprived of the opportunity to determine its rightful place in the world community.* In response, the President called a constitutional referendum to be held on the following 19 February. Parliament obviously opposed it, vetoing Dudaev's decree. However, he was willing to go ahead and turned his referendum into a *sociological survey with no legal effects.* Parliament sensed the trap, and in any case forbade the holding of the vote. Dudaev then reacted by declaring that the poll would take place anyway, and that it was not within the powers of Parliament to prevent a sociological consultation. Parliament held an extended session at the Constitutional Court and the Public Prosecutor's Office, in which the defendant institutions condemned the President's initiative, as this contradicted the Constitution of the Chechen Republic. Among the conclusions of the assembly, it was made clear that, in the event of a constitutional crisis, the Parliament could call new elections. Finally, a special emergency commission was set up to study the presidential decree. Parliament could have called new elections. Finally, a special emergency commission was set up to study the presidential decree.

On February 18, Parliament officially vetoed the presidential decree, and set the date for an updated version of the referendum proposed by Dudaev: it would be held in official form on March 27, and citizens would be asked to decide if they preferred a parliamentary or presidential republic, and whether or not they wanted to be part of the Russian Federation. Dudaev in turn vetoed the provision, declaring that the consultation would expose the Chechen state to the risk of self-dissolution in the Russian Federation, a prospect that in any case, according to him, was absolutely to be avoided.

On February 19, the *sociological survey* was held. Four hundred thousand ballots were distributed, somewhat in bulk, between government offices and DVP headquarters. To the "survey" 117,000 people attended, and official figures reported just 3861 "NO". Hussein Akhmadov immediately contested the validity of the referendum, which was participated by just a fraction of the voting population and in any case not authorized by Parliament. Although devoid of legal effects, the popular pronouncement was a major political victory for Dudaev, who had gathered his supporters and had obtained a good result: in the face of the criticisms and attacks he had received, he and his people had proved able to ask for and obtain the support of more than one hundred thousand Chechens in the space of two weeks. Soslambekov, Akhmadov and Mezhidov, together with the majority of the deputies formulated a formal request for resignation from Dudaev, declaring their distrust and calling for the establishment of a *Government of National Trust*. If Dudaev had accepted the invitation to establish a government appreciated by Parliament, the assembly would have withdrawn the call of the referendum for March 27. Dudaev replied by declaring that on March 19 he would hold a National Congress of the Chechen People to which he would submit the question of the referendum on March 27 and in general of the proposals made by the presidential staff on the modification of the Constitution.

The tones were heated, and the peaceful President of Parliament, Akhmadov, seemed unable to resist the overflowing personality of his opponent. Unable to manage the tug-of-war with the general, he decided to resign in favor of the more grim and combative Yusup Soslambenov. Ever since he formed his parliamentary group and switched to the opposition, the President's former right-hand man had stood in the way of any initiative of his old leader. As a member of Parliament he had systematically attacked all his proposals, as head of the Foreign Parliamentary Commission he had carried out negotiations and talks without seeking an understanding with him. As leader of the Confederation of Peoples of the Caucasus, he also stole the media scene from him.

The worsening of relations gave Soslambekov the possibility of taking the confrontation with the President to a new level. On February 17, two days before Dudaev held his "poll" on constitutional reform, Soslambekov founded the *Committee for the National and Civil Agreement*, a sort of grouping of opposition groups of all kinds, a political platform from which to launch a electoral offensive against Dudaev and overthrow his regime[178].

---

[178] In its plans, the Committee should have been a re-edition of the Popular Front, a heterogeneous formation from which the

The Mugadaev government

As soon as he had achieved the political success he expected with the more than one hundred thousand adhesions to his reform program, Dudaev began working on an executive that could allow him the freedom of maneuver he had lacked until then. With the divorce underway between Dudaev and Mamodaev, a crackdown in the government was increasingly necessary for the President, starting with the premier. Mamodaev was not only accused of wanting to unload the general and set up a new government in agreement with Parliament, but also that of being inefficient and corrupt: in fact, a year after his inauguration, economic reform had not yet been seen, nor the privatization, now necessary and no longer postponed if the republic was to be prevented from continuing to wallow in insolvency. Of course, an important part in this inaction was played by Parliament and by Dudaev's stubborn opposition to any measure that smacked of capitalism, but surely Mamodaev had not fought like a lion in defense of his theses. Even the promised foreign investments never arrived, and the country's economy sank into lawlessness. And still talking about illegality, there were rumors about Mamodaev's

---

protagonists of the Chechen Revolution had emerged with the same objective: to overthrow the tyranny and hand over power to the people. The first thing the Council for the National and Civil Accord should have done was to ensure that the referendum proposed by Soslambekov was held on time. The law just approved by Parliament with the approval of the Constitutional Court provided that the referendum could be called at the request of the Parliament, at the request of the President or at the request of one hundred thousand citizens with the right to vote. According to his memoirs (Chechnya, an inside view) Soslambekov did not trust many of the deputies, and tried to secure the necessary signatures to continue even without the support of this. So he set up an "initiative group" that would collect one hundred thousand signatures.

alleged misappropriation of oil shares, during the period in which he had disposed of the sector at his discretion. He returned all charges to the sender, and indeed openly accused the President's entourage of enriching themselves behind the public budget[179].

From February 1993, Dudaev therefore began to work for a replacement at the top, which would guarantee greater freedom of maneuver to his government and give a breath of renewal to the executive. On the table were two aspirants to Mamodaev's succession. The first was *Musa Doshukaev*, a company manager from the same background as the other. He had been Minister of Industry and Consumer Goods in Zavgaev's time, and even before Mamodaev's appointment he had been floated as a viable alternative[180]. For some time it seemed that Dudaev had chosen him as his deputy, though it is true that he began holding closed-door meetings in his personal office. It seemed, because as the General often did, within a few weeks he changed his mind, opting for support for another candidate: *Mairbek Mugadaev*. He was another similar manager, who had cut his teeth in the past as the director of a state-owned company that was involved in building pipelines across the length and breadth of the Soviet Union. A few years before the

---

[179] Soslambekov echoed this theme: "*Meanwhile, taking advantage of the republic's "suspended" state, Dudaev and his entourage, along with the corrupt structures of the Russian government, used the territory of the Chechen republic for questionable operations, later referred to by Shakhrai as "a pomp for the transfer of wealth." (but these proceeds were not pumped into the budget of the Chechen Republic, not for the needs of the Chechen people, but to the foreign accounts of those who, with Dudaev's help, created an uncontrolled zone in Chechnya). At the same time, the Chechen population was plagued by the Kremlin's blockade of finance, economy, transport and information.*"

[180] Doshukaev was an exponent of Teip Benoy, the most numerous and influential Teip Chechen. He was, however, disliked by some of the high-ranking members of Dudaev's entourage, particularly the Minister of Justice Imaev. It also seems that in October 1991 he sided against the Executive Committee of the OKChN, even if he categorically denied any kind of accusation.

Chechen Revolution he had returned to his homeland to run a construction company. In May 1992 he was invited by Mamodaev himself to take part in the work of the government[181]. The "resigned" premier did not take the President's initiative well and ran to Parliament to ask for his resignation to be revoked, obtaining the support of Soslambekov and the veto on the dismissal order.

But the President didn't seem willing to stop his crackdown: firmly regaining control of the executive, Dudaev began to put into practice one of his most ambitious goals: the creation of a national currency that would surpass the Russian ruble and guarantee the country monetary sovereignty. Until then, this had only been discussed at the beginning of 1992, when, with the Decree of entry into force of the Constitution, Parliament had established the circulation of the ruble and recourse to the ex-Soviet monetary system *until the creation of its own monetary credit system or its unification with systems of other states*. This state of "permanent suspension" had left Chechnya within the Russian monetary system, which in those years was facing an unprecedented crisis. The ruble had devalued enormously, and so Chechnya found itself, in addition to its problems, also having to face the problems deriving from the transformations of a monetary system over which it had no power. Issuing a new currency into circulation, however, was not child's play. In the first place this had to be designed to have

---

[181]Mamodaev had previously worked under Mugadaev's direction, and this must have played an important role in Dudaev's last-minute choice to prefer him to Doshukaev. Probably he intended in this way to influence Mamodaev and persuade him not to go to the parliamentary branch. The choice to prefer Mugadaev was also motivated by the fact that he enjoyed the informal support of the Command of the *Shali Armored Regiment*, the only military unit under Dudaev's orders actually capable of maneuvering at that time, which had emerged from the reorganization of the apparatus. military left in Chechnya by the Russians in June 1992. His appointment would have pleased the army too.

exchange value, otherwise it would have remained little more than waste paper. With respect to this issue there was a heated confrontation between Dudaev, anxious to put the new currency into circulation as a propaganda means, and the Minister of Finance, Taymaz Abubakarov, who objected that without hedging the new banknotes would have no appreciation on the currency market and would soon be reduced to mere worthless pieces of paper. In order to build up enough assets to guarantee a minimum of stability to the new currency, Abubakarov calculated the capital needed by the Chechen National Bank at 50 billion rubles in 1993, a figure higher than the annual budget of the entire Republic. The project was therefore, in fact, impracticable. But Dudaev did not give up and began to make contacts with foreign companies, planning the creation of the first Chechen national currency.[182].

The institutional crisis

While Soslambekov maneuvered the parliament, the extra-parliamentary and pro-Russian grouping of Umar Avturkhanov organized ever more impressive raids directly in Grozny. The mayor of the capital himself, Gantamirov, opened the gates of the city to him. He too, during 1992, had developed a profound disillusionment with the President, who over time had become open opposition. At the origins of his discontent there was not only a crisis of personal confidence. Since his

[182] This should have been called *Nahar*, and Dudaev set out to design the details: how it should be made, what cuts could be made available, what should be pictured on it. For him, as well as a possible means of financial stabilization, the national currency was a means of showing the world the independence of his country. Any reader wishing to deepen the subject can consult the article *A currency for Ichkeria: the Nahar* available on the website www.ichkeria.net

inauguration as mayor, in fact, Gantemirov had worked to consolidate his power in the city, asking for great autonomy in the investment of public funds and arming his own private army. To finance his business he had had access to substantial shares of the proceeds from the production and export of petroleum products. The use of these quotas in theory should have been controlled, in order to prevent public officials from enriching themselves in the folds of budgets. In early 1993, the judicial authorities had begun to verify that state bodies were using public funds in a transparent manner. Gantamirov seemed to have used most of the funds not for the functioning of the bureaucratic apparatus of the state, but for the arming of its Municipal Police. Furthermore, substantial oil quotas were "vaporized", a phenomenon for which Gantamirov risked being accused. When Parliament sent Dudaev a specific question about the oil quotas for Gantamirov, and he in turn turned the request to the Mayor of Grozny, he not only did not reply, but declared that he did not recognize the authority of the President and joined the opposition.
On March 24, the first public meeting of the Round Table took place, a grouping of the opposition movements in Dudaev, from which the first protests in the square arose[183]. Faced with the impossibility of bringing Parliament back to milder councils, with the extra-parliamentary opposition on a war footing and

---

[183] Its exponents publicly declared that Chechnya was on the verge of social explosion: *The discontent of the people under Dudaev's regime has reached such proportions that at any moment masses of people could take to the streets and demand that the government be removed* one of these told the press. One of the leaders of Daymokh, academician Dzhabrail Gakayev, excluded any compromise with the government, and hoped for the resignation of the President and new elections. On the same day, many professors and students of the University of Grozny, who had already been on strike for more than a month, declared that they wanted to take to the streets to demand the resignation of Dudaev and his government.

members of the same presidential entourage who were taking a stand against him, Dudaev was left with nothing but forceful action. The right moment came towards the end of April, when the eyes of the world and of Russian citizens turned to the referendum on trust in the President of the Russian Federation.

In fact, in Moscow the fragile understanding between the President and Parliament had cracked in a surprisingly similar way to what was happening in Chechnya. Here too, in fact, the friction between the two powers manifested itself in a "struggle for investitures" and a consequent paralysis of the legislative activity of the State. Between 26 and 28 March both Elstin's and Khasbulatov's resignations were put on the table. Neither won the majority necessary to proceed, but the political significance for the two leaders was profoundly different: for Elstin it was a victory, which showed how the President could still govern parliamentary activity. For Khasbulatov, however, it was a defeat, because as many as 339 deputies voted to resign, making it clear that the presidentialist party was strong, and that a room renewed by new consultations would see him regain control of Parliament. To capitalize on the political result, Yeltsin resolved to undergo a referendum test of trust, scheduled for April 25, 1993.

Taking advantage of the state of fibrillation of Russian public opinion, on April 17 Dudaev gathered a crowd of supporters in front of the Presidential Palace, and in front of it he read the decree that *suspended* the activity of Parliament, entrusting its tasks to the Constitutional Court, it officially *dissolved* the Mamodaev government and *placed* the entire territory of the Republic *under presidential authority*. Finally, he *entrusted* Mugadaev with the formation of a new government by 15 May. Finally, given the exceptional gravity of the crisis, he instituted a curfew throughout the country and scheduled new parliamentary elections for September / October of that year. In the following hours, the National Guard took control of the Parliament building, the Prosecutor's Office and State TV. If it was not yet the coup d'état, we lacked very little. In a single decree, the President had suspended the main constitutional guarantees, and established a de facto dictatorship that would inevitably have inflamed the streets. And so it was. The following day the opposition began a permanent rally in Theater Square in Grozny, demanding the protection of the institutions and the resignation of Dudaev. The crowd was stirred up by Salambek Hadjiev, Khasbulatov's favorite at the time of the November 1991 State of Emergency, who called for the dissolution of all republican authorities and the organization of new elections. Defending it was Gantamirov with his private army. The demonstration was attended by Daimokh, the Movement for Democratic Reforms, the "Marsho" movement, the "Civic Agreement" group and the Association of Intellectuals.

As the square began to fill up with protesters, the Constitutional Court inevitably canceled the presidential decrees passed the previous day. The Mayor of Grozny echoed this by canceling the curfew on the city with a *municipal decree*. Dudaev also called his people together. On April 19, Freedom Square was filled with supporters of the President (about twenty thousand according to press agencies). Dudaev ordered the army to take sides between the two demonstrations, within which the first firearms were already beginning to be seen. On the same day he dissolved the Gantamirov militia by decree, ordering the delivery of all weapons to the National Guard.

Meanwhile, a referendum on trust in the President was being held in Russia. The consultation was based on four questions. The first and second were related to trust in the person of Yeltsin and in the politics of the government he supported[184]. On both points, Yeltsin would have had enough 50% + 1 of the valid votes to be reconfirmed. The second two questions instead asked the Russians to express themselves on the need or not to hold early presidential and parliamentary elections[185]. In these last two questions, the principle established by the Congress was to consider the "YES" valid only with a majority of votes in favor of all those entitled to it. The referendum was an institutional and political victory for Yeltsin: the majority of voters confirmed their confidence in the President (59.9%) and in government policy (54.3%), rejected the proposal for new presidential elections (48.8%) and strongly supported the need to renew the parliament (69.1%). The last question in particular demonstrated the controversy of the voting system. Despite an overwhelming majority in favor of the elections, in fact, this was not enough to force the constitutional mechanism, as 69.1% of the voters, corresponding to 46 million people, however, it did not represent 50% + 1 of those entitled, who were 107 million. However, the political victory was overwhelming, and Yeltsin appealed to the popular will to continue with the dissolution of Parliament and its renewal, certain of winning an absolute majority of seats. On April 29, Yeltsin published his proposal for a revision

---

[184]Question number 1: *Do you trust the President of the Russian Federation Boris Yeltsin?* Question number 2: *Do you approve of the socio-economic policy pursued by the President of the Russian Federation and the Government of the Russian Federation since 1992?*

[185]Question number 3: *Do you think it necessary to hold early presidential elections in the Russian Federation?* Question number 4: *Do you think it necessary to hold early elections for people's deputies of the Russian Federation?*

of the constitution, and called a special assembly to finalize a draft of the new fundamental text. The project that came out of the work of the Council provided for the dissolution of the Congress and its replacement with a bicameral system centered on the figure of the President of the Federation. The idea was strikingly similar to the one presented by Dudaev a few weeks earlier, and was unacceptable to the Russian parliament, as well as the Chechen parliament[186].

While Yeltsin took home his referendum victory, the situation in Chechnya had become explosive. On April 27, Dudaev sent a letter to the President of the Constitutional Court urging him to give his opinion[187]. At the same time he sent a proposal to Parliament, in which he offered to hold both parliamentary and presidential elections by the autumn. The opposition responded to the General's openings to dialogue by increasing the intensity of the demonstrations against him. On the same April 27, the movements of the Round Table signed a resolution in which they returned to demand the resignation of Dudaev, the dissolution of the

---

[186] In fact, it seems that between the two leaders there was a community of political vision. Regarding the friendship (whether real or interested) shown by Dudaev towards the Russian leader, there is no doubt: on many occasions, both publicly and privately, the General sympathized with him, advised him to resolve the institutional crisis to his advantage and he warned of the parliamentary branch that was maneuvering to make him fall. He even sent letters in which he demonstrated his closeness as a politician and as a man to the Russian President. Elstin, for his part, never answered, and we don't know how deeply he could appreciate the figure of the Chechen leader. But surely the way in which they both faced the institutional crisis, the way in which they resolved it, trace two almost parallel paths.

[187] The text of the letter read: *In a difficult period of a real threat to the independence of the Chechen Republic and its constitutional system, please express an opinion [...] the current situation has been determined by the Parliament which, despite the Constitution of the Chechen Republic guarantees the division of powers, has effectively acted on the formation and control of the majority of executive bodies. [...].*

Mamodaev government and new elections as soon as possible.[188]. Parliament accepted the requests of the square, calling a referendum for June 5 organized around 3 questions: *Does the Chechen Republic need an institution of Presidency? Do you trust the President? Do you trust Parliament?* If the population had spoken out against Dudaev, or against Parliament, or against both, new elections would have been called. If the President had objected, Parliament would have voted impeachment. The negotiation plan was now completely compromised: Dudaev would never have accepted a confirmatory referendum on his person, much less a question concerning the abolition of the institution of the presidency. The 12 deputies loyal to him left the parliament, in order to make the assembly lack the quorum and to render any acts of formal notice to the President null, but the latter replied by summoning the two deputies elected as reserves and thus restoring the necessary quorum. With the opposition in the square on the warpath and the parliament that flanked it, Dudaev was left only to continue on the way of government by decree.

The coup d'état

So on April 29, in a speech on state TV, the President read two new decrees: in the first he called new parliamentary elections, in the second he ordered the dissolution of the City Council of Grozny, in the meantime passed bag and baggage to the opposition following the Mayor Gantemirov and ready to host the

---

[188]The opposition's demands also included the abolition of the institution of the Presidency, the convening of the Constituent Assembly and free access to the state media, under the control of the National Guard since April 18. In addition, it was required to reactivate the military detachments deployed in the city.

sessions of the Parliament "suspended" by Dudaev twelve days earlier. With this last measure, the President abolished yet another constitutional organ of the republic: by now, with the exception of the government and the Constitutional Court, there was no longer any political authority capable of opposing his will. The authoritarian turn hit full force on the Speaker of Parliament Akhmadov who, unable to contain the overflowing personality of his opponent, ended up handing over the presidency of the chamber to Soslambekov on 10 May. He was a much more combative man than his predecessor, and as his first act he proposed again the constitution of a government of trust, expression of the will of Parliament. To train him he called Mamodaev, who had been fired by Dudaev a few days ago and now was ready to support the parliamentary cause body and soul.

If at the moment the advantage in the institutions was on the side of Dudaev, who had the nascent regular army on his side, in the squares there was a substantial balance, with the two demonstrations (Loyalists in Freedom Square, opposition in Theatre Square) that showed no sign of dissolving and risked degenerating into guerrilla warfare at any moment. In early May, the President ordered the permanent rallies to be dissolved to avoid armed clashes between opposing factions. The maneuver was also political, because the general knew that his people would obey him, while the opposition would refuse. And so it was: after the promulgation of the order to dissolve all the demonstrations, the loyalists left the square, the opponents did not. The situation was aggravated by a group of armed strangers who attacked the television center at night, triggering a shooting with the Presidential Guard. There were no casualties or significant damage, but Dudaev had an easy time accusing the opposition of wanting to unleash an armed rebellion. Mamodaev, having arrived in Parliament and accepted the proposal to form an alternative government, tried to organize a cabinet meeting, but only obtained the blitz of Dudaev's supporters in the government building, during which he was almost lynched. On May 17 he issued a note in which he condemned Dudaev's actions as anti - constitutional, hoping for calm and a political solution to the crisis that did not lead to a bloodbath, and refrain to pursuing political initiatives that further degenerate the situation, awaiting instructions from Parliament.

By now, however, the limits of the institutional clash had largely been passed, and Dudaev demanded the application of his decree of suspension of parliamentary activity. On the evening of May 17, a squad of the National Guard occupied the hall, dispersing the deputies. About twenty of these, led by Soslambekov, took refuge in the building of the City Council of Grozny, also formally dissolved but still in the hands of Gantemirov and his Municipal Police. The National Guard took up a position a short distance from the town hall, ready to occupy it. On May 25, the first deaths arrived. Four people died in a fire fight between the opposition and loyalists, including a nephew of Dudaev himself, Shamil. In response, the National Guard stormed the Grozny City Council, re-occupied Parliament and dispersed the opposition protesters. In Theatre Square the permanent rally showed no signs of dispersing, despite Dudaev's warnings and threats. And just near the square on May 30 an unknown hand fired at the President, as he was returning home. The presidential procession was hit by numerous gunshots. Dudaev did not let himself be intimidated, got out of the car and headed towards the stage, intending to calm the crowd, but the first rifle was joined by others, and soon more shots reached him and his bodyguards. One of these was hit in the neck, while the General hurried back into the car and the procession left at full speed.

The attack on Dudaev brought even greater speed to the evolution of the crisis. On 3 June, faced with yet another refusal by the Constitutional Court to recognize his initiative, the General decreed his dissolution. By now almost no institutional structure of the state remained standing. The remnants of the democratic system, gathered in the building of the City Assembly in Grozny, awaited the showdown, which came on the night of June 4. There were only a few hours left before the opening of the seats for the referendum of 5 June, called a few weeks earlier by Parliament. The Electoral Committee was working at full capacity and was packed with people. But none of them had any illusions: Dudaev would never have allowed the referendum to take place. It was dark when the loyalists, led by Shamil Basayev, they entered the building and opened fire on the defenders. Within minutes, the headquarters of the Electoral Committee was stormed and devastated, and opponents were killed, captured or expelled. After wiping out the City Council, the armed militiamen headed towards Thatre Square, to put an end to the permanent rally "by crook". The opposition representatives declared *we will remain standing until the end, an attempt to drive the demonstrators from the square will lead to numerous victims, whose responsibility will rest entirely on President Dudaev and his supporters: instead of holding a national referendum, the president has declared war on his own people.* At the first light of dawn in the square there was no one left. The next day there were 15 dead and 33 wounded. All that remained of the parliamentary and extra-parliamentary opposition had been wiped out. The Regime was beginning.

Dudaev's Regime

With the establishment of the dictatorship Dudaev was able to complete the constitutional reform, introducing state presidentialism and reducing Parliament and the Constitutional Court to mere appendages of his power: the presidency of the first, suitably purged of anti-Dudaevite elements, was appointed a loyalist of the President, Ahkyad Idigov*[189]*. The second was replaced by a *Constitutional College* whose seven member judges would be appointed by himself[190]. Now free to make and break the executive as he pleased, Dudaev launched himself with renewed vigor into the promised and never implemented reform program. The new government began to operate in the first weeks of June: for the most part this was made up of members of the previous executive, but there were some new appointments. *Hussein Ferzauli*, manager of a large metalworking industry, was appointed Minister of Industry, while Taimaz Abubakarov passed from the finance department to the economy department, replaced by *Rizvan Guzhayev*[191]. *Akhmed Zakayev*, theater actor and President of the Union of Chechen Theatrical Workers, made his appearance in the political arena as Minister of Culture. The Ministry of the Interior, which until then had been a

---

[189] Member of the Parliament of first call, exponent of the Dudaevite faction, he was President of the *Commission for Industry and Construction*. With Akhmadov's resignation from the office of President of Parliament and the appointment of Soslambekov in his place, Idigov had obtained the position of Vice-President, in an extreme attempt to reconstitute a parliamentary dialogue between the two souls of Chechen independence.

[190] Commenting on Dudaev's coup, experts Pain and Popov wrote: *Having accused the leaders of parliament and the entire opposition of pro-Russian conspiracy and national treason, Dudaev was able to dissolve the elected parliament together with him without apparently suffering any damage to his popularity.*

[191] Former finance officer of the Chechen – Ingush RSSA.

"snake in the grass" was abolished, and its functions were taken over ad interim by Dudaev himself. The President then proceeded to abolish all those dual dicasteries that had made Chechnya a diarchy. All the agencies that dealt with state security were reorganized into the *State Security Department,* which was entrusted with the functions of police, intelligence and counter-espionage.[192]. At its top, Sultan Geliskhanov was appointed[193].

Mugadaev, officially appointed head of the government, identified three lines of action: seeking consensus in civil society, maintaining good relations with neighboring Russian provinces, economic and social reform. The director of the new government policy would have been the Minister of Economy Abubakarov, who already at the beginning of '92 had contended with Mamodaev for the deputy premier and who now, having disappeared the uncomfortable competitor, was returning to the fore. Under his advice it was decided to establish a mixed economic system, based on private property but in which the state would control some strategic sectors.[194].

---

[192] The crackdown in the system led to a real purge within the repressive apparatus of the state: 172 police officers were fired, presumably because of their opposition to Dudaev's leadership.

[193] *Sultan Geliskhanov* (Kazakhstan, 1955) was a traffic police officer. Having supported the Executive Committee during the Chechen Revolution, at the end of 1991 he was promoted to head of the State Traffic Inspectorate of the city of Gudermes, the main railway hub in Chechnya. In this capacity he had had access to most of the freight traffic in and out of the country, and according to some he had taken advantage of it to manage the looting racket that he should have been fighting instead. Appointed senior official of the Ministry of the Interior in April 1993, upon its dissolution he proved to be the most faithful Dudaevite of the ministry's senior figures, thus obtaining the appointment to the operational direction of the security forces.

[194] Abubakarov reports in his memoir, The Dudaev Regime: *The question of property reform through its partial privatization was planned to take place around 2000 in accordance with the law" On property in the Chechen Republic ", the project of which was already was developed on the basis of the principle of a mixed economy. The project envisaged that the state would retain ownership of the subsoil, oil refining and energy infrastructure (in the case of*

To introduce the market economy, however, it was necessary to break the Russian economic siege. For this reason it was decided to reopen the negotiations interrupted at the end of January with Moscow. Given the failures of all previous negotiations, the government proposed a different policy: instead of getting nailed on the question of independence, it should have tried to reach an agreement through a dense network of secondary agreements that progressively linked Russian interests to Chechen ones. This network of sectoral agreements should have been obtained not only, or not mainly through agreements between the Chechen Republic and the Russian Federation, but through local agreements that made the economic blockade increasingly "uncomfortable" for the Russians themselves.

Another fundamental point was the formal rejection of populism as a form of government: no more subsidies, no more donations. Public resources were to be used to make the state function and finance the recovery. The saved resources should have served as the basis for a plan to modernize the republic's infrastructures and industries. An investment of 100 million dollars was even planned through which the American company *Enforce Endgy* would refurbish the republic's oil plants, bringing them back to production efficiency and increasing the revenue in the state coffers. New infrastructures were designed, such as a new road connecting with Georgia, through the mountain pass from the Chechen town of Itum - Khale to the Georgian village of Shatili.

The market segment that was mainly intended to enhance was that of small businesses. In this sense, a subsidized credit was established to finance the opening

---

integration with Russian companies, ownership of the stakes necessary to control them) of the infrastructure as well as nationally owned cultural properties.

and restructuring of family businesses, whose impact on the national economy should have become between 15 - 20% of GDP by 2000. In the drafting phase of the program, it was a reform of the social and welfare system was also prepared, which was entrusted to the Deputy, as well as President of DVP, Zelimkhan Yandarbiev. From the end of June 1993 Dudaev announced the resumption of the work of the dispersed Parliament but *without the right of legislative activity*. About twenty deputies agreed to return to meet, but most refused to attend. MPs who refused to return to work, including Akhmadov and Soslambekov, they were deprived of parliamentary powers. In the midst of the tide of problems that opened the establishment of an authoritarian regime, at least one actually solved it: for the first time since independence in the country there was a single power, free to operate. And indeed, in some fields the state seemed to be starting to function better. At stake, first of all, was the survival of a state that was not even able to pay regular pensions and salaries. The arrears amounted to a staggering figure of about thirty billion rubles. The first thing to do to solve this contingent problem was to understand precisely who and how much he had to receive from the central state. In the last three years the system of public money contributions had never been reformed. A chaotic development ensued for which different wages were in effect in each state company[195]. The same chaos was taking place in the pension system[196].

---

[195]Taymaz Abubakarov reports that, for example, a difference of up to 30% on the average wage could insist between one factory and another. This was the case of the biochemical plant in Grozny (inactive due to the lack of workable raw material) in which the wages were a third higher than the nearby Lenin refinery, which instead worked non-stop. A similar situation was found in public offices, where in some wages were expected up to six times higher than in others.

[196]This remained the same as that provided for by Soviet law,

The Audits of the Ministry of Finance found that some public managers had deliberately avoided updating the lists of workers and retirees, so that in 1993 the State still had over thirty thousand "ghost" salaries and as many pensions in charge. Furthermore, the leakage of confidential public documents was frequent, for which those responsible for the violations were regularly bribed. Dudaev dealt with this personally, initiating at least a dozen criminal proceedings and dismissing those responsible whom he managed to catch red handed. To avoid the bleeding of the state coffers in supporting a bureaucracy that has become useless, Dudaev personally took charge of reducing the number of state salaries to the indispensable.[197].

In addition to spending cuts, centralizing cash flow was essential. An attempt was made to identify two / three credit institutions that could be connected to the already existing (but practically inactive) *National Chechen Bank* through which to organize a homogeneous payment

---

and was based, rather than on the job position, on the degree of affiliation to the now dissolved Communist Party. Dudaev would have wanted a "hierarchical" system based on position levels (worker, manager, director, etc.), but if this was applicable to factories and farms, it was much less so to the tertiary sector, where personal skills brought different economic incomes . For this reason it was decided to set the payment of pensions on the declared income, on which the workers would pay adequate tax. The intervention in question could not be decreed in the middle of the year, so it was decided to foresee it for the beginning of 1994. For the fiscal year 1993 - 1994, only the adjustment of the salaries of government officials was foreseen, calculated on a decreasing basis with respect to the salary of the President. This was first set at $ 300 a month, then it was reduced to $ 100 at Dudaev's initiative, proportionally reducing all the others. The figures in question were really very low, and risked a proliferation of corruption in the upper echelons of the state.

[197]How much of this was motivated by budgetary needs and how much a consequence of the "purge" carried out following the coup is difficult to say. Certainly such a cut eased the pressure on state finances and made it possible to adjust the salaries of "surviving" employees to the changed economic situation.

system at least in the main public companies and in the pension-welfare system. The path was tortuous, because the banks operating in Chechnya were based in Russia, and were under pressure from the Moscow government. Attempts to agree with Russian credit institutions such as *Credobank* were made throughout '93, without achieving tangible results. However, the path was useful in making the Chechen Central Bank operational, which until then had been little more than a propaganda entity. The application of a Dudaev decree dated July 4, 1992, in which public enterprises were obliged to pay their earnings into the deposits of the Chechen National Bank, allowed the government to manage income and expenses more effectively. During 1993, the government succeeded to significantly reduce the amount of arrears with employees, making up for a delay of between 2 and 3 months of wages, for the equivalent of 10/15 billion rubles. In essence, the control of spending and a more efficient income / expense management system made it possible to almost halve the debt deriving from non-payment of six wages[198].

Setting up the tax system and rationalizing the tax collection system was another important necessity. But this action was far from easy, considering that it was heavily influenced by Russian fiscal policy. In particular, recovering the claims accrued by state-owned companies and public entities against Russian debtors was impossible, because the courts of independent Chechnya were not recognized by Russia. Then there was the problem of the enormous amount of debt accumulated by public bodies and companies with respect to which

---

[198] The influx of more resources, combined with a clever idea by the Minister for Commerce, *Roza Zabrailova*, who promoted the creation of "special" shops capable of supplying low-cost (but still marketable) basic necessities to the population, it allowed a certain improvement in the quality of life.

there was no other way for the government to operate than by loading them into the state coffers. These debts amounted to 54 billion rubles, 8 billion more than the entire annual state budget. Using the tool of tax amnesties, through which the state renounced to recover part of its credits, and by increasing the squeeze on recoverable credits, the disastrous fiscal situation of the country slowly began to improve, so much so that, according to the words of Minister Abubakarov, more than half of the 54 billion rubles of debts would have been recovered or amnestied by the autumn of 1994. A critical situation, however, remained that of the primary sector of the Chechen economy, that of agriculture. The global debt of agricultural enterprises amounted to 15 billion rubles, 11 of which were, so to speak, "structural", that is, linked to the sector's dependence on lubricants and fuels. The agricultural economy had always benefited from non-repayable funding from the Soviet government, and this state of affairs had moved to independent Chechnya. In theory, the loans were supposed to increase the productivity of the funds, but in reality they ended up decreasing it sharply, in the face of a constant increase in production costs. State welfare and popular price policy had done the rest, preventing the agricultural sector from remaining competitive and displeasing both those who wanted to boost production (who saw their products purchased by the state at low cost as a counterpart to the subsidies paid) and those aiming for state economic support (who accumulated a budget deficit that they were unable to repay). The solution to the problem could have been agrarian reform, land privatization and the end of subsidies, but Dudaev strongly opposed this choice.[199].

---

[199] The reader who wants to deepen the history of agriculture in the Chechen Republic of Ichkeria can consult the economic insights

Another sector in which the inefficiency of the state generated enormous losses in the public budget was that of petroleum products. Since the end of 1991, as we have seen, Dudaev had placed under his direct written authorization every export of oil from the plants of the republic. In fact, however, he had never been able to handle it. Thus, with the birth of the Mamodaev government, he entrusted the management of the system to them. However, the real drama was represented by the continuous thefts of crude oil that occurred along the route of the pipelines through illegal withdrawals, or through the looting of tankers loaded with raw materials, often with the connivance or active participation of the guards placed for their protection.[200]. Dudaev intervened first of all by centralizing production in a single plant, the Lenin Refinery, closing all the others. This certainly implemented production and reduced costs, but led to a new wave of layoffs. The storage and distribution of petroleum products were also centralized. An area was identified near the Zavodskoy district, in the western suburbs of Grozny, which was declared "reserved" and constantly manned by road checkpoints[201]. The centralization of the system and the introduction of a more disciplined control service faithful to Dudaev's leadership produced its results: within a few weeks the

---

available on the site www.icheria.net in the *in-depth section/economics and finance*.

[200] Emblematic in this sense is the account of Minister Abubakarov with respect to an event that occurred in the spring of 1993: *[..] We ran into employees of the Ministry of the Interior, who, instead of organizing the protection of the object entrusted to them, were covering up the looters. [...] it all ended in a compromise: the two Kamaz loads of petroleum products were confiscated, and the looters were let go. When we reported this incident to Dudayev, he periodically ordered to change the guards.*

[201] The "Borz" ("Wolves") Battalion, a unit of veterans selected from the Second International Brigade who had served in Abkhazia, under the command of the aforementioned Ruslan Gelayev, was called to protect the oil district.

thefts of petroleum products fell to a minimum, and the republic was able to enjoy a flow of constant cash. This centralization in the management of the oil sector gave important arguments to the opposition in accusing Dudaev of wanting to manage oil as a personal asset. Dudaev's detractors, Khasbulatov in the lead, always scrambled to declare that Dudaev would personally enrich himself from the illegal sale of oil, and that the members of his inner circle would do the same. Considering that during his presidency his lifestyle was not very different from what he had in the days of the Red Army, it seems difficult enough that he pocketed the large sums he was being charged. And knowing the character, it seems unlikely that he pocketed even a single ruble: for Dudaev, glory (at any cost) was worth much more than material wealth[202]. In May 1993 he himself commissioned a government report that charted the cash flows from the production and sale of oil and derivatives.[203]

---

[202] Surely this did not happen for the oil extracted and sold by state plants whose production in 1993 could hardly hope to reach a billion dollars in turnover, and which had to support the purchase of 300,000 tons of wheat, 6 billion cubic meters of natural gas, 350 million kW-hours of electricity, 500,000 tons of coal, as well as financing a lot of other services, such as the purchase of medicines for the state's health centers. Furthermore, there is no trace of this money in Dudaev's checking accounts, neither in Chechnya nor abroad, just as nothing of this money seems to have remained after his death.

[203] Abubakarov, in his memoir "*The Dudaev Regime*", Summarizes in great detail the cash flow deriving from oil revenues deriving from the analysis of the report. In his book, among other things, we read: *In fact, 65-70% of the revenues of the Republican budget came from the oil industry. Unlike my opponents, I can always demonstrate the objectivity of my data. Regarding the sale of petroleum products to the world market, we have never hidden the available data. We are talking about the sale in 1992 of two hundred thousand tons of Siberian oil and one hundred thousand tons of diesel under the contract between the Groznefteorgsintez association and the German trading company Stinnes Interiil, which brought the country to 36 million gross and about 24 million dollars. net. The difference between gross income and net income was made up at that time up to one third of gross income due to the deduction of customs fees, as well as the costs of transport, storage, transshipment,*

The intent was to silence the rumors about the misappropriation of raw material or capital from its sale. The opposition, while noting the full traceability of the flow, contested that a number of state structures, including the Parliament, the Grozny Mayor's Office and the Ministry of Agriculture had not reported to the commission on the use that they had made certain "quotas" assigned to solve economic problems related to the functioning of their dicasteries. The eyes of the opposition fell on a decree by Dudaev authorizing the office of the Mayor of Grozny, who at the time was Bislan Gantamirov, to take advantage of a share corresponding to about 5 million dollars from the sale of 200,000 tons of diesel to replenish the city's coffers and support social projects. It seems that in reality a large part of these resources ended up financing his private army. As we have already told, questioned on the matter by the Attorney General of the Republic, Gantamirov not only refused to provide the data and invoices, but sided against the government and occupied the town hall of Grozny, from which he was evicted following the coup of June 4th.

As Dudaev built his regime and put the government into operation, the old and new members of the opposition began to count themselves. In addition to the parliamentarians, who at this time represented little more than themselves, to the north were the anti-Dudaevites of all time, perched in Upper Terek, under the orders of Avturkhanov. Militias loyal to *Ruslan Labazanov*, a "new

---

banking services. 16.6% of the revenue went directly to the Republican budget and was used strictly for budgeting purposes. Another $ 4 million was received in the foreign account of the National Bank of the Chechen Republic and was spent on printing the national currency, passports, postage stamps and other state activities. The remaining 16 million was used by oil workers for their production needs. Some of these funds went to the purchase of road construction equipment from the German company Wirtgen, drilling equipment from the American Enforce Energy, communication equipment through the FADI company.

entry" of the opposition, which we will discuss shortly, were gathering in Argun. In Urus - Martan there was the former Mayor of Grozny Gantamirov, who hastily fled the capital after the assault by the loyalists on "his" City Council and taking refuge in Urus - Martan, a city that has always been critical of the President. Many of his militiamen had followed him, and while the others licked their wounds, Gantemirov was already preparing his revenge. And the first signal came on August 8, just a couple of months later. That morning an armed commando opened fire with machine guns, rifles and grenade launchers on the ninth floor of the Government Building, home of Dudaev's offices. Gantemirov's signature was found almost immediately: two cars owned by the Grozny Town Hall were abandoned a stone's throw from the site of the attack. Informants later reported that some militiamen wounded by firearms had been hospitalized in Urus - Martan. two cars owned by the Town Hall of Grozny were abandoned a stone's throw from the site of the attack. Informants later reported that some militiamen wounded by firearms had been hospitalized in Urus - Martan. two cars owned by the Town Hall of Grozny were abandoned a stone's throw from the site of the attack. Informants later reported that some militiamen wounded by firearms had been hospitalized in Urus - Martan. Dudaev took it out on the Russian secret services: *Even if he had been Gantamirov, he would have acted as a mere executor. According to our information, the order to remove me was given by the Russian General Aleinikov. All these diversions are prepared in the offices of the Special Forces in Moscow.* The reaction of the Presidential Guard, however, was immediate. A squad of loyalist forces headed for Urus - Martan, while another paced the administrative border of Upper Terek in combat gear, demanding and obtaining a declaration of loyalty from every village on the way to the district capital, *Znameskoye*. For Dudaev it was time to arm a real army with which to assert his political supremacy once and for all and defeat the armed opposition.

Assault on the White House

We had left Yeltsin struggling with the Russian Constitutional Crisis, busy consolidating his power after the April 25 referendum. In the summer of 1993, the Russian president began to work to capitalize on the success he had just achieved. In particular, he railed against the decision of the Congress not to recognize the will of the voters, who had expressed themselves in an overwhelming majority for a renewal of the legislative bodies and declared that he would put in place all means, including the avoidance of the constitution, to obtain new parliamentary elections. The point of no return in the conflict between the President and Parliament came when Yeltsin decided to suspend Vice - President *Rutskoi*, a member of the parliamentary party, in favor of the unpopular Gaidar. Faced with yet another outcry from Parliament, Yeltsin proposed to undergo a new electoral exam if Parliament decided to do the same. His proposal hit a rubber wall, so that on September 21, Yeltsin forced his hand, declaring the Supreme Soviet dissolved in open violation of the Constitution[204]. The

---

[204]The decree represented a clear forcing of the current constitution, which in article 121 clearly stated: *The powers of the President of the Russian Federation cannot be used to change the state organization of the Russian Federation, to dissolve or interfere with the functioning of any elected body of state power. In that case, his powers cease immediately*. Yeltsin, for his part, motivated his choice with these words: "*Attempts have already been made for more than a year to reach a compromise with the body of deputies, with the Supreme Soviet. The Russians know well that how many steps have been taken by my side during the last congresses and among them. [...] The last days have destroyed once and for all the*

dissolution of the Supreme Soviet went hand in hand with the project of a constitutional referendum, and of a new electoral round to be expected by December. The reaction from the parliamentary front was predictably angry. Rutskoi called Yeltsin's gesture *a step towards the coup*. The next day the Constitutional Court declared Yeltsin prosecutable, having openly violated the constitutional provisions. During the night, after the Congress had been held in an extraordinary session, Khasbulatov declared the decree of dissolution of the Supreme Soviet to be null and void, and the nomination of Rustkoi as President voted. Rustkoi was sworn in immediately afterwards, thus establishing a diarchy *in Chechen sauce*: a "parliamentary" and a "presidential" leadership. What had happened in Grozny four months earlier was being repeated in Moscow.

As news of a clash at the top of the state began to circulate, crowds of supporters of the respective factions took to the streets. On September 28, the first clashes took place between demonstrators loyal to Parliament and the police, loyal to Yeltsin. By 1 October the Parliament building was besieged by the security forces, with inside, as well as numerous deputies, about six hundred parliamentarian militants. The next day, as sterile negotiations followed, Moscow was filled with barricades as a grouping of armed civilians, supported by elements of the security forces belonging to the Ministry of the Interior and passed to the parliamentary cause, tried to break the encirclement of the loyalists in the White House. It seemed that the popular reaction was on

---

hopes of a resurrection of at least constructive cooperation. The majority of the Supreme Soviet goes directly against the will of the Russian people. [...] The laws, which Russia urgently needs, have not been approved for years [...] Power in the Supreme Soviet was seized by a group of people who turned it into an uncompromising opposition headquarters. [...] I, as the guarantor of the security of our state, must propose an exit from this dead end, we must break this vicious circle."

the side of Khasbulatov and Rutskoi, who exhorted civilians to arm themselves against *the criminal and usurper Yeltsin*. As the riots mounted, Yeltsin proceeded on the road of direct confrontation, and on the evening of October 3 he declared a State of Emergency in Moscow. At the same time, armed units loyal to parliament attacked the main television center of the city, from which the state TV was operating. The battle lasted all evening, but the loyalist security forces eventually repulsed the attack. There were 62 civilian and military deaths. The attack put the Supreme Soviet and the parliamentary faction in a bad light, and the next day an appeal from Vice-President Gaidar was picked up by numerous prominent figures in politics and culture, as a crowd of Yeltsin supporters gathered under the Town Hall Building.

The situation was now compromised, and only the intervention of the armed forces would have determined the fate of the crisis. The army was the entity that had suffered most from the heavy spending cuts made by the Gaidar government. Especially the lower middle cadres of the army were starved and demoralized, and in general the federal armed forces were the shadow of what had been the glorious Red Army. However, the situation was quite different when looking at other army cadres. Senior officers were well paid, and with the end of the USSR they had a free hand in divesting Soviet military assets on the black market. Corruption was rampant in the upper echelons, and no military or almost no military had any intention of handing the country over to a Khasbulatov, or a Rutskoi, that could have put an end to their Cockaigne. Thus it was that only a few officers responded to the appeals of the parliamentarians, and even those few then avoided taking the initiative. Those who effectively carried out the orders were the loyalists, who at dawn on October 4 surrounded the White House with their units and began bombing it.

At noon the special forces began the assault, occupying the building within a few hours. By mid-afternoon the resistance had been suppressed. Elstin was again master of the square and the institutions and was able to proceed with the dissolution of Parliament. On October 12, he officially declared it's fall, and on 15 he arrested Rutskoi and Khasbulatov. Finally, he called a constitutional referendum for December 12, to coincide with the new parliamentary elections. The new Constitution, which obtained popular support for the referendum, established a Presidential Federal Republic, in which Yeltsin guaranteed ample freedom in terms of government formation and appointment in the main offices of the state, first of all military ones.

The Zviadist uprising

If in Russia, as in Chechnya, the situation evolved towards a victory of the presidents over the parliaments, in Georgia the situation went in the opposite direction. President Ghamsakhurdia, kicked out at the end of 1991, had lost control of the state, and at the end of 1993 he tried one last time to take it back. Made confident by the defeats the Georgian army was suffering in Abkhazia, he prepared a blitz to regain power. The opportunity presented itself when the Georgian armed forces collapsed in the face of a new, massive offensive by the separatists.

After the successful June-July campaign, Ardzimba's forces had moved the front to a line that ran along the Kodori River, some forty kilometers south of Sukhumi. Beyond those lines the Abkhazians had since October 1992 a besieged enclave, left cut off at the time of the first Georgian offensive, and gathered around the town of Tkvarcheli, leaning against the mountains in the north of the region. The Georgians had tried several times to storm it without success, also due to the fact that the federal air force regularly supplied the defenders and kept open a sort of humanitarian cordon for the evacuation of the wounded and refugees. On September 16, supported by a large squadron of federal helicopters, the Abkhazians simultaneously launched an attack on Sukhumi, against the front on the Kodori and against the besieging units in Tkvarcheli, taking by surprise the Georgian National Guard, still weak and badly organized after the defeats of the previous months. Within two weeks, all three goals were achieved. The first to fall was Sukhumi, on September 27th. *Eduard Shevardnadze,* the Georgian leader who succeeded Gamsakhurdia, had rushed to the city to urge the defenders to resist, but had to leave in a hurry, while members of the pro-Georgian government barricaded themselves in the government quarter for one last stand. By the late afternoon, the attackers controlled most of the city. In the evening the last stronghold of the defenders also fell, and the attackers indulged in a frightening ethnic cleansing[205]. Also in the other sectors of the battle the Georgian front was completely destroyed[206].

The collapse of the Georgian army left Shevardnadze's regime vulnerable, opening hope for the dethroned Gamsakhurdia. The former president, as we have seen, was far from resigned to the idea of losing power. And so were many of his supporters, mainly concentrated in

[205] The first to be executed were government officials who were unwilling or unable to leave. Over the next forty-eight hours, hundreds of civilians of all ages and sexes suffered violence, torture and murder. It was the beginning of a terrible massacre that would have led, over the next few months, about two hundred and fifty thousand Georgians, Greeks, Estonians, and anyone who did not have Abkhazian ancestry to flee the country.

his native region, the *District of Sarmegrelo*, which was precisely located close to Abkhazia. In this region the activity of the supporters of Gamsakhurdia had never stopped, and the political-military movement in favor of the resettlement of the deposed president (called *Zviadist* after the first name of Gamsakhurdia, *Zviad*) was taking advantage of the situation to reorganize and recover. the power. As soon as the remains of the Georgian army began to abandon the front line to regroup, Gamsakhurdia reached his native region, being greeted by an enthusiastic crowd. Collecting all the weapons he could find, he organized an armed insurrection, and within a few weeks he managed to take control of a large area in western Georgia, threatening with his militias the second city of the country, Kutaisi.

After the defeat in Abkhazia, Shevardnadze no longer had the opportunity to carry out the pacification of the country alone. He therefore had to come to terms with the Russian authorities, who offered him a compromise agreement: they would have kept him in the saddle if he had agreed to bring Georgia back into the Commonwealth of Independent States and had granted the federal army a series of military bases on everything. the Georgian territory. In return, Moscow would cease to support the separatist forces and help the loyalists take out Gamsakhurdia once and for all. Shevardnadze, despite himself, had to accept the agreement, and at the end of October 1993 the Georgian National Guard was able to launch a violent counter-offensive against the Zviadist rebels. In November of the same year the last rebel forces were defeated. Gamsakhurdia took refuge in the mountains east of the city, where he continued to fight in hiding until the end of December. On December 31, he finally died in mysterious circumstances.

With the suffocation of the Zviadist uprising, the Caucasus experienced, after three years, the end of armed conflicts. During this period, conflicts occurred in Azerbaijan, Armenia, Georgia, Ossetia and Ingushetia, in addition of course to the Chechen Revolution. At the end of 1993, each of these regions could be said to have been pacified, and Russian supremacy re-established. Only Chechnya stubbornly continued to oppose Moscow. It was time for the Kremlin to take the "Chechen question" seriously.

The Provisional Council

1993 was drawing to a close. It had been a defining year for both Russia and Chechnya. The authoritarian turnarounds in Moscow and Grozny had created quite a few problems, but they also offered some opportunities. In fact, as never before, a two-way dialogue between Yeltsin and Dudaev could have produced a peaceful solution to the crisis. In March 1993, two months after the Russian Constitutional Referendum, Dudaev had tried to open a direct channel with a letter, in which he urged the Russian president to recognize Chechnya and to start a joint negotiation process[207]. A few days later he

---

[207] The letter read: *"Dear Mr. President, I express my deepest respect, I wish you and your family well-being and good luck, peace and prosperity for the people of the Russian state. I appeal to you in the name of all the Chechen people on an issue that has crucial significance for relations between our states [...] I appeal to you [...] to discuss the question of the recognition by the Russian Federation of the sovereign Republic Chechen. The solution of this question would remove all barriers in the path of solving many problems in the mutual relations between our states. The Russian Federation could acquire an important partner and guarantee political stability for the entire Caucasus. I am sure that you, president of a great power, it will show the political wisdom that characterizes it and will do everything possible to resolve the question of the recognition of the Chechen Republic by the Russian Federation. Our consciences will be clean, both in front of our peoples and in the face of history, if we are able to soften relations between our peoples and guarantee equality and mutual*

had sent another letter, in which he recommended that Yeltsin dissolve the parliament as Dudaev was about to do with the Chechen one. Yeltsin never answered and refused to keep that channel of correspondence open. For both, however, the opportunity existed, and could be seized by committing to resolve the political crisis in a series of face-to-face talks. Negotiations, on the other hand, were interrupted. Yeltsin's philosophy was to let time pass, *cook the Chechens in their soup*, and wait for the economic blockade to bring the small republic into chaos. At that point, public opinion would have abandoned Dudaev, now isolated, and an internal branch would have brought him down. The independence front had already broken for the first time with the assault on the Supreme Soviet, then a second time with the quarrel between Dudaev and Mamodaev and then another third, with the quarrel between Dudaev and Parliament. Moscow therefore chose to negotiate with all those who in some way were in crisis with the President, without ever involving him in person, with the only evident purpose of overthrowing him and establishing a more "docile" government.

Following the coup, Sergei Shakhrai, who as we have seen had been the main director of this policy, began to reap the rewards of his work. In mid-December 1993, after the consolidation of presidential power, the opponents were left with no other solution than to attempt an insurrection. That was what Yeltsin and Shakhrai were waiting for: on December 16, all the main opposition figures gathered in Znamenskoye, in Upper Terek, and founded the *Provisional Council of the Chechen Republic*. At its top Avturkhanov was elected, while Gantamirov was appointed commander of the armed forces. The first decision taken by this "shadow government" was to hold a national congress that would give legitimacy to the new organization. Meantime, the available militias would be organized into a real army, with which, if necessary, the Provisional Council would besiege Grozny. The initiative was also joined by *Ibrahim Suleimenov*, Member of Parliament and former President of the National Security Service of parliamentary appointment, who passed to the opposition at the end of 1992 in the Soslambekov current, and then went underground after the coup. From that moment he had animated a political - military organization called the National Salvation Committee. It was he who devised the first force action of the opposition aimed at demonstrating to Dudaev how ephemeral his power was. Suleimenov had actively participated in the Chechen Revolution, gaining a place of respect and a certain esteem among the separatist militants and then among the soldiers of the National Guard. As Director of the National Security Service, he had been in control of one of the main armed contingents of the republic, and his passage to the opposition had led to a certain disorientation among the departments and among some militiamen who had just returned from the war in Abkhazia. When he decided to organize a "military pronouncement" in Grozny, many of them joined him. On the evening of December 16, Suleimenov concentrated his armed militiamen a short distance from Dudaev's home and had it surrounded. Then he rounded up Basayev and Gelayev and convinced them to show themselves on state TV. The two declared that they were in favor of a definitive separation between the powers of the President and the Prime Minister. They demanded that Dudaev leave the leadership of the government, that he establish a Security Council and a Ministry of Defense (a department that the General had always kept to himself) and that he hold parliamentary elections by the end of March 1994. They finally declared that they would not take part in actions directed against other Chechens, and which in any case would have avoided a civil war. The message was clear: if Dudaev had wanted to impose his power with violence, his military leaders would not have been with him. For the General it was a cold shower. However, he managed to reconcile hostilities, meeting both Basayev and Gelayev separately and regaining their trust.

The time was ripe for an open confrontation which, as we shall see, would tear Chechnya to pieces throughout 1994, and fear began to spread among the people. The first effect of this state of affairs was the onset of mass emigration, especially by the Russian-speaking minority. Between mid-1992 and mid-1993 about one hundred thousand people, corresponding to 7% of the republic's population, had already left Chechnya. After the war, numerous documents were produced (some true, some invented from scratch) about the pressure that the Chechen government exerted on citizens of Russian origin. Certainly the government never put in place a program to eradicate the Russian-speaking population, but it certainly did nothing to stop the spontaneous manifestations of anti-Russian hatred that were mounting among the population.[208]. If we add to this the progressive criminalization of society due to rampant misery, it is evident that the Russian component of the population found itself to be the weakest and most defenseless.[209]. The second effect of the climate of

---

[208] In 1992 alone, the Chechen Ministry of the Interior counted 250 murder cases and 300 disappearances among the Russian population. If these are not genocidal numbers, they certainly give an idea of the climate of terror and general impunity that existed in the country.

[209] According to what is reported in the "White Book", published with the participation of FSK (the Russian state security agency,

uncertainty and fear now endemic in the Republic was a dizzying increase in crime. In 1993 alone, 600 murders were counted, the same number as those estimated in the Rostov region, five times as large. And this only according to official data, which according to some sources would have been spoiled by the "theft" of at least seventy corpses from the Grozny morgues. The third effect was a collapse of public finances.

Totally focused on defending itself from Russia, from the opposition, from internal fronds, the Grozny government, which had also begun a good job of streamlining the accounts and offices, gradually lost even those few men capable of representing an added value, by militarizing itself more and more and making decision-making power converge in the hands of Dudaev and his most loyal militants[210]. Constantly trying to get

---

which recently succeeded the KGB) in 1995, there are numerous testimonies on the matter. Witness I. Bibaeva says: *Being originally from Baku and having many relatives in Russia, I often use the services of the Caucasian railway [...] in front of my eyes the passengers of the train, regardless of nationality and religious affiliation, were subjected to unprecedented humiliation and abuse by Chechen militiamen armed with machine guns, who stopped the train and broke into the wagons. Passengers were stripped, their belongings were taken away, their jewels were taken from women, while the attackers gave free rein to their hands, degrading the dignity of women. [...] Until my death I will not forget the face of an old man who, under the grin of the rebellious young men, tried to cover his nakedness, a woman sobbing over her empty bags. A fur jacket had been taken from her luggage and, as a punishment for the resistance she had shown, she had been pushed out of her bags and everything she wanted to take to her relatives in Russia had been trampled on. [...] And how many looted freight trains have appeared in our eyes, and in the same place Chechen women with bags near the wagons carrying the stolen goods.* " *as punishment for the resistance she had shown, she had been pushed out of her bags and everything she wanted to take to her relatives in Russia had been trampled on. [...] And how many looted freight trains have appeared in our eyes, and in the same place Chechen women with bags near the wagons carrying the stolen goods.* " *as punishment for the resistance she had shown, she had been pushed out of her bags and everything she wanted to take to her relatives in Russia had been trampled on. [...] And how many looted freight trains have appeared in our eyes, and in the same place Chechen women with bags near the wagons carrying the stolen goods.*

[210] Researcher Fiona Hill commented: *The new Chechen elite [...]*

out of his isolation, Dudaev began to turn to the Islamic clergy. He had done a first "pleasure" by planning to re-establish the Sharia courts in the Republic, and even if they were still not operational at the end of 1993, this first step towards the Islamic Republic was aimed precisely at winning the support of the religious. In 1993 he invited the well-known and influential Islamic leader *Abdul - Baki* to Chechnya in the hope of making him the confessional pillar of his power. Baki accepted the invitation, and in 1993 he went to the country. After a few months of stay, however, the dramatic situation he found made him change his mind, so much so that, in a statement on state TV he said: *a state in which even a single child, or an adult, they are starving while the rulers are well fed cannot be called Islamic. Even less, if in that country Islam and Adat are used not for constructive purposes, but for the destruction of society, law and order, this is dangerous for the people who inhabit it.* The next day Baki was defined by Dudaev as *a spy of the Russian secret services*, referent *of the world mafia organizations* and *traitor of the faith*. The general revoked his citizenship, giving him a month to leave the country. The same fate befell another spiritual leader, the former mufti of Chechnya, *Mukhamed Bashir - Hadji*. When asked why he left, he replied: *If I tell the truth I fear Dudaev, if I don't, I fear Allah*.

In a state of creeping civil war, the country's economy, already stressed to the brink of bankruptcy, could only get worse. The main index was oil production. In that sector, the use of skilled labor was essential. And the skilled labor was mostly Russian. And the Russians were

---

was made up of radical nationalists on the fringes of politics, with no previous administrative experience; by the leaders of the so-called "Chechen mafia", specialized in extra - legal activities; by members of the Chechen diaspora and a handful of idealistic intellectuals whose reform proposals were systematically opposed. They were all terribly ill-equipped to face the multiple challenges of creating a new Chechen nation state and creating a functioning market economy.

leaving Chechnya *en masse*. Crude oil production, which had been 4 million tons in 1991, had dropped by 2.6 million in 1992, and then to 1.2 million in 1993[211]. At the start of the First Chechen War, only a hundred out of 1500 wells would have been able to produce usable crude oil. The raw material extracted then became the favorite target of the looters. In 1993 alone, 47,000 tons of oil were withdrawn from pipelines without permission[212]. At the same time, all the other sectors also recorded dizzying drops between 1992 and 1993. In 1992 alone, industrial production fell by 30%, when the average of post-Soviet countries in that year was -18%. An almost double drop, which in any case is still decent if we consider that of 1993 (-61.4%, when in Russia the trend already stood at -16%). Same situation in agricultural production: in 1993 food production fell by 46% (against the Russian average of -18%). Unemployment, which was already an endemic problem in Chechnya, grew steadily, up to a jump of 16% in 1993.

The increasingly impoverished population retreated from Grozny. Those who had relatives in the villages moved to the countryside to work the land and find sustenance. But even in the countryside the situation was far from rosy. The collapse of Soviet-era collective farms had paved the way for the looting of properties, and their distribution on the basis of customary law. Some models of mechanized agriculture survived in the flat north, but

---

[211] Readers wishing to learn more about oil production in Chechnya can consult the in-depth study entitled *The black gold of Ichkeria* available on the website www.ichkeria.net.

[212] If we want to give credit to the estimates produced by Salambek Hadjiev, between 1991 and 1994 between 1991 and 1994 were subtracted from 10 to 15 million tons of oil, obviously considering not only that produced locally, but also that "transit" through the Chechen pipeline , through which also the oil that reached Russia from the Azerbaijan fields passed.

the chronic lack of funding with which to buy spare parts for machinery made production less and less efficient. Criminal activities had become endemic, starting with the thriving market for counterfeiting debt securities. Suffice it to say that in 1993 alone, of the 9.4 billion rubles in counterfeit government bonds in Russia, 3.7 billion came from Chechnya. Smuggling of goods and drugs flourished, and Grozny's black arms market was at that time the largest market in the whole of the former Soviet Union. The looting of trains was now out of control: between 1992 and 1994 there were 1354 attacks on freight and passenger trains[213].

---

[213] According to data reported by news agencies and the Chechen Ministry of the Interior, 559 trains were attacked at the Grozny station of the North Caucasus Railway in 1993 alone, about 4,000 wagons looted for a value of about 11.5 billion rubles. In the first 8 months of 1994, 120 armed attacks were committed, which resulted in the looting of 1156 wagons and 527 containers, for over 11 billion rubles in damage. In the two-year period 1992 - 1994, 26 railway workers lost their lives in armed attacks. In his "Political Monitoring" Timur Muzaev wrote: *Today the trains bound for Chechnya are attacked by thieves from the first kilometers. This happens mainly when starting from Kargalinskaya station and continuing to Chervlennaya - Uzlovaya. The methods of robbery are different: some enter the train at one of the railway stations [...]. Then, when the train leaves the village, the thieves start maneuvering axes and picks, opening the containers and throwing the moving objects, so that they can later be picked up and taken away by the cars. [...] There is another way of robbery. The robbers wait for the train to stop, then block it and threaten the operator with firearms. Then some KAMAZ trucks flank the train and the goods are loaded directly from the wagons [...]. Gradually bands of thieves formed, each with its own place. The most famous are in Staroshedrinskaya and Starogladkovskaya. In each village there can be several gangs [...]. The goods are immediately put up for sale in flea markets or sold to professional merchants for half the price. [...] Where are the police, the guards, the army, the National Security Service? They pretend to be busy watching the trains, while some of them break in along with the thieves.*

CHAPTER 7

THE CIVIL WAR

At the end of September I ran into one of the deadliest battles to date: 20 to 30 Chechens died fighting each other under the scorching sun, on a hill outside the village of Tolstoy Yurt. A tank and a transport vehicle were blown up, and columns of black smoke snaked up into the beautiful late summers sky. This battle caused a real shock. The next day in Tolstoy Yurt hundreds of men gathered for funerals, standing around the open graves. A Man, a relative, tried not to cry as the fresh earth flew of the shovel with a rustle. Everyone was praying, their palms facing the sky: "There has been a betrayal" a peasant with a deeply tanned face told me. "This has never happened in Chechnya [...]". Going back to Grozny, everyone I spoke to even Dudaev's men, [...] felt the same shock. "How many killed? 30? This is terrible," said a restaurant owner and avid Dudaev fan.

Anatol Lieven: "Chechnya: tombstone of Russian power"

The Chechen Republic of Ichkeria

On January 19, 1994 Dudaev performed an act with a strong symbolic value: he renamed the State as *Chechen Republic of Ichkeria* (in acronym ChRI). As we have seen, this term derived from the ancient Turkish name of a specific region of Chechnya corresponding to the districts of Vedeno and Shatoy, the southernmost of the country. From a political point of view, the measure was a recognition of the highlanders' support for the Dudaev regime. The new banners of the Chechen Republic of Ichkeria flew in the wind for the first time at Gamsakhurdia's funeral. In Grozny, the death of the former Georgian president, a personal friend of Dudaev, had been experienced with great apprehension: Gamsakhurdia was the only head of state to have reconquered independent Chechnya, albeit after being deposed. In the capital Dudaev organized a state funeral, with a military parade in honor of the deceased. In the lead, the procession walked through the streets of the city, and then stopped in front of the memorial to the victims of Ardakh, just inaugurated: a square strewn with ancient tombstones between which stood a hand that raised a Caucasian dagger to the sky. In the background was written in large letters: *We will not cry! We will not be discouraged! We will not forget!* [214] Leading the parade was the new Chief of Staff of the Chechen army, *Aslan Maskhadov*.

Artillery colonel of the Soviet army, Maskhadov had returned to Chechnya from Leningrad, after having taken his leave with merits of service. Appointed as chief of civil defense by Dudaev in November 1992, during the

---

[214] Any reader wishing to learn more about the history of the memorial, which has now been demolished, can consult the in-depth study on *The Tombstones of Ichkeria* on the website www.ichkeria.net.

spring of 1993 he entered the General's good graces, earning his trust as he tried to take control of the institutions. In the summer of 1993, following the June coup, he had participated in the actions of the loyalist army, displaying his military skills and his loyalty to the President. At that time in command of the armed forces was Lieutenant General *Viskhan Shakhabov*. The latter, appointed at the beginning of 1992, had done little or nothing to set up an army worthy of the name, and in the spring of 1993 he had underground passed to the opposition. In the months preceding the coup of 4 June he had "lost" a lot of weapons and ammunition, which had ended up in the hands of the anti - Dudaevite militiamen, provoking the ire of the President, who had put him at the door. Maskhadov had taken his place "ad interim" immediately after the coup, setting to work to give a minimum of framing to that jumble of corps, militias and armed bands that made up the regular Chechen army. It was on his initiative that the Chechen government attempted to open a new negotiating channel with Moscow. Maskhadov proposed setting up a unitary commission to organize and train the nascent Chechen army. The proposal was intelligent, and could have paved the way for a series of understandings from which even a political agreement could have emerged. The Russian delegation invited to the confrontation promised to provide for the arming, training and maintenance of the Chechen army, and explicitly renounced the use of force against the Chechen Republic. For its part, Grozny made itself available for an alliance with Russia. Furthermore, Chechnya would have refrained from joining blocs of hostile alliances, such as NATO for example. The agreement reached by the two delegations would have been an excellent compromise if Yeltsin had agreed to continue the talks directly with

295

Dudaev. But from Moscow now the prerequisite for the resignation of the Chechen President and the restoration of the old institutions were essential to conduct any kind of negotiation. This condition was unacceptable for Dudaev, therefore the draft agreement, in itself good, was not ratified, and the negotiations were wrecked for the umpteenth time.

Those who ratified was Tatarstan, the last republic left out of the Federative Treaty beyond Chechnya. On February 15, the Tatar republic signed a bilateral agreement with Moscow, obtaining the right to negotiate foreign trade agreements on its own, the right to independently decide on matters relating to the ownership, use and distribution of the land and natural resources in its territory. Now Chechnya was alone, and Moscow's voice grew harder. Shakhrai declared: *The situation in which one million and two hundred thousand Russian citizens live outside the Russian constitution and outside Russian law is no longer tolerable. The explosion of crime is something in which a man's life and future are not safeguarded. Hundreds of families are forced to flee their homes. Obviously the federal authorities cannot remain indifferent.* Yeltsin's rough appeal to Dudaev followed: *Stop accusing Russia of having imperial ambitions, and take the treaty signed with Tatarstan as the basis for a possible meeting in Moscow.* This proposal excluded from the outset the possibility of dialogue with Dudaev, who considered himself a President in the fullest of his political capacities, and not the head of a semi-independent republic. Yeltsin's position was publicly formalized by Shakhrai a few days later. The conditions placed by them on the Chechen Secretary of State, Aslambek Akbulatov, were the following: 1) immediate interruption of any media action aimed at defaming or attacking the Moscow government 2) Recognition of Chechnya as a federated subject with Russia 3)

Acceptance of the same federal treaty signed by Tatarstan as the basis for the federal accord between Chechnya and Russa.

Despite the harsh words of the "hawks", there was in Russia moderate positions on which the Chechens could have leveraged, such as those of the Secretary of the State Duma, *Vladimir Shurnienko,* who proposed that the decree by which the Supreme Soviet had declared the Chechen elections of 27 October 1991 illegitimate and to recognize the government of Dudaev, in exchange for the recognition of Chechnya as a subject of the federation. The negotiations could have been supervised by a foreign commission to oversee their proper conduct. Even if Yeltsin had wanted to align himself with the positions of the moderates, however, the wave of nationalism that seemed to pervade public opinion would still have prevented him from taking any concrete steps in this direction.

If ever in Moscow the moderates had managed to move the government a few millimeters regarding the reopening of negotiations, a series of terrorist actions on Russian territory definitively tipped the scales in favor of a direct or indirect intervention towards the overthrow of Dudaev. Between April and July 1994 four terrorist attacks, the last of which was particularly bloody, struck the south of Russia. In two cases, in particular, armed commandos took hostage buses that transported Russian citizens and policemen to the town of Mineralnye Vody, in the Stavropol territory, robbing passengers of everything, taking them hostage and demanding a substantial ransom and a safe conduct for the Chechnya. The attacks had not been hatched nor by Dudaev, who was unjustly blamed for them, nor by the anti - Dudaevites, who ended up in the regime's crosshairs with the accusation of wanting to provoke a civil war. Most likely it was the initiative of criminal groups based in Chechnya, or which intended to disappear from circulation once the coup was carried out, taking advantage of the chaos taking place in the separatist republic. In some cases the Grozny government actively collaborated in the capture of the perpetrators, in others it refused to let them enter Chechnya. The fact is that the Russian press began to present those tragic events as the consequence of the dramatic situation in which Chechnya lived, conditioning public opinion to consider it "out of control". Chechnya began to be described as a criminal paradise.

While the negotiation option was wrecked for the umpteenth time, the anti-Dudaevite opposition carried out its first armed attacks. On February 4, 1994, an armed squad led by Commander Ibragim Suleimenov attempted to take Grozny with a blitz, but was stopped by the National Guard, who managed to repel the attack and arrest Suleimenov. On May 27 a car bomb exploded as the presidential procession passed through the center of Grozny. It was a coincidence that the General, that day, got into a different car from the one he usually occupied. In his place, Undersecretary of the Interior *Magomed Eldiev* and his deputy blew up. The attack further strengthened the general belief that the Chechen President was not in control of the situation.

On Yeltsin's recommendation, General *Aleksandr Kotenkov* was sent to create an anti - Dudaevite army by recruiting it from among the members of the Provisional Council established in Upper Terek. The secret services, for their part, began to bring in undercover agents and to supply the opposition with small arms, ammunition and money. As we have seen, the Provisional Council was made up mainly of members of the old Soviet nomenklatura, members of the Zavgaev clan, administrators of the Upper Terek District and escaped from the loyalist front. This jumble of characters still lacked valid popular support. This is why Avturkhanov called a *People's Congress of Chechnya*, along the lines of the one convened at the time of the Revolution, which would discourage Dudaev. After a long preparation, the Congress was held between 3 and 4 June in Znameskoye, the capital of Upper Terek. According to the organizers, more than two thousand delegates participated, mostly from the northern districts and the city of Grozny. Congress revoked trust in Dudaev and recognized the Provisional Council as the only legitimate authority in the country. Following the indications of the assembly, the Provisional Council issued a *Decree on Authority* in which it proclaimed the general removed from the Presidency and assumed full powers in the Republic. Avturkhanov then promoted the formation of a *National Awakening Government* to organize new parliamentary elections. The Provisional Council requested official recognition from the federal government, proclaiming the firm will to sign the Federative Treaty.

Dudaev, for his part, called his followers to another National Congress: as many delegates participated in his *anti - congress*, this time mainly from the southern districts of the country. In response to the proposals of the "Northern Congress", the "Southern Congress" asked Dudaev to proclaim a general mobilization against the *enemies of the Fatherland* and to prosecute Avturkhanov for *high treason*. Towards the opposition leader, the tones were particularly heated. Avturkhanov was even sentenced to death in absentia. Dudaev also took up the invitation of his followers, introduced martial law and proclaimed general mobilization.

Strange alliances

While loyalists and rebels organized their congresses, two "non-aligned" characters took up positions on the chessboard: Ruslan Khasbulatov, whom we already know, and Ruslan Labazanov, of whom we are about to speak. The latter deserves attention not so much for his political role, in itself almost irrelevant, as for the caliber of the character, indicative of the typology of the subjects who made their way taking advantage of the situation to conquer spaces of personal power.
Ruslan Labazanov was born in Kazakhstan in 1967. He moved to Krasnodar and became a martial arts master. From the circuit of fighters Labazanov had selected a criminal gang dedicated to extortion and racketeering. In 1990 the Rostov police had arrested him on charges of robbery and murder. Sentenced to 10 years in prison, he had been transferred to the Grozny prison from which he had witnessed the early stages of the Chechen Revolution. In September 1991, taking advantage of the caos that war erupting in che country, Labazanov led a prison uprising obtaining to be released with his henchmen. Back at liberty, he had placed them in an armed detachment and placed himself under Dudaev's orders. The General, impressed by the spirit of initiative and his aggressive character, he had gladly accepted his offer, going so far as to appoint him head of his personal guard. Labazanov had set about recruiting subjects of dubious extraction, mostly cellmates and common criminals, and within a few months he had turned them into one of the best-trained units in the loyalist camp, earning him the nickname *Rambo*. But the price to pay for his "professionalism" was the freedom to "express" his criminal vocation: in the role of presidential security chief, Labazanov had had a free rein in all sorts of illegal

traffic and activities.[215] As his power increased, his methods became more and more violent and mafia. Labazanov took possession of a palace in the Grozny and fortified it until it became a real fort.

His behavior began to embarrass the regime, which after the coup d'état of June 1993 needed to shake off certain characters, who have now become uncomfortable. This did not go unnoticed by the Russian secret services, who began courting Labazanov. He must have begun to realize that his Cockaigne was about to end, if it is true that the criminal activities began to combine a close correspondence with the federal authorities, probably in the hope of being able to continue to manage his traffic undisturbed. In early June 1994, the Chechen police arrested four of his men and opened a file on Labazanov for illegal trade in petroleum products. *Rambo* had by now built a good circle of supporters both among the militiamen and among the population, to whom he donated part of the proceeds of his illicit activities, and found it possible to force the government to release his men, threatening to go into opposition and overthrow Dudaev. So, having gathered a hundred fully armed militiamen and got their hands on some armored vehicle, he organized a "demonstration" in Sheikh Mansur Square, demanding the resignation of Dudaev and the holding of new elections. The claims were flimsy, and his

---

[215] Anatol Lieven from this description of Labazanov: *The first time I met Labazanov was in February 1992, when he was still serving as Dudaev's bodyguard [...] his general appearance suggested that he was not the right man to argue with. [...] He wasn't a particularly tall man, but he was so solid that he looked much bigger, with huge forearms and fists, and on the rare occasions when his little eyes weren't covered by dark glasses, they had some sort of encroachment, and a reddish reflection, as if it were a large, ferocious animal congratulating itself on the fact that it could eat you whenever it wanted, but didn't want to bother doing it. He carried two huge pistols in his gold-encrusted belt and a black sash, and when we met again in August 1994 he had added to this a large gold watch with rubies, a gold ring [...] a heavy golden bracelet and a gold chain around the neck.*

interest was certainly not to restore the rule of law to Chechnya. Labazanov just wanted to prove his power, but he must have miscalculated. Dudaev not only did not bow, but ordered the army to end the rebellion. At dawn on June 13, the loyalist forces, under the command of the new commander-in-chief, Aslan Maskhadov, they surrounded the Labazanov fortress in the center of Grozny and put it under siege. It took a day of bombing before Labazanov, wounded, fled, proclaiming a blood feud against his former protector. According to Russian media reports, some of the militiamen who surrendered at the end of the shooting were publicly executed and their bodies exposed to the public.

Retired to nearby Argun, Labazanov settled at the entrance to the main access bridge to the town, seizing all vehicles that could contain values or public officials, who were systematically robbed or killed on the spot. His raids plagued the eastern outskirts of Grozny until September, when Maskhadov managed to track him down. Hunted again, Labazanov took refuge in Tosltoy - Yurt, north of Grozny, where in the meantime Ruslan Khasbulatov had made his base.

He had just been released, and as soon as he was released from prison he had returned to his homeland Chechnya, where he hoped to gather some political consensus and rebuild his position. Khasbulatov was still one of the most popular men in the country, and arguably the only one capable of competing with Dudaev on the political arena. However, he had to face two major difficulties: the first was Yeltsin, who would never have supported his new descent into the field. The second was the country's political situation, now deteriorated and on the verge of exploding. As we have seen, the opposition had already launched a military assault on Grozny in early February, an attack nearly blew up Dudaev in May, and in June the rebel Labazanov attempted to overthrow the government by force. The room for maneuver, for a politician not accustomed to the use of force, was reduced. The first meetings of his "peacekeeping mission" had attracted the interest of thousands of people, generating apprehension both in the Provisional Council and in the loyalist camp. But without adequate armed protection, Khasbulatov's initiative would have ended up being wiped out by the Grozny government, or by the pro Russian opposition itself.

So the former President of the Russian Supreme Soviet welcomed, albeit with some reluctance, Labazanov into his ranks. The presence of such a person in a mission that called itself "peacekeeping" sounded rather grotesque[216]. But given the tense climate and the need to protect his person, Khasbulatov could not help but get him on his chariot, hoping that it could be useful if things got bad.[217]. The feeling that Khasbulatov had about Dudaev was that of an isolated monarch and now despised by the population[218]. Returning to Moscow on

---

[216] Anatol Lieven recounts Labazanov's apparition to Tolstoy Yurt thus: *Labazanov then set out in search of new allies, and in August he aligned himself with Ruslan Khasbulatov and his " peace mission ", for which he provided armed protection. I saw him as he rode with his men in the Khasbulatov procession, which paced bumpy streets with flagpoles fluttering from antennas, rifles and machine guns aiming from the windows, horns blaring, men screaming, rows of lights burning from the roofs of the great Nissan jeeps, Cherokee and Pajero. Minor vehicles veered off the road to avoid them. Reporters and camp followers panted behind them. While Khasbulatov spoke from behind a truck about a "peaceful and civilized solution to Chechnya's problems", Labazanov stood behind him with an AK – 47 with his hands on his hips, the barrel outlined against the merciless August's sky [...].*

[217] When asked about Labazanov's presence at his rallies, Khasbulatov replied embarrassed: *I too think Labazanov is a great bandit, but what can I do? A peacekeeping group has to talk to everyone, both the Gandhis and the bandits. I don't think so. no one blames me for talking to a bandit and telling him not to shoot.*

[218] In his memoir on the Chechen crisis he wrote: *In the spring / summer of 1994, the social base of Dudaev's supporters was reduced to a minimum. Ninety percent of the population was angry. In this context, the parasitic clique that ruled in Grozny generated widespread hatred. This was*

18 July, he issued a declaration *On the situation in the Chechen Republic* in which he hoped for a peaceful solution to the political conflict[219]. On 8 August he returned to Chechnya again, where he would remain until the outbreak of the war. Having just been released from political captivity, his figure could be considered neutral, and in any case certainly not a puppet in the hands of the Russian President, as Avturkhanov was perceived. The problem was that, precisely by virtue of the fact that he was hated by both Dudaev and Yeltsin, he could not be a

---

immediately visible to anyone who analyzed the situation.

[219] The text of the declaration read: *[...] I have seen thousands and thousands of people who wanted only one thing: a quiet and peaceful life [...] These people only wanted one thing: that their children do not die, that they can study in schools and institutes, that they can work and that they can have honest sources of income for life. They were deprived of all this by Dudaev's criminal regime. The economy has been destroyed, factories have been looted, workers and engineers leave Grozny, Guderemes and other villages in search of a piece of bread. [...] I am a firm supporter of the peaceful resolution of the protracted drama in the republic. So: first of all I declare that I do not claim any position, neither elective, nor administrative, neither in Moscow nor in Grozny. Secondly, knowing that virtually the entire population of the Chechen Republic - Chechens, Ingush, Russians, Cossacks, Armenians, Jews, and others, are placing their hopes on the ordering of the situation in the country, with the authority of my name, I declare the my willingness to undertake peacekeeping and mediation functions. Consequently, I propose the following mechanism to resolve the crisis: together with the most authoritative informal spiritual authorities of the republic (10-12 people), I could be the guarantor of the strict implementation of the agreements reached between the current regime and the broad opposition [...] Taking into account the current heat of public passions and the total rejection by the population of the "president" and "vice president" figures, my proposals can be carried out on condition of immediate resignation from their posts. I, in turn, could, in my opinion, persuade people not to raise the issue of criminal and other proceedings against them. [...] Other representatives of the current Chechnya administration could count on participation in the provisional government (before the elections), as well as take part in subsequent electoral campaigns without any violation of their rights. They could obtain guarantees against any legal proceedings. [...]. " Chechnya's current administration could count on participation in the provisional government (before the elections), as well as take part in subsequent election campaigns without any violation of their rights. They could obtain guarantees against any legal proceedings. [...]. " Chechnya's current administration could count on participation in the provisional government (before the elections), as well as take part in subsequent election campaigns without any violation of their rights. They could obtain guarantees against any legal proceedings. [...].*

mediator[220]. At best he could have constituted his own political bloc, but as things were degenerating, he would hardly have had time to do so.

Khasbulatov's intervention, in essence, did nothing but further fragment the already jagged front of the opposition: Avturkhanov, who was on the front line from the beginning, was not interested in recognizing him as a political leader[221]. In mid-September 1994, when the civil war had already exploded in all its violence, Khasbulatov had to surrender to the evidence and join the initiatives of the Provisional Council. His efforts did not achieve the desired results, and when it came from Moscow at the hands of the Deputy Minister of Nationalities Alexander Kotenkov, a telegram in which he was openly warned against *endangering Russia's efforts to help the Chechen opposition*, he had to to stand aside and accept that the solution of the armed conflict would run its course. The return to the arena of such a popular leader would probably have given the Provisional Council enough time to build a support front capable of bringing about the dissolution of the regime, or in any case to force Dudaev to make substantial compromises with the moderates. But Yeltsin's fear that Khasbulatov

---

[220] Also in his memoirs, Khasbulatov writes: *After my speech [of July 18, ed.] When the Provisional Council had been recognized by Moscow, Avturkhanov began to avoid meeting me, citing the fact that Moscow forbade him to see me and advised him to oppose me as much as he opposed Dudaev [...] In the words of Avturkhanov, Chernomyrdin [then Prime Minister of the Russian Federation, Ed.] said to him: "don't think about bringing Khasbulatov to power.*

[221] When questioned by a journalist about the Khasbulatov mission, Avturkhanov declared: *this man carries out his moral duty towards the Chechen people. In the autumn of 1991 [...] he made a political mistake and objectively contributed to the coming to power of the conspirators. [...] Now Khasbulatov considers it his duty to contribute to the restoration of constitutional order in the Chechen Republic. Using his public authority he can go a long way. [...] There is no "Khasbulatov Factor" in Chechnya. There is a citizen Khasbulatov who fulfills his civic duty to destroy the fascist dictatorship in Chechnya.*

would win back the sympathy of the people, that he could be credited throughout Russia as *the man who had solved the Chechen crisis* prevailed.[222].

Dudaev seeks consent

While the opposition was compacted, by will or by necessity, around the military solution of the crisis, Dudaev was desperately trying to shore up his consensus. With the negotiations at a standstill and the civil war about to explode, flying around the world seeking unlikely recognition was just not the case. The General then concentrated on domestic politics. After a year of dictatorship, the country needed to be reintroduced some of the republican organs abolished by decree in June 1993. The first of these was the Ministry of the Interior. Dudaev had dissolved it because since its constitution it had behaved like a real counter-power: during the attempted coup of March 31, 1992, the Minister of the Interior had publicly dissociated himself from the government. During the following year's institutional crisis, the units dependent on the Ministry had never intervened. Given the impossibility of influencing the work of his offices, Dudaev proceeded to assume his powers ad interim. In the summer of 1994 the President decided to gradually begin to reintroduce the elements of the democratic state, to try to stop the crisis and recover

---

[222] Yeltsin Payin and Popov's former advisers, in their memoir on the Chechen crisis, suggest that the whole Russian strategy in early autumn 1994 may have been hastened in order to anticipate Khasbulatov's success: *If the main point was to get rid of Dudaev* they state *then the marginalization of Khasbulatov was probably a mistake in any case. Khasbulatov's prestige among ordinary Chechens at that time far exceeded that of the Provisional Council, as they were seen by most Chechens as Russian stooges and he was not, or not to the same extent.*

at least part of the members of the opposition to the independence cause. So he appointed *Ayub Satuyev*, former Deputy Director of the State Security Service, as Minister, and then replaced him in October with *Kazbek Makhashev*. From August 1994, Dudaev restored the legislative functions of Parliament. In exchange for the restitution of powers, Dudaev requested and obtained an amendment to the Constitution that prevented the assembly from removing the President. The new legislative assembly was constituted for the most part by loyalists of the regime, since none of the members of the opposition wanted to return to participate in its work.

Meanwhile, the Mugadaev government was trying to function. In a climate of increasingly fiery tension, trying to keep state offices open and running ordinary administration was already an achievement, but Dudaev wanted something more: he wanted the government to be even more active, proactive and daring than it had been in the past. The general threw the issue of monetary sovereignty on the table again, relaunching the idea of giving a national currency to the country. From his point of view, the issue was strategic: Dudaev was interested in the coins of independent Chechnya circulating among the people, that the Chechens recognize them as "their" coins. As we have seen, the project to put a national currency into circulation was strongly opposed by the Minister of Economy and Finance, Taymaz Abubakarov. The General, however, did not lose heart, and gave a mandate to the Governor of the Chechen National Bank, Usman Imaev, to design the new monetary system. Imaev contacted a series of Western companies, obtaining the interest of the French *Oberthur*, which designed two series of banknotes, the *Nahar* and the *Som*, copying left and right from Bolivian and Iranian banknotes. The contract with Oberthur, in the end, did not go through, because Dudaev, trying to find a balance between the position of the Governor of the National Bank (who wanted to introduce banknotes at face value into the monetary circuit) and Abubakarov (who asked that at least the new currency be linked to the circuit of a currency appreciated on international markets) he proposed to impose a nominal exchange rate of the new currency at par with the dollar. This could have produced a dual-rate monetary taxation model, with a strong banknote for the foreign market and a weak one for the domestic market. A new banknote project was then commissioned to the German firm *Giesecke & Devrient*, which actually managed to print and deliver around 100 tons of small denominations (1, 3 and 5 Nahar) designed to resemble the US dollar. Together with the banknotes, Dudaev ordered the printing of passports, insignia, pennants, badges, banners and any other signs of recognition of the Chechen Republic Of Ichkeria.

While the utopian project of monetary sovereignty continued as we have seen, the Chechen state continued to wallow in insolvency. After a 1993 marked by structural reforms, aimed at limiting the cost of the state and rationalizing spending, 1994 was seeing the beneficial effects of these interventions waning due to the worsening of the political crisis. Yeltsin's decision to effectively block deliveries of crude oil from Russian pipelines to Chechen refineries, after two years of substantial laissez faire, gave the coup de grace[223].

---

[223]Until then, the Russian economic blockade had not affected the deliveries of crude oil from Siberia to Chechnya, partly because the Grozny refining center was the only one capable of supplying Russian industries with strategic products (such as lubricants for l 'aviation) in part because the "oil tap" could serve as an instrument of pressure with the Grozny government to obtain negotiating advantages. Since late 1993, however, the decision to overthrow Dudaev was increasingly perceived as the only viable solution to bring Chechnya back to the Russian Federation. From this point of

Chechnya's modest domestic production, insufficient to supply the Grozny refineries, could not have borne the weight of the state machinery alone, even after the draconian public administration reforms launched in 1993.

The opposition is compacted

Let's go back to the rebel camp. We had left them struggling with the formation of a National Awakening Government. At the end of July, Yeltsin recognized the Provisional Council as the only legitimate authority in Chechnya, warning Dudaev against taking any military action against the opposition, under the threat of armed intervention. On July 29, the federal government issued a declaration in which it defined the situation of the republic as *out of control*[224]. Shakhrai warmly welcomed the members of the Provisional Council, and publicly

---

view, the flow of crude oil to Chechen refineries no longer had any strategic role, and from the first months of 1994 the Siberian oil pipelines were closed.

[224] *Dudaev's political ambition* the statement read, *which attempts to present Russia as an" aggressor "and an" enemy "of the Chechen people, has led the Chechen Republic to isolation from the Russian Federation. The policy of the current leadership of the Chechen Republic has become a destabilizing factor in the North Caucasus, preventing the regularization of the Ossetian - Ingush conflict*. The Provisional Council echoed him: *The lessons from the experience of a three-year nightmare in Chechnya have been learned from the people, the opposition and the Provisional Council. [...] The civil war in Chechnya has not yet become universal in nature just because our centuries-old traditions have hindered the insane bloodshed. Whenever there were conflicts between Chechens who threatened to turn into bloody clashes, the mediators took on the difficult mission of reconciliation between the parties and woe to those who refused their efforts and chose the path of war. [...] Dudaev's regime has not simply crossed the line beyond which there is war. He has shown everyone that he does not want and does not accept any other solution to the intra - Chechen conflict, other than resolving it by force. Dudaev and his clique have taken the blame and responsibility for all the blood that has been shed and still is shed in this struggle. [...]*.

declared that *the possibility of political dialogue with Dudaev* was *exhausted*. He claimed that the General actually controlled *only in the center of Grozny* and pointed out that the Russian government *was carrying out consultations with the Provisional Government in Chechnya, which controls a significant part of the territory*. On August 11, Yeltsin spoke on television. Compared to Chechnya, he categorically denied a direct intervention by Russia, marking it as *unacceptable*. However, he also stated: *Intervention by force is inadmissible and must not be done. If we had exerted pressure by force in Chechnya, it would have awakened the whole Caucasus, there would have been such confusion, there would be so much blood that no one would ever forgive us. It is absolutely not possible. However, the situation in Chechnya is changing. The role of the opposition to Dudaev is increasing. So I wouldn't say we're not influencing at all.*

Strengthened by federal support, the rebels had continued to form the government, whose team was formalized on 11 August: the former director of a Soviet kholkhoz, *Ali Alavdinov*, was appointed to the presidency, Badruddin Jamalkhanov, former Vice-president, was named to the vice-presidency of the Provisional Council. The government itself was of little use, if not to claim its existence. Avturkhanov was reassuring himself that the Provisional Council was a Chechen creation and not a Moscow puppet[225]. The only act for which the National

---

[225] To the objection a journalist, who remarked: *People are frightened by the Russian boot, whose entry could be foreseen in the near future* Avturkhanov replied: *This is a fairy tale for the naive. First of all, we members of the Provisional Council are Chechens like everyone else. The fate of all people and the good name of the Chechens are as dear to us as anyone else. Furthermore, we do not want the stigma of the traitors of our people, if we got the support of the Russian authorities, it was only after we received the firm assurance that the Russian troops would not enter Chechnya. Yes, we asked Russia for help, but not military. From our point of view, the help was given to allow us at least occasionally to tell our people the truth about the state of affairs in Chechnya through the Russian mass media. Chechen TV, radio, newspapers are under Yandarbiev's control. And there is nothing but praise to the regime.*

Awakening Government stood out was an arrest warrant issued by the Attorney General, Bek Baksanov, against Dudaev. The real opposition leaders, Avturkhanov and Gantemirov, continued to meet privately, carrying out plans for an armed insurrection. It was at one of these meetings, held on August 29 in Znameskoje, that they agreed to give Gantemirov command of the rebel armed forces and to plan an assault on Grozny. Gantemirov went to work, and between July and August reorganized the rebel militias in Upper Terek and in the Urus-Martan district. In early September his units began to operate some blitzes to test the reactivity of the Dudaevite army.

The civil war

In September 1994 the civil war entered its "hot" phase. Until then there had mostly been skirmishes on the borders with the districts of Upper Terek and Urus-Martan, as well as fighting with Labazanov's militia in Grozny and Argun. But with the birth of the National Awakening Government and the mobilization of rebel troops, the actions of the opposition became more daring. After Gantemirov consolidated his forces southwest of Grozny, in the Urus-Martan District, it became clear to Dudaev that if he did not intervene firmly, the capital would soon be the subject of a mass attack. So he decided to launch a series of local counter-offensives that put the rebels on the defensive. The loyalist units positioned themselves on the outskirts of

---

We asked for help to pay for pensions, allowances and honestly earned salaries. For Russia itself, the armed invasion would not be profitable in any respect. Or does anyone think that Dudaev's "army" is preventing him from doing so?" armed invasion would not be profitable in any respect. Or does anyone think that Dudaev's "army" is preventing him from doing so?

Urus - Martan, while others took up positions just outside the Dolinsky, along the main route that reached Grozny from the north of the country. At the end of August these forces carried out an offensive against the anti-Dudaevite contingent barricaded in the village. The attack was unsuccessful, and there were copious losses on both sides. The operations moved to the town of Tolstoy - Yurt, headquarters of the militias loyal to Khasbulatov: Dudaev's units tried to take it unsuccessfully, using ten tanks and numerous armored vehicles. and there were copious losses on both sides.

As the loyalist offensive gained momentum, the Russian government was gaining credit in supporting a "peacekeeping" intervention to restore order to the Republic. The comings and goings of agents and military in northern Chechnya, although resolutely denied by Moscow, did not go unnoticed. Between the end of August and the beginning of September, two intelligence officers, *Stanislav Krylov* and *Sergei Trekhov*, ended up in the hands of the Dudaevites, who showed them on state TV and forced them to confess that they were on a mission for Moscow. In the same days, departments of the rebel army supported by armored vehicles were hired by the loyalists and forced to retreat to Upper Terek. Again, the Grozny government claimed to have captured Russian "contractors" sent from Moscow to support the opposition. The news was not a cure-all for the Provisional Council, which already smelled of collaboration. The actions of the regular army continued throughout the first half of September, only to be exhausted as soon as the rebels arrived in support, according to Avturkhanov's own admission, *A good number of MI - 24 and MI - 8 helicopters* supplied by the army federal.

The civil war was now a fact, and for the Chechens it was a shock. Spilling Chechen blood in the struggle for power was not the habit of these people, and the disorientation was great. Moscow intensified its support, hoping to turn the tide of the civil war upside down and to overthrow Dudaev by the local opposition. Yeltsin had four leaders at his disposal, each with his own militia, capable of carrying out an attack on Dudaev. In Upper Terek was the historic opponent Avturkhanov, with his armed force that had hitherto been able to repel the timid offensives of the loyalists. In Urus - Martan there was Gantemirov, with the remains of his Municipal Police and in Tolstoy - Yurt there was Khasbulatov, with his Peacekeeping mission, defended by the small private army of Labazanov. Soslambekov and the remains of the old parliament dissolved by Dudaev, still in favor of a political solution to the crisis, could in no way influence the course of events. For Moscow's plan to succeed, it was necessary to strengthen the anti-Dudaevite militias with heavy weapons and provide them with air support. It was the opinion of the Russian high command that the regime, however weak, was rather well armed. In particular, there was fear of the use of the nearly 250 civilian and military aircraft that Dudaev had found in the Soviet hangars when the Russian army had demobilized. The support of air weapons, therefore, was essential to ensure peace of mind for the militias to be able to descend on Grozny without risking being destroyed by the loyalist air force.

From 5 September the Northern Caucasus Military District, the local military authority of the Russian Federation, went on high alert. As armed units deployed at the border, supplies began to arrive plentiful in Upper Terek. 10 tanks and 6 combat helicopters were delivered, all equipped with trained crews. The loyalist offensive was running out, and Dudaev's units, after a failed attempt to take Tolstoy-Yurt on September 17 and an unsuccessful raid into Upper Terek on September 27, went on the defensive. The opposition was able to return to besiege Grozny, and by the end of the month a detachment from Urus-Martan reached the outskirts of the capital, captured the Attorney of the Republic Usman Imaev and returned to their starting positions. The operation was supported by the Russian air force, wich bombed the Severny airport, north of Grozny, destroying five civilians and two military aicrafts [226] and bombing the training center of the nascent Chechen national air force, in the military base of Kalinovskaya. At the end of September the loyalists launched their latest offensive against the opposition, attacking the Gantamirov base near the village of Gekhi, west of Urus-Martan.[227].

---

[226] Readers wishing to deepen the subject of civil aeronautics in the Chechen Republic of Ichkeria can consult the *Ichkeria in the sky* study available on the website www.ichkeria.net.

[227] According to reports Mairbek Vatchagaev, in his book *Chechnya: the inside story* Maskhadov planned an attack from three different directions. The action was supposed to be carried out in tandem with Ruslan Gelayev, who was supposed to come early in the attack and lock Gantamirov's men in a vice. However, Gantamirov was informed of the impending offensive, and was able to take appropriate countermeasures. His men intercepted Maskhadov's column along the road connecting Urus - Martan to Gekhi at night, forcing it to stop. The clashes lasted until dawn, when Maskhadov's vanguards reached the Gantamirov base. At the time of the attack, Gelayev's men who were supposed to block the defenders from the west did not arrive. Their delay allowed the Gantamirov garrison to keep a convenient escape route open. The attacking departments found themselves under fire from the defenders without cover, and the formation began to skid. At that point, according to what Vatchagaev reported, *Aslan Maskhadov spoke to his troops, telling them that it would be shameful to return to Grozny without having captured the base, given the losses they had already suffered, and this would have strengthened the opposition if they were withdrawn. [...] He pulled out his gun, urging all those who considered themselves men to follow him; and without looking back he began to cross the esplanade in front of the base.* Maskhadov's example inspired his men, who resumed the advance. After about an hour of skirmishes, Gantamirov ordered his men to

On October 15, the opposition counter-offensive began. The rebel militias managed to penetrate deep into the capital, and it appeared that they had managed to take it. However, in mid-afternoon, Avturkanov and Gantamirov ordered the forces of the Provisional Council to withdraw. It remains unclear why, on October 15, 1994, the opposition forces, which had captured Grozny with the loss on both sides of just 7 men, left the city.[228]. The fact is that the action turned out to be more of a demonstrative move, not decisive for the evolution of the conflict. The front calmed down for a fortnight, giving both sides time to prepare their move. In the loyalist camp, a certain optimism reigned, fueled by the fact that the opposition, alone, was unable to achieve anything more than some limited local success, and at

---

leave the base, having learned that in the meantime the Gelayev column was arriving late. In Vatchagaev's words there is no sign of boldness: *In their words, none of Geckhi's fighters were elated. They felt bitterness and guilt. It was the first battle in which Chechens fought Chechens for the future of the country.*

[228] *The city* wrote Khasbulatov, *could have been taken de facto on October 15, but then Avturkhanov and Gantamirov withdrew at 4 pm, leaving their popular militia and equipment behind. What happened?* It happened that, apparently, when Avturkhanov telephoned Moscow saying that he had virtually taken the city, orders came from Moscow to withdraw. According to Khasbulatov: *Moscow reasoned on the fact that in the absence of the clash between the militias, there was no reason for a solving intervention by Moscow. And without the resolving intervention there could have been no legitimate dismissal of Dudaev*". Other historians are of different opinion, such as Maria Esimont, a journalist from Segodnya, who believes instead that the initiative to penetrate the city with the opposition militias belonged to Khasbulatov, with the support of Gantamirov. Esimont writes: *On October 15, 1994 Khasbulatov, with the support of the commander of the armed opposition Gantamirov, carried out his own attempt to conquer the city of Grozny. Gantamirov's units, supported by Khasbulatov's "peacekeeping group", entered Grozny. They met almost no resistance and managed to occupy a number of administrative buildings. However, neither Avturkhanov, nor the air force of the North Caucasus Military District [the federal army, ed.] Provided any kind of support, and on the same day Gantamirov ordered his troops to leave the city.* However things really went, it is clear that there was no agreement among the opposition representatives, there was no mutual respect, and there was not even the intention of collaborating.

most it could land a few raids in the capital, without being able to take any. control. The climate in the rebel camp was similar: after Dudaev's violent offensive between August and September, the loyalist forces seemed to need time to reorganize, and this gave Avturkhanov and Gantemirov the opportunity to launch a decisive attack on the city. However, given the failures of the previous weeks, it was clear that this was not going to happen unless Russia vigorously supported the rebel offensive, providing the Provisional Council with heavy weapons and air cover. It was enough to ask the Russian Ministry of Defense to get all the necessary support: Minister Pavel Grachev made available the base of the 33rd Motorized Regiment of Prudboy, near Volgograd, to train the backbone of the anti - Dudaevite army: 120 men in all, which would have formed the footed support for 40 Russian T-72 battle tanks, complete with crews. By mid-November the armored detachment was ready, and Avturkhanov went to the federal base of Mozdok, where his militiamen were setting up, to prepare the plan for the final attack on Grozny. Grachev demanded and obtained that the direction of the offensive be directed by one of his trusted men, and appointed the Deputy Commander of the VIII Corps, *General Zhukov*, to lead the operations. By now the Russians could no longer hide their massive support for the opposition, nor their military maneuvers at the borders. Even just a year earlier, this kind of approach would have put Yeltsin in serious trouble in the face of his public opinion. But the political balance in Moscow had changed. After the collapse of the USSR and a period of "political settling" and general mistrust of institutions, the test of strength won by Yeltsin in October 1993 and the dissolution of the post - communist currents of parliament had opened the way to nationalism, represented by *Vladimir*

Zhirinovsky and his *Liberal Democratic Party*. The latter, in the parliamentary elections of December 1993, had obtained 23% of the votes, relying on the frustration of the Russians at having lost their "empire" and on the desire of many citizens to see the reconstitution of a strong Russia capable, first of all, of impose his reason on the turbulent Caucasian suburbs. Elstin wanted and had to pursue this nationalist turn of the Russian electorate in order to secure victory in the presidential lectures scheduled for 1996, and began to clean up the liberal-inspired presidential entourage that had served him until then to seize power and put economic reforms are finalized. Presidential advisors such as *Emil Pain* and *Arkadi Popov*, in favor of a negotiating approach with the Caucasian republics, they were put at the door, in favor of officials from the "hawk" wing, which would be journalistically defined "the war party". They represented the reaction to the ultraliberal wave that had led to the dissolution of the USSR. They weren't nostalgic, but they regretted Russian imperialism, and they wanted to recover as many "pieces" that had left with the collapse of the Soviet Union. Finally, the signing in October 1994 of an agreement between numerous Western oil companies and the Azerbaijani government regarding the supply of large quantities of oil by exploiting the only oil pipeline of a certain size available, the Baku – Novorissijsk Line, which crossed Chechnya from east to west, and wich could have guaranteed the Dudaev's regime the possibility of intervening in a gigantic oil deal, contributed to further accelerating the events.

In Moscow it was believed that Dudaev now represented little more than himself. In fact, the strength of his government was endangered not only by the opposition, which in any case remained on the outskirts of the country, but also by the bankruptcy of the state, by rampant poverty and by the dramatic social situation. Consensus in Dudaev had dropped dramatically following the outbreak of the civil war. But who, in fact, could have replaced him? Most tolerated the regime because there was no alternative. Avturkhanov was virtually unknown, and yet he represented the former Soviet apparatus, the Russian and Cossack minority, and those who had grown rich on the collapse of the USSR. The average Chechen, if he ever knew him, did not believe in him. The only personality capable of competing with Dudaev was Khasbulatov, but his constant intrigues and the fact that he had severely attacked Dudaev when everyone liked him, made him an unlikely alternative, in addiction to the fact that Yeltsin would never allow him to return to power.

The November Assault

With the support of public opinion and confident that he could capitalize on an easy political victory, Yeltsin gave *carte blanche* to preparing a military attack by the opposition. It was important that Moscow emerged as a simple supporter, in order to prevent the fear of a military invasion from spreading among the Chechens. On the other hand, it was clear that without the support of men and weapons, the rebels would not be able to overthrow Dudaev. Thus it was that the FSK began to recruit mercenaries from the ranks of the federal army. Given the dramatic situation of ordinary soldiers, paid little and in fits and starts, it was not difficult to obtain the adhesions of a hundred tankers, infantry personnel and combat pilots.[229]. The attack plan was quite simple:

---

[229] The contracts prepared for the hiring of mercenaries provided for the payment of 1 million rubles (equivalent to about 325 dollars) and compensation from 25 to 75 million for any injuries, as well as

an armored column, flanked by numerous footed infantry and under air cover would enter Grozny from the north, would occupy the government quarter and the Presidential Palace, where the provisional government would be installed. Two other minor contingents, coming from Tolstoy-Yurt and Urus-Martan, would have prevented the Dudaevites from leaving the city, capturing the notables of the regime and, if possible, Dudaev himself. Once in office, the government would have asked for Russian intervention to support the restoration of constitutional prerogatives and, if successful, would have put Dudaev under arrest, or ordered his execution. The backbone of the attacking army would have been a unit of forty T - 72 battle tanks, already available at the Mozdok military base in North Ossetia. At this base, the training of the crews, mostly Russian, began. By November 20, the armored unit was ready and able to maneuver.

The attack was scheduled for November 26, but it was far from a surprise for the defenders of Grozny. As early as the 24th, in fact, "unidentified aircraft" (therefore Russians) had bombed the airport, blocking the loyalist air force on the ground. On the same day, rebel units had taken control of some crossroads on the outskirts of the city, alerting the defenders. This had given Maskhadov the opportunity to calmly arrange his units according to a cynical but effective defensive scheme, borrowed from the experiences of urban guerrilla warfare. Maskhadov knew he did not have the resources for an open-field confrontation. He therefore decided to have the attackers penetrate deeply, allowing them to reach the city center. This was mostly made up of tall buildings with four or

---

compensation of 150 million rubles (about 50,000 dollars at the time) to family members in the event of death. The commanding officers of the units to which the enlistments were made were either silenced, or turned away.

five floors, equipped with basements whose windows opened to street level. The elevation of the guns of the Soviet tanks was not sufficient to allow them to reach the top floors of the buildings and basements, and this would have nullified their usefulness in urban combat. Not only that: if the defenders had managed to destroy the head and tail of the convoy, the clumsy and heavy armored vehicles of the rebels would not have been able to maneuver, forcing the crews to go out and expose themselves to snipers. For the defense plan to be successful, however, it was imperative that the attackers did not realize they were entering a trap. So Maskhadov ordered some units to offer some resistance. This would have strengthened in the Russian – Chechens the conviction that they have a small and demoralized army in front of them.

At dawn on November 26, the assault began. 110 armored vehicles, 40 battle tanks, 20 self-propelled howitzers, supported by 40 combat helicopters and the air support of fighter-bombers penetrated the suburbs of the city. 1,500 infantry units followed the armored strike force. Confident that a simple show of muscles would disperse the loyalist forces, the attackers entered the city in columns, as if parading, with tanks leading and infantry troops in line. The Russians had already experienced the consequences in Afghanistan of overconfident behavior in the superiority of their army. Unfortunately for them, the separatist commands had a commander in chief who Afghanistan had done so, and an excellent second in command, Maskhadov, who knew well the potential of his men. And so it was. The attacking columns converged on the city center in the middle of the morning of November 26, quartering near the government buildings, almost without encountering resistance, except for a skirmish, which occurred around

9 at the north entrance of the city. By 11:00 the tanks were stationed in front of the Presidential Palace, and Avturkhanov declared victory.

After an initial moment of optimism, the rebels began to understand that something was wrong. There was too much silence and too little resistance. However scarce and unmotivated, the loyalist forces could not have completely abandoned the field. And in fact Dudaev and his best men were gathered in the Oktiabrsk residential district, not far from the Presidential Palace, and were preparing to counterattack. Around the government buildings occupied by the attackers, loyalist snipers had been stationed since the previous night. At 11 o'clock, Dudaev ordered the counterattack: from the upper floors of the buildings and basements a storm of bullets hit the armored vehicles unable to defend themselves and the disoriented infantry. Within an hour the the attacking army had already dispersed in all directions, without command and coordination. Most of the vehicles were immobilized or destroyed, and the air support was unable to operate effectively in that chaos of men fleeing in bulk. The few aircraft that attempted to approach the theater of operations were hit by a shower of RPGs. Those who could tried to save themselves with their means by retreating to the north, while many Chechens attached to the attacking army began to loot shops and warehouses and then flee on foot or on makeshift vehicles. For seven hours since the start of the counter-offensive, the loyalists tormented the rebels with a continuous manhunt, at the end of which almost all the endowment of the Russian - Chechen army had been destroyed or captured. 68 Russian mercenaries ended up in the hands of the Dudaevites. What remained of the rebel army retreated to Upper Terek, leaving 32 tanks out of 42, 17 self-propelled guns (12 of which captured), 4 combat helicopters and a fighter-bomber, about 300 dead and 200 wounded. In mid-afternoon a triumphant Dudaev regained possession of the Presidential Palace, and publicly announced that the attack had been rejected. The defeat was a disaster for the opposition. Although Hadjiev and Khasbulatov gave an almost optimistic reading of the event, tending to present the assault as a "demonstration", the failure was there for all to see, and the direct involvement of Moscow as well. The regime took a military victory which was also a political victory. His most valuable booty was the 68 Russian prisoners who were irrefutable proof of the involvement of the federal army. Thousands of people gathered in the streets of Grozny, demanding the dissolution of the opposition movements, while Dudaev threatened to shoot the prisoners if Moscow did not recognize them. Russian Defense Minister Pavel Grachev, up to his neck in this affair, kept his bronze face declaring that the hypothesis of Russian involvement in the assault on Grozny was *delusional*[230]. Moscow's official response came on November 29, with an ultimatum in which Yeltsin demanded the disarmament of *the illegal armed militias*. The Russian President declared that *the safety of citizens* would be guaranteed by the federal army at any cost, opening up to the hypothesis of direct armed intervention. Two days after the Grozny debacle, the Federation Security Council met to discuss the Chechen crisis. The invasion plan was ready and had only to be approved. According to the reconstructions of those present, not everyone was in favor. There was a substantial part of the Council that

---

[230] *I have no interest in what is happening over there* He declared. *The armed forces have not been involved in conflicts there, although I look and feel that perhaps some people have been taken prisoner [...], I would never have ordered the tanks to enter the city. This is pathetic ignorance. And secondly, if we had to fight, we would do it with a regiment of paratroopers to decide the whole thing in two hours.*

feared a second war in the Caucasus, or at least the rise of a guerrilla war that would transform Chechnya into another Afghanistan.

However, the issue of Russian prisoners captured by the Dudaevites was nevertheless embarrassing the Kremlin to the whole world. Dudaev paraded them in front of the cameras and circulated interviews in which the soldiers claimed to be in the pay of the Federation's secret services, showing that the debacle of November 26 had been wanted, prepared and conducted by the Moscow army. Journalistic investigations began to bring the first results. On December 2, the Izvestia newspaper published the first documents proving the hiring of mercenaries by the FSK, and after a week of embarrassed silence, the Counterintelligence Service had to acknowledge that it had recruited mercenaries to support the opposition, and that it had provided men, vehicles and air cover.

The ultimatum

The invasion plans were pulled out of the safes and rewritten. Everyone more or less agreed on the need to reach and take the capital as soon as possible. It was planned to conquer Grozny, install a collaborationist government there and delegate the task of winning the war on the territory to Chechen forces, limiting themselves to supporting them with logistical, technological and intelligence support. Thus, Yeltsin returned to order the *illegal armed groups* to demobilize within 48 hours, and the next day he ordered the creation of a military intervention group. Obviously, one could not speak of "invasion": Chechnya was formally an autonomous republic of the Federation. Dudaev, always formally, was nothing more than a criminal posing as

President. Therefore the operation could not be defined as "war". And without war there would have been no invasion. We had to speak of a "police operation", an action, albeit an important one, aimed at restoring order in a turbulent province. Control should have remained in the hands of the Ministry of the Interior, and not that of Defense, because there was no "external" enemy to fight: the Chechens were Russian citizens, and whoever commanded Chechnya was a common criminal, a conspirator, an abusive occupier of institutional authority. Whatever action Grachev had planned should have been lightning-fast, aimed at restoring legitimate authority as soon as possible. And it had to lead to the arrest or elimination of the "criminals". "Lightning-fast" meant an operation that could wear out in a couple of weeks. And this was no small detail, considering the service that the Dudaevites had reserved for the army of the Provisional Council a few days earlier. On November 30, before the ultimatum expired, Yeltsin signed the decree on measures to restore constitutional legality and law and order in the territory of the Chechen Republic, which provided for *the disarmament and liquidation of armed formations on the territory of republic.*

After the drafting of the plan, Grachev introduced it to Yeltsin. This included four phases: in the first, to be completed by 6 December, the concentration of the operational units at the military bases of Mozdok, Vladikavkaz and Kizlyar should have been completed, in order to establish a North front, a West front and an East front. At the same time, the air forces were supposed to secure control of the skies and block the airspace. The second phase should have consisted in the blockade of Grozny, presumably between 7 and 9 December, simultaneously with the blockade of the administrative borders of Chechnya. The counterintelligence services were supposed to identify and locate the leaders of the Dudaev government and the main political figures who supported him, in order to prevent their escape. Meanwhile, the air forces, master of the skies, they would begin the hammering of military infrastructure. In the third phase, the federal troops would occupy Grozny, concentrating on the government quarter and then radiating towards the suburbs, disarming any armed formation they encountered in their path. The fourth and last phase would have been to introduce units dependent on the Ministry of the Interior and transform the military operation into a police operation, establishing a pro-Russian government and delegating to it the "cleaning" of the peripheral districts.

On paper, the plan was straightforward to implement, and posed no problem for one of the strongest forces in the world. But the situation of the Russian army was, in many ways, very different from the public image it gave of itself. The state of moral exhaustion of the military was terrible. The military had not been paid regularly for months, the officers were selling the equipment on the black market, and in general a climate of such defeatism reigned that the federal army would not have been able to even carry out a drill, let alone a military attack. The departments lacked weapons, ammunition, logistical equipment, and not least of officers and motivated non-commissioned officers[231]. The situation of the officers

---

[231] According to the Commander, then Minister of Internal Affairs, Lieutenant General Kulikov, the salaries of the officers were paid with a delay of two or three months. The militia at the disposal of the Ministry of the Interior had only 50% of its supply of weapons and equipment. Two out of five command posts were vacant due to a shortage of officers. At the Ministry of Defense The situation wasn't much better. This had been confirmed by Grachev himself. Ten days before the start of the military campaign, he read a directive, number D-0010, entitled *Regarding the state of preparedness of the armed forces of the Russian Federation and the corrective measures to be taken for 1995* in which he called the Russian army *unprepared for*

was catastrophic. Poor living conditions, non-payment of wages and rampant corruption were forcing the best-trained officials to leave military service to seek work in commercial enterprises.[232]. The Ministry of Defense responded to the alarmed reports by confirming the irrevocable decision to "break the back of Chechnya". Grachev was convinced that the failure of the assault on November 26 was the fault of the Chechens, and that the operation, suitably "improved", was well thought out.

Russian troops concentrated in Belsan and Mozdok airports. Due to the shortage of personnel and the lack of combativeness, the Russian command found itself constituting mixed regiments formed by units gathered on the right and left of the most varied weapons of the army. The situation ensued in which most of the units that carried out the invasion of Chechnya were understaffed, untrained, and without a well-established chain of command. Following the military came hundreds of military police officers (called OMON in acronym), mostly lightly armed and totally unaware of what was happening. Once the federal troops had reached the arrival airports, evidently taking only the light armament with them, the Federal Headquarters gave orders to the depots of the Caucasus Military District to prepare the units and to supply the gold for the heavy armament. However, the deposits were largely empty, and the workshops had not carried out adequate maintenance on the vehicles, so that the endowment of the departments was immediately inadequate. Even the choice of the moment was not happy: launching an invasion in the middle of winter is not in itself a good

---

combat actions. The best units rarely had 70% of the workforce. Most of the units had just 20-30% of the workforce.

[232] According to the appraisal report, most officers were not only unfamiliar with the combat readiness requirements set by the control documents, but also did not know their personal duties.

idea, because the low temperatures and muddy terrain reduce the performance of the vehicles, and the aircraft undergo greater wear. Furthermore, December was a difficult time for the Russian army, because in that month the turnover of the line units took place: the veteran soldiers were put to rest and replaced with replacements lacking in training and discipline. On November 28, even before Yeltsin issued his 48-hour ultimatum, the Russian air force launched a raid on the Grozny military airport, destroying the small Chechen air force on the ground. And not only the military one, but also any aircraft that could take Dudaev and his people out of the country. The two highways leaving the city were also affected. Since 1 December Grozny has been under aerial bombardment almost every day. The Ministry of Defense denied having given the order to bomb the city, but a delegation of Russian opposition Deputies, which arrived in Grozny to evaluate the possibility of reopening the negotiations and found themselves under the air attack, reported having witnessed in first person to the bombing. The delegation met with the loyalist authorities and obtained the release of two prisoners, then another 7, on condition that the deputies were the bearers of a petition to reopen the negotiations. Once again the issue of Russian soldiers in Dudaev's hands became topical again, and to reassure public opinion Grachev was forced to organize a meeting with the Chechen General. The meeting was obviously unsuccessful.

Dudaev's relaxing actions provoked bitter discussions in the Duma, where the opposition pressed for a "political" solution to the crisis and emphasized the General's willingness to recompose the negotiating table. The latter, for his part, knew that a Russian invasion of Chechnya would not be rejected as had happened with the Provisional Council: however courageous and motivated his men might be, the Russian Federation was still the second military power on the planet, and even if she got bogged down in a long guerrilla war, she would have reduced the country to a heap of ruins. It was clear, therefore, that Dudaev's will was to be able at the last minute to fix the situation. In this sense, the Chechen President asked for only one thing: a summit meeting with Yeltsin, to open a round of official negotiations and avoid war. But Yeltsin had neither the interest nor the political opportunity to proceed down that path. On December 5, Grachev met in Mozdok with the Minister of the Interior, *Jerin* and the director of operations, *Stephasin*. Despite the serious shortcomings of his army, Grachev approved the operational plan and agreed to the assault. By that date the first Russian military interventions had already taken place: on November 29, as we have said, the federal fighter-bombers had carried out the first raids on Chechen airports, destroying several civil and military aircraft on the ground[233]. In the afternoon of the following day, then, the air strikes were renewed: all that remained of the Chechen military and civil air force was destroyed in the hangars, while the runways of the civilian airport of Grozny were cratered and rendered unusable. A few bombs also fell on Grozny, causing the first civilian victims of the conflict. On 2 December a new wave of air strikes hit the airports, the base of the Shali Armored Regiment, the Gudermes railway station and the residential districts of Grozny again. To start the hostilities, only a "casus belli" was needed: on 6 December Grachev met Dudaev in Slepcovsk, Ingushetia, and again listed the terms of the

---

[233] One of the attacking aircraft had been hit and crashed not far from Serverny airport. The news did not cause much sensation, as it was now clear that Russia would intervene in force against Dudaev.

ultimatum: demobilization of "illegal armed groups" and elections for the renewal of Chechen institutions. The meeting was obviously provocative, because Dudaev was referred to as a criminal and no kind of negotiation was put on the table, but only a series of unacceptable conditions. On December 8, the North, East and West assault groups were declared ready for combat. On the same day the State Duma and the Federation Council met behind closed doors, decreeing the military solution, not without the strong opposition of numerous deputies. On December 9, Yeltsin signed Decree 2166 *On measures to curb the activity of illegal armed groups on the territory of the Chechen Republic and in the area of the Ossetian - Ingush conflict*, in which he instructed the government to *use all means available to the state to guarantee the security, legality, rights and freedoms of citizens, the protection of public order, the fight against crime and the disarmament of all illegal armed groups*. On the same day, the government adopted resolution 1360: *To ensure the security of the state and the territorial integrity of the Russian Federation, the rule of law, the rights and freedoms of citizens, the disarmament of illegal armed groups on the territory of the Chechen Republic and of the neighboring regions of the North Caucasus*. December 10, 30.000 between soldiers and policemen, supported by 500 armored vehicles, positioned themselves close to the Chechen borders. Meanwhile, the Russian Air Force had begun bombing targets on Chechen soil again, destroying an armored vehicle shed near the Grozny airport and once again bombing the city's residential districts. On that occasion, the Federal Air Force once again embarrassed the Kremlin, when the "targeted" bombings on the Presidential Palace and the TV Station building missed their objective, mostly hitting the neighborhoods of the city center, mainly inhabited by Russian civilians. On December 11, Yeltsin appeared on television and gave a short speech in which he stated: *[...] Our goal is to find a political solution to the problems with one of the subjects of the Federation - the Chechen Republic - and to protect its citizens from armed extremism. Today, however, peace talks and the free expression of the will of the Chechen people are blocked by the real threat of open civil war [...].* On the same day, federal troops crossed the border. The First Chechen War began.

*Bibliography, name index and insights available on
www.ichkeria.net*

Contacts: libertaomortechri@gmail.com

Printed in Poland
by Amazon Fulfillment
Poland Sp. z o.o., Wrocław